Art and History

Art and History

Images and Their Meaning

**Edited by ROBERT I. ROTBERG and
THEODORE K. RABB**

Contributors:
Jonathan Brown
Christoph L. Frommel
Raymond Grew
J.R. Hale
Diane Owen Hughes
Elizabeth Johns
Richard L. Kagan
Barbara Miller Lane
Peter Paret
Simon Schama
Antoine Schnapper
Randolph Starn

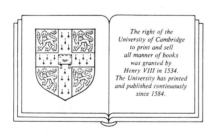

The right of the
University of Cambridge
to print and sell
all manner of books
was granted by
Henry VIII in 1534.
The University has printed
and published continuously
since 1584.

CAMBRIDGE UNIVERSITY PRESS

CAMBRIDGE

NEW YORK   NEW ROCHELLE   MELBOURNE   SYDNEY

Published by the Press Syndicate of the University of Cambridge
The Pitt Building, Trumpington Street, Cambridge CB2 1RP
32 East 57th Street, New York, NY 10022, USA
10 Stamford Road, Oakleigh, Melbourne 3166, Australia

First published 1988

Printed in the United States of America

Library of Congress Cataloging-in-Publication Data
Art and history : images and their meaning edited by
Robert I. Rotberg and Theodore K. Rabb.
p. cm. – (Studies in interdisciplinary history)
Includes bibliographical references.
Contents: The evidence of art / Theodore K. Rabb and Jonathan
Brown – Representing the family : portraits and purposes in early
modern Italy / Diane Owen Hughes – Papal policy : the planning of
Rome during the Renaissance / Christoph L. Frommel – Reinventing
heroes in Renaissance Italy / Randolph Starn – The soldier in
Germanic graphic art of the Renaissance / J.R. Hale – Philip II
and the art of the cityscape / Richard L. Kagan – Enemies of flattery /
Jonathan Brown – The domestication of majesty / Simon Schama – The
King of France as collector in the seventeenth century / Antoine
Schnapper – Picturing the people / Raymond Grew.
 1. History in art. 2. Art and History. I. Rotberg, Robert I.
II. Rabb, Theodore K. III. Series.
N8210.A65 1988
704.9′4994–dc19   87-35474
                       CIP

British Library Cataloguing in Publication Data
Art and history : images and their meaning.
 – (Studies in interdisciplinary history).
1. Historiology. Influence of visual arts
I. Rotberg, Robert I., 1935–   II. Rabb,
Theodore K., 1937–   III. Brown, Jonathan,
1937–   IV. Series
907′.2

ISBN 0-521-34018-7 hard covers
ISBN 0-521-33569-8 paperback

Contents

The Evidence of Art:
Images and Meaning in History

Theodore K. Rabb and Jonathan Brown

The Evidence of Art: Images and Meaning in History

It may be that historians and art historians will forever maintain distinct sets of priorities when they examine works of art—the first seeking evidence for conclusions that go beyond the objects at hand, the second going beyond, if at all, primarily in order to reach conclusions about those very objects or their creators. But such differences can be misleading. Their interests repeatedly converge and, in the approaches that are taken, the questions that are asked, and the concerns that are pursued, there are common preoccupations that often blur the disciplines. Five of those preoccupations were particularly salient in the papers and discussions that constituted a 1985 conference at the Rockefeller Foundation's Villa Serbelloni, in Bellagio, Italy, partially funded by the Samuel H. Kress Foundation. The proceedings of the conference have been revised to form this special issue of *The Journal of Interdisciplinary History*. By considering the issues that these articles raise, we can elucidate some of the assumptions and burdens that both disciplines share, and thus point to areas where their interaction may be especially fruitful.

The first, at the simplest level, is the powerful appeal of the written text. This preoccupation might seem paradoxical amidst a series of efforts to comprehend non-verbal materials, but it is all the more noticeable for that very reason. Let there be some phrase on a painting, or statement from an artist, and it receives intense, almost disproportionate, scrutiny. Such attentiveness may be no more than natural to scholars who are, after all, trying to comprehend meanings and purposes, and who therefore welcome any explicit message, however fragmentary, that can clarify what is otherwise often a world of nuance and allusion. Words can sometimes be as elusive as pictures, let alone buildings, in con-

Theodore K. Rabb is Professor of History at Princeton University and is co-editor of *The Journal of Interdisciplinary History*. Jonathan Brown is the Carroll and Milton Petrie Professor of Fine Arts at the Institute of Fine Arts, New York University, and guest co-editor of this issue of the *Journal*.

veying some specific intent, but the exceptional interest that they arouse indicates that the verbal often takes precedence over the pictorial in the eyes of most scholars.

What this emphasis suggests is that, despite the growing fascination that both historians and art historians find in hidden messages, in teasing out the complex implications of symbols, mental patterns, and cultural structures, the hope for the tangible and the concrete flows eternal in the land of the implicit. In some cases, such as in Jan van Eyck's *Arnolfini Marriage,* the less ostensible references can transform surface appearances; but always, in that quest for the deeper framework that will supply the right context for individual acts of expression, the open, direct, and unambiguous signpost is especially cherished. When the subject matter consists of works of art—by their nature frequently undefined and indeterminate in purpose—the need for a form of guidance that is verbalized, and thus less inconclusive, is particularly strong. In their fondness for the written text, and in their willingness to weigh it so heavily even when they focus on images and representations, the two disciplines reveal their common methodological predispositions and their closely related agendas.

Yet the fundamental assumption for both groups—and this is a second area of agreement—is that painters, sculptors, and architects are able to give us clues (and sometimes answers) about the universe that they inhabit that are available nowhere else. In the absence of words, artifacts can point us in directions we could not otherwise imagine. For art historians, this exploration is the meat of the enterprise; increasingly, however, it is also becoming a staple for historians. The power that visual evidence possesses to define what a society considers both normal and eccentric is an asset that no scholar can ignore. By forcing observers to ask whether some detail would have been taken for granted or dismissed as peculiar, images help shape our inquiries, even if only by sending us back to written sources with new objectives. The queries that they prompt might be as simple as: Why *do* dogs appear in portraits? How and why does their representation change? What does their presence tell us about those who wanted to see them in the pictures? The answers may lead to new ways of perceiving patronage, family life, styles of portraiture, gender relations, and other such seemingly remote topics. The appeal of this means of penetrating the assumptions of an age crosses disciplinary boundaries.

The third common feature derives from the first two. Like history, art history still betrays its origins as a branch of rhetoric. Giorgio Vasari was no less well trained than Francesco Guicciardini in the skills of style and persuasion that were cultivated by the humanists. The fact that their successors are still united by the need to master the rules of plausibility, to convince readers, and ultimately to tell a story, may be the clearest sign of the distinct bond that brings them together. The problems that beset their narrative enterprise are also shared: How, despite the inevitable gaps in information, does one maintain the possibly conflicting virtues of momentum and accuracy, and how long can shortcomings of evidence be tolerated when the chief aim is to keep a progression of events convincing? To the extent that an uninterrupted and developing account is difficult to construct, is coherence a virtue in its own right, or only as a means of strengthening an argument? And what is the effect of the seemingly self-sustaining flow of a story on the logical or evidentiary connections that it is making?

These are not simple issues to resolve, but they apply equally to descriptions of the architectural policies of successive popes or to surveys of the political propaganda of English monarchs. And they indicate that each discipline can draw on the strengths of the other as it addresses these dilemmas, whether it be historians paying closer attention to coherences of form and manner, or art historians displaying a heightened awareness of the coherences that emerge from detailed textual comparisons.

That proposal of strengthened alliances—illustrated though it is by a distinction that may exaggerate the differences between the two fields—leads to a consideration of the fourth mutual preoccupation: the role of causation. As arguments and narratives are established, it becomes necessary to explain the emergence of B out of A: unique portrayals of soldiers out of sixteenth-century Germany, for example, or certain types of royal collecting out of the courts of the seventeenth century, not to mention the policies or paintings of one individual out of those of another, or a nineteenth-century engraver's subject matter out of his politics. On a much more cosmic scale, one is occasionally called upon to give reasons for the outbreak of the French Revolution or the transformation of the Baroque into the Rococo.

At the conference, a wide variety of mechanisms was brought into play to deal with this constant demand for causes. There were invocations of the standard political, social, and economic customs and pressures; references to the constraints of convention; and (appropriately for children of rhetoric) citations of the power of styles, whether they were artistic forms or lifestyles. What happens all too rarely, in either discipline, is an effort to make the causal pattern explicit. A linkage may seem convincing in its own terms, but only in the absence of alternatives. When a divide is reached, it is all too easy to give the road taken the air of inevitability. Yet the negative decision at a moment of choice may be as interesting as the positive. And here the interaction of diverse scholars may prove fruitful, because it can suggest alternatives that might otherwise be ignored. If historians these days are sensitized to the psychological, demographic, climatic, or anthropological influences that they once neglected, they should be all the more prepared to accept the force of artistic traditions and worldviews. On a topic like the changing role of France's monarchs before and after the Revolution, such a perspective provides an additional means of understanding that clearly enhances a scholar's analyses. For art historians, similar benefits must accrue when there is a borrowing of explanatory patterns from colleagues who have such similar purposes.

Yet, in the end, it has to be their interest in the same subject matter that unites the two fields. The reasons for examining Spanish city views may differ widely, but the fascination of the objects themselves, and their potential as a means of insight into a larger world (richer, in some ways, than that of words) are the foundations for any study that they may inspire. As soon as such visual materials are treated as evidence, however, a problem arises that seems likely to evade a quick or simple resolution. It is a concern that affects anyone who investigates the work of artists. Yet this fifth preoccupation that is common to the two disciplines may well be the most important, for it threatens, unless addressed vigorously, to tarnish the very promise that the field is beginning to offer.

How does one come to terms with the meaning of a program of paintings or buildings? Works of art may provide a unique way of seeing the past, but, because they are so much less specific, are they not harder to penetrate, and thus to trust, than words? Whereas we have learned to explain the effectiveness of a piece of written rhetoric, such as Queen Elizabeth's Tilbury speech, we are less certain about judging the effects of visual rhetoric. Why does one picture succeed better than another—Titian's *Charles V at Muhlberg*, for instance, more than Peter Paul Rubens' *Cardinal-Infante Ferdinand at Nordlingen*? Some paintings have to work hard to convince (as does the Rubens to bestow glory on Ferdinand), while others, such as the evocations of the motherliness of Queen Victoria, achieve their aims with consummate ease. To some extent their effectiveness depends on the way that their message relates to their political and social context. Their actual content seems less decisive; images can be as powerful when they attempt to defend or exalt the status quo as when they seek to change or reshape the outlook of their age. But part of the explanation for their power also lies in the analysis of the form and style of the images.

This understanding derives from the recognition of art as a special class of evidence, shaped by imagination as well as tradition and purpose. Unlike a file of state papers, the contents of a parish register, or a set of commercial accounts, a work of art is a subjective creation. Furthermore, the artist often seeks to provide something that is difficult to quantify but dangerous to dismiss—a sense of delight, awe, and beauty.

But surely historical studies demand something more tangible and hard-headed than a response to beauty? This claim seems obvious, but it is not entirely correct. Most art historians are drawn to the field because they respond to the allure of beautiful man-made objects. It is not surprising that many of the methods of investigation were developed to accommodate the evocative, many-leveled properties of art. Thus, the orientation to an object or group of related objects and the special techniques for interpreting allusive evidence distinguish art history from other types of history and need to be understood by those who wish to use the evidence of art.

Beyond this truism is another point of fundamental importance: that style possesses meaning; that, to some extent, form is content. The operational implications of this observation are complex and not entirely clear; in fact, they are now at the center of far-reaching discussions in the field of art history. The very way in which artists represent man and the world can be as meaningful as the objects they choose to represent. It is relatively easy to describe the stylistic differences in landscape paintings by Claude

Gellée and Claude Monet, but to attribute these differences merely to technique, or to regard them as of secondary importance, is to minimize the value of art in understanding the past.

Yet despite the difficulties of drawing art and history together, there is perhaps no enterprise that is more deserving of major and united effort; in a time of increasing interdisciplinary contact, moreover, there is an expectation that it will indeed be pursued.

If the need seems particularly urgent at present, it is because of the current state of crisis in the two fields. In both history and art history, the reaction against what is regarded as a specious certainty—among historians often identified with quantification, and among art historians often associated with historicism—has been a flight from the traditional canons of verification. In their present revisionary mood, both fields are in danger of converting self-doubt into disdain for established methods of gathering and evaluating evidence. This attitude can lead to what Johns has called "temporal imperialism," which seeks to deny the independent validity of past human experience on the grounds that it is inevitably transformed and consumed by the changing concerns of individual, or classes of individual, scholars. From this position it is but a short journey to the anarchical realm of personalized and politicized scholarship where only might makes right.[1]

But even less extreme efforts to renew the disciplines have their pitfalls. As scholars have tried to rely on personal responses, structural models, semantics, and other self-enclosed systems, they have been unable to bridge the gap that separates them, or that they seek to open, from the forms of discourse that have anchored their fields for generations. The resultant fragmentation has brought few benefits, if any, and the time is thus ripe for building bridges in another direction. As the examples multiply of interdisciplinary studies that rely on the skills of both historians and art historians to provide new insights into the significance of visual artifacts, it will become apparent that this is indeed an essential means of enriching both disciplines, and thus our ability to explicate the past.

1 Elizabeth Johns, Review of Bryan J. Wolf, *Romantic Re-Vision: Culture and Consciousness in Nineteenth-Century American Painting and Literature* in *Art Bulletin*, LVI (1984), 707.

Diane Owen Hughes

Representing the Family:
Portraits and Purposes in Early Modern Italy

Family history has from its beginnings been shaped by artistic
representations. Ariès, who drew the family into history in his
remarkable *L'enfant et la vie familiale sous l'ancien régime,* discovered
childhood in medieval representations of Jesus nursing at his
mother's breast, saw it develop in the games of putti that ornament Renaissance art, and traced its full bloom through seventeenth-century family portraits in which naked or lightly clad
children were allowed to inhabit part of the canvas. A variety of
more traditional documentary evidence served merely to illustrate
his primarily iconographic vision: a religious concept of childhood
was appropriated by a laity that gradually discovered its own
children and helped them invent a private and discrete period of
childhood.[1]

Ariès discovered childhood as a way of focusing attention on
a new and dangerous domesticity that let it flourish—a domesticity that changed both the family's self definition and its attitude
toward the community. For, he argued, domesticity weakened
the concept of lineage on which the family's strength had earlier
depended and reduced its members' participation in a larger sociability outside the household. It created instead the conjugal
cell, whose links with the lineage were easily broken and whose
members were increasingly isolated from the body social. It also
inspired countless domestic scenes that not only express the sti-
fling warmth of household life but also reflect a new structure of
authority within the reduced family, as husbands seized authority
to become domestic monarchs. Although Ariès alluded to the
legal deterioration of the wife's position in the households of
seventeenth-century Europe, he found his most evocative and
telling expression of the husband's growing strength in the new

Diane Owen Hughes is Associate Professor of History at the University of Michigan.

1 Philippe Ariès (trans. Robert Baldick), *Centuries of Childhood* (New York, 1962).

domestic authority of Joseph, whom artists began to rescue from a cuckold's obscurity to head the fully conjugal Holy Family of the Counter Reformation.[2]

Ariès' discovery of childhood has been questioned, but his charting of the course of family history remains a standard guide. Historians now tend to describe that history with reference to demographic statistics and legal arguments, but Ariès' confidence in the validity of iconographic evidence has not been challenged. Although it is not an essential form of evidence in *Family, Sex and Marriage,* portraiture, according to Stone, reflects and confirms the family changes that his study describes: the proliferation of family portraits in the seventeenth century mirrors the rise of an "affective individualism," just as the affectionate and playful family portraits of the eighteenth reflect a new permissive mode of child-rearing that grew out of companionate marriages in which wives finally achieved domestic equality.[3]

Furthermore, Ariès' vision has given art historians new ways of beholding by placing artistic production in the context of family change. The popularity of marriage portraiture in seventeenth-century Holland has been assessed, for example, in light of "the new centrality of marriage and domesticity" in that bourgeois, Protestant land, and the portraits themselves have been seen to reflect both the marital relations and marital desires of the couples that they portray—"the growing appreciation of . . . warmer, more intimate bonds between husband and wife." Art historians have generally been more aware of the role of artists in popularizing and promoting such change—whether making love a domestic virtue by admitting cupid into their marriage portraits or raising motherhood to a domestic cult through their approving

2 Joseph's rise began in the fifteenth century with the help of Jean Gerson, but it was Johannes Molanus, ardent reformer of the iconography of the Counter Reformation, who, by pointing out that the Gospels did not describe Joseph as an old man, encouraged the domestic scenes in which Joseph takes an active part: *De Historia Sacrorum* (Louvain, 1570), II, xxv. As Carlo Saraceni's *The Holy Family in the Carpenter's Shop* shows, however, he was also portrayed in this period as an old man caught up in his work. See Richard E. Spear, *Caravaggio and His Followers* (New York, 1975; rev. ed.), 160–161.
3 Examples of challenges to Ariès' theories include David Herlihy, "Medieval Children," in Bede K. Lackner and Kenneth Roy Philp (eds.), *Essays in Medieval Civilization* (Austin, 1978); Urban T. Holmes, "Medieval Children," *Journal of Social History,* II (1968), 164–172; Klaus Arnold, *Kind und Gesellschaft in Mittelalter und Renaissance* (Paderborn, 1980). Lawrence Stone, *The Family, Sex and Marriage in England 1500–1800* (New York, 1977), 226, 411–412.

portrayals of ecstatic mothers nursing their children in pure and verdant countrysides and conversely condemnatory scenes of sullen wetnurses enclosed in squalid quarters with their unloved charges. But for art historians and historians alike, the composition of family scenes seems clearly to respond to and reflect changing ideals and realities of family life in the West, which can be "read" in a work of art.[4]

This article discusses problems in finding an isomorphic reflection—a direct mirroring in domestic scenes and family portraits of values and relationships existing in family affairs. It turns away from northern Europe, where family history has been presumed to follow Ariès' schedule of transformations, which its art apparently heralded and chronicled. It concentrates instead on the less explored familial world of the Italian peninsula, where, some have argued, the domestic impulse was born. According to Goldthwaite, the Florentine patriciate withdrew in the fifteenth century from the demands of lineage and turned its back on the public sociability of the neighborhood to create in its new palaces a private internal space designed to house and to celebrate the conjugal family. Their internal plans testify to the weakened lineage, their imposing facades to the withdrawal of the shrunken patrician family of the Renaissance city from the life and inhabitants of the district with which it had earlier been more intimately involved. The conjugal families that built and occupied these palaces thus turned from lineal claims and community rites to throw their energies into the elaboration of those domestic rituals that became a mark of the Renaissance and that have come everywhere to characterize the bourgeois family.[5]

At the center of the conjugal family is the couple, a husband and wife joined in a marital relationship that is in a fundamental way transforming; for it binds them more tightly to each other and to the offspring of their union than blood ties bind them

---

4 David R. Smith, *Masks of Wedlock* (Ann Arbor, 1978), 24–25. See, however, the conflicting "lineal" interpretation of many of the same works by Berthold Hinz, "Studien zur Geschichte des Ehepaarbildnisses," *Marburger Jahrbuch für Kunstwissenschaft*, XIX (1974), 139–218. Carol Duncan, "Happy Mothers and Other New Ideas in Eighteenth-Century French Art," *Art Bulletin*, LV (1973), 570–583.

5 Richard A. Goldthwaite, "The Florentine Palace as Domestic Architecture," *American Historical Review*, LXXVII (1972), 977–1012; but see also the different interpretation of family development by Francis William Kent, *Household and Lineage in Renaissance Florence* (Princeton, 1977).

individually to their respective kin groups. It is just such a marriage that the Gregorian church had defined and championed, both in its canon law that insisted on the primacy of consent of the partners and made the union difficult to dissolve, and in its artistic representations that substituted a priest for the woman's father, the church door for the private chamber, and a wedding ring for the marriage contract. Such art, ecclesiastical rather than secular in its inspiration, began in Italy with Giotto's portrayal of the marriage of the Virgin at the Arena Chapel in Padua. It remained popular throughout the sixteenth century when the church of the Counter Reformation, by insisting that the marriage rite be public, tried to solve the problem of clandestine marriage that had plagued the post-Gregorian church. But unlike Protestant reformers, who insisted on parental approval as a means of public and lineal control, the Roman church never officially bowed to the authority of the lineal blood tie. It thus awarded a fuller authority to husbands over wives than it did to fathers over daughters who were about to leave the household.[6]

The relationship of women to their fathers and husbands in a competition between lineal and conjugal bonds is central to an understanding of the nature of domestic life and kinship organization at the social level of the urban patriciate. Patrician practices conflicted with ecclesiastical prescription. Far from adopting the church's insistence on consent, most urban law denied to daughters who married contrary to their fathers' will the dowry that they would ordinarily take into marriage and on which, by the fifteenth century, marriages had come increasingly to depend. Property law further strengthened lineal ties that bound wives to their own kinsmen even after marriage had taken place by insisting on a policy of separation of goods. Although Italian husbands used and controlled their wives' dowries (as indeed they were meant to rule their wives) during the marriage, wives did retain ownership that might be exercised at a husband's death. In the event of the wife's demise, the dowry reverted to her children or, in their absence, to her lineage.[7]

6 Christiane Klapisch-Zuber (trans. Lydia Cochrane), *Women, Family, and Ritual in Renaissance Italy* (Chicago, 1985), 199–209; Beatrice Gottlieb, "The Meaning of Clandestine Marriage," in Robert Wheaton and Tamara K. Hareven (eds.), *Family and Sexuality in French History* (New York, 1980), 49–83; Jean-Louis Flandrin (trans. Richard Southern), *Families in Former Times* (Cambridge, 1979), 131–136.

7 Hughes, "From Brideprice to Dowry in Mediterranean Europe," *Journal of Family History*, III (1978), 262–296.

Nor did wives share in the economy of the husband's lineage. Whatever gifts, jewels, and clothes were awarded a wife by her husband remained the real possessions of his own kin group. Klapisch-Zuber has indeed imagined wives of the patriciate of Renaissance Florence as Griseldas who entered naked into their husbands' homes where they were decked out with finery that served to mark and claim them for that lineage—clothes and jewels of which they were systematically stripped when they had fully served the lineage by producing its children or had left it as widows. A lineal separation of wife and husband, which incest rules helped to ensure and for which dotal separation of goods stood as a symbol, thus qualified the completion of conjugal union.[8]

Pictorial representation in the later Middle Ages and Renaissance explicitly recognized the dangerous ambiguity of the woman's position and was used in a variety of ways to assuage it. Fathers as well as husbands understood that women had to undergo the profoundly transforming act of marriage as the means through which society not only reproduced itself but also extended its social bonds. Such a message was encoded in scenes of classical and Renaissance subjects that adorned the great marriage chests, the *cassoni,* filled with the bride's trousseau, that were publicly carried through city streets from her house to that of her husband in the days before the consummation of the marriage. The decoration of the *cassoni* is exceptional in its commitment to secular themes recorded in a highly contemporary idiom, so that even antique heroes would be recognized as Renaissance Florentines whose stories might speak directly to that society. Their scenes, almost allegorical in their expression of both collective and individual destinies, are a suggestive illustration of a neglected aspect of social representation that I stress throughout this article. That is, they exemplify ways in which pictures are both created and viewed not as reflections of social and personal reality but rather as idealized or admonitory representations of what is desired or what is feared.[9]

8 Klapisch-Zuber, *Women, Family, and Ritual,* 247–260.
9 On the *cassoni,* see Paul Schubring, *Cassoni* (Leipzig, 1915), 2v., suppl. (Leipzig, 1923). For interpretations of their themes, see Ellen Callman, "The Growing Threat to Marital Bliss as Seen in Fifteenth-Century Florentine Paintings," *Studies in Iconography,* IX (1979), 73–92; Brucia Witthoft, "Marriage Rituals and Marriage Chests in Quattrocento Florence," *Artibus et Historiae,* V (1982), 43–59. I am also indebted to an unpublished paper by

Altieri, a Roman humanist, located the origin of Roman marriage in an initial act of violence, the rape of the Sabines, which its later ceremonies were designed both to conceal and to symbolize. The often brutal and threatening themes that decorated Tuscan marriage *cassoni* suggest a similar and earlier awareness of the violent origins of marriage and of the larger social violence that it had the potential to create or to relieve. Thus the story of the rape of the Sabine women proposes that collective submission to enforced carnal knowledge is necessary to the continuation of the race, the stability of society, and to the process of civilization itself. The demographic plight of the ancient Romans may have given the story a particular poignancy in plague-ridden Tuscany, and at least one chest portrays the plump products of the union. Although that outcome is clearly implied in any of the renderings of the theme, its social and moral aspects seem more important. On a chest designed in 1465 for a marriage that united the Davanzati and Redditi families, for example, the ultimately reconciling and civilizing outcome of the act is stressed: amid the arms of the two marrying families, a celebratory feast follows the collective rape. Even the chest that records the children sets them in the moral context of a scene depicting the refusal of the Sabine women to return to their own people. It is women's submission to male desires that allows for that exogamy that Augustine saw as the means of extending charity outside the family and that provided throughout the medieval period a means of reconciliation—a path to social peace. Yet as the chest suggests, that submission could ultimately transform the victim into a passionate defender of the new order.[10]

Such illustrations are idealized or threatening images, but we can also see that these panels, if read as narratives or stories, point to double or complex relationships between the picture, its subject, and its beholder. The story of Nastagio degli Onesti, as told

Elisabeth Welles, who connects the decoration of *cassoni* with the decoration of houses on the occasion of a marriage. On the contemporaneity of idiom, see Erwin Panofsky, *Renaissance and Renascences in Western Art* (Stockholm, 1960), 162–172; Ernst Gombrich, "Apollonio di Giovanni, a Florentine Cassone Workshop Seen Through the Eyes of a Humanist Poet," *Journal of the Warburg and Courtauld Institutes*, XVIII (1955), 16–34.

10 Marc Antonio Altieri (ed. E. Narducci), *I Nuptiali* (Rome, 1873), 15–17. For a sensitive account of the author and his work, see Klapisch-Zuber, *Women, Family, and Ritual*, 247–260. The *cassoni* panels appear in Schubring, *Cassoni*, Table LXXII, 298–299; Table LXXXVII, 377–378.

by Boccaccio, might seem brutally inappropriate on a chest that carried into marriage the jewels and clothes of a pure, young bride. Yet it was a popular theme. The story has a strangely dreamlike and repetitious quality. Nastagio happens in the wood upon the pursuit by a knight of a naked girl who has rejected his love. As his hunting hounds hold her to ground, the knight, in Boccaccio's words, "slashed open her loins, and plucking out her heart with its surrounding organs threw them to two mastiffs, who, ravenous with hunger, devoured them instantly." She then arises and the hunt resumes. That repeated attack and evisceration in the wood is a *tableau vivant* that Nastagio shows to his own beloved—at a feast in the wood to which he has invited her kin and other friends—as a warning that she should abandon her disdain and agree to love him; and her viewing and capitulation acts as a constant warning or reminder to the bride who bore the chest as an emblem of her submission to a new and unknown knight/Nastagio (Fig. 1). The admonitory nature of the story is made explicitly in four beautiful panels painted for the marriage in 1487 of Giovanni Bini to Lucrezia di Francesco di Giovanni Pucci. On a tree in the wood to which Nastagio invited the disdainful maiden and her relatives and where the guests are transfixed by the chase of the naked woman that has upset the feast are affixed the Pucci arms. At the wedding feast that celebrates the submission of Nastagio's bride appear the arms of both Pucci and Bini.[11]

The submission of the woman to the designs of her lineage and to the desires of her conjugal partner emerges as a theme in a number of narratives, particularly in the stories of Penelope and Griselda, whose extraordinary and exemplary devotion to distant or unreasonable husbands might simply be read as a recommendation of cheerful, wifely submission to the conjugal ideal. But if fathers selected the decorations, they might also have served as a warning and a solace: a preparation for young daughters whom lineal needs had sacrificed to the conjugal demands of older, distant, and suspicious husbands and a solace to the fathers who had let them be sacrificed.[12]

11 Giovanni Boccaccio, *Decameron*, V, 8. Schubring, *Cassoni*, Tables XCIV–XCV, 398–400. The illustrated *cassone* panel (Fig. 1), from the Johnson Collection in Philadelphia, bears the Del Nero arms.

12 For the Penelope and Griselda themes, see *ibid.*, Tables XXXIX, LV, LXI–LXII.

Fig. 1 Master of the Brooklyn-Johnson Cassoni, Panel from the Story of Nastagio degli Onesti.

SOURCE: Reprinted by courtesy of the John G. Johnson Collection, Philadelphia Museum of Art, Philadelphia.

The illustrations of these chests, which furnished the bridal chamber, served, then, to remind brides of their conjugal duties; but they may also have served to alert husbands to the lineal strength that stood behind their brides. The separate but mutually reinforcing stories in panels that represent the rape of Helen and the Trojan War as well as the story of Aeneas' abandonment of Dido show the need for patrician males to rise above and leave behind the claims of female desire and demands if they are to fulfil their political and historical destiny. They also suggest, however, the strength of female provocation and the catastrophes that might ensue from it in the form of blood vengeance and enduring enmity—catastrophes that arranged marriage and the gift of a daughter were ideally designed to avert, even to amend. If these illustrations instructed the couple to bow to the conjugal tie, they clearly also alluded to the lineal power that it served.[13]

The multiple messages of the marriage chests should encourage us to look with more care at the marriage portraits that attained considerable popularity in northern Italy in the following century. These portraits might seem at first glance obvious illustrations of the growing independence and mutuality of the conjugal pair, for they apparently record and celebrate the conjugal union to the exclusion of the lineage. The emergence of the genre may indeed respond to a new conjugal demand, for it owes a debt to devotional donor portraits of husbands and wives that Italians had begun to commission in Flanders in the fifteenth century. Pope-Hennessy is correct to stress the individuality of the donor form, "distinct from the commemoration of the family in frescoes." Yet the presence of *couples* is also striking. Even in the Portinari Altarpiece, executed in 1476 by Hugo van Goes for Tommaso Portinari, a Florentine merchant, the children are dwarfed by the presence of the parents and by their name saints. If Pope-Hennessy is right to see in this altarpiece that adorned the family altar at Santa Maria Nuova an inspiration for Filippino Lippi's altarpiece at Santo Spirito, painted in 1488 for Tanai de' Nerli and his wife Nanna Dina de' Capponi, their appearance as a single couple on each side of the Virgin and Child may indicate

CXXII. On the demographic pattern of older men marrying young brides, see Herlihy and Klapisch-Zuber, *Les Toscans et leurs familles* (Paris, 1978), 204–209.
13 Schubring, *Cassoni,* Tables XXXIV, XLIX–L, LXIV, CXLIV.

the extent to which the couple visually dominated the earlier work.[14]

The complementarity of the couple in such donor portraits is strikingly delineated in one of the earliest examples executed for members of the Italian patriciate. This triptych, of which only the wings portraying the donors survive, was painted in Bruges in the middle of the fifteenth century by Petrus Cristus for two members of the large Genoese community resident in the Flemish city (Fig. 2). The absence of full-scale guardian saints emphasizes the individualized portrait nature of the donor wings, giving them almost the quality of pendant portraits that would become fashionable in northern art in the sixteenth and seventeenth centuries, a form that the triptych donor wings may have suggested.[15]

Did the rich and stunning clarity of Flemish art prompt Italians resident in the northern cities where it flourished to commission these conjugal portraits before they were fully ready to accept their conjugal implications? In the case of the Cristus triptych, lineage abruptly inserts itself into the coupling, through the coats of arms affixed to the rooms in which the subjects kneel in prayer. The arms serve to identify both husband and wife; but since it was the lineal identity of the wife that a marriage chiefly threatened to efface, her coat of arms appears to reassert and preserve her separate identity. Further details reinforce that impression. Although the husband's name is not indicated by a personal saint, the colored woodcut on the wall probably indicates his wife's first name, as well as suggesting, through St. Elizabeth of Hungary's notorious charity, a life beyond the conjugal house and its restrictions. Her husband acknowledges the sanctity of the conjugal space by taking off his clogs, as Joseph does at the stable in the Portinari altarpiece and as the groom does in Van Eyck's *Arnolfini Marriage* of 1434. He is, in a sense, more enclosed within that space. The door leads out to yet another part of the building that opens on tamed, directionless hills. Her piety, however, is more exalted, reminiscent of contemporary renderings of the An-

14 John Pope-Hennessy, *The Portrait in the Renaissance* (Princeton, 1979), 263–264; M. Salmi, "Ugo van der Goes nel trittico della Cappella Portinari," in *L'Italia e l'arte straniera: Atti del X Congresso internazionale di storia dell'arte* (Rome, 1922), 223–227.

15 For many suggestions, genealogical and iconographic, about these panels, I am indebted to Martha Wolfe of the National Gallery, where the panels hang. On pendant portraits in the north, see Smith, *Masks of Wedlock*, 2–3.

Fig. 2 Petrus Cristus, *Portrait of a Male Donor* and *Portrait of a Female Donor, c 1455.*

nunciate Virgin, who also knelt with a prayerbook before a prie-dieu. Her world seems more open: to the world of active charity through her saintly patroness, to learned piety through her book, and even to the world she knew in Genoa through the canal beyond the window that might take her home.[16] The Genoese patriciate may have served and cherished the lineage more fervently than any except the Venetian. Should we see in these lineally distinct pendant panels a further sign of their stubborn reluctance to yield to a conjugal melding that might encourage domestic harmony but might, at the same time, extinguish links between the lineage and its daughters? Or did a different impulse encourage a Lomellini husband to acknowledge the lineage and exalt the individuality of his Vivaldi bride? If St. Elizabeth functions in this portrait as a name saint, Cristus' right panel may portray Battina Vivaldi, whose father Luca had dealings with the Genoese community in Flanders. She married, as his second wife, Domenico Lomellini, a member of that community, who had three daughters but no heir. Is her pose reminiscent of the Annunciate Virgin merely coincidental or does it reflect the fact or hope of pregnancy—the expectation of the longed-for male heir that Battina did, in fact, produce?[17]

Although the wife's delivery of an heir, especially a male heir, ultimately bound her more tightly to his lineage, it briefly relaxed within the household the authority of the husband. Throughout the early modern period, that event signaled the moment when she became the focus within the household of the attention of the world beyond its walls. In Venice silken sheets spun with gold and silver were spread on her bed, from which she received delegations bearing gifts, a practice that sumptuary law tried—in vain—to limit and which at least one contemporary painting has managed to record (Fig. 3).[18]

16 Panofsky, "Jan van Eyck's *Arnolfini* Portrait," *Burlington Magazine*, LXIV (1934), 126. The openness of the wife's world is different from later Dutch portraiture, where the wife's enclosure is emphasized: Smith, *Masks of Wedlock*, 56–58.

17 Natale Battilana, *Genealogie delle famiglie nobili di Genova* (Genoa, 1825), Lomellini genealogy, 26. For their activities in Bruges, see Renée Doehaerd and Charles Kerremans (eds.), *Les relations commerciales entre Gênes, la Belgique et l'Outremont (1400–1440)* (Brussels, 1952), docs. 242, 244, 261–262.

18 For sumptuary control of the practice, see Giulio Bistort, *Il magistrato alle pompe nella Republica di Venezia* (Venice, 1912), 339. Although the painting supposedly records gifts born to the mother of Catarina Cornaro, an extremely privileged child who would become

Fig. 3 Anonymous Venetian or Austrian Artist, Birth of Catarina Cornaro.

SOURCE: Reprinted by courtesy of the Isabella Stewart Gardner Museum, Boston.

Among the gifts presented were special birth platters or salvers, many of which were decorated with antique scenes in a way and for a purpose reminiscent of the *cassoni* that the same bride had not long before brought to the marriage and in which her clothes were probably still stored. But the scenes on the salvers told different stories and conveyed different messages. When Giovanni d'Amerigo dei Benci commissioned such a commemorative plate in Florence on the birth of his daughter in 1452, he specified the theme, allowing male wisdom, represented by Solomon, to be briefly overshadowed by female splendor, represented by the Queen of Sheba. Others let Venus triumph, or, in a clear reference to extraordinary wifely dominance and husbandly subservience, let Phyllis ride Aristotle. The gifts offered in this interlude thus suspended momentarily the accepted order of the household, a period of suspension to which Cristus' portraits may more gently allude.[19]

Double portraits that celebrate the marital union itself—portraits that attained considerable popularity within the Italian patriciate in the sixteenth century—seem to suggest the abolition of lineal or authoritarian concerns. The best known and the most conspicuously conjugal of the genre is Lorenzo Lotto's *Engagement Portrait* of 1523. As Flemish artists in the north seem to have purveyed in the fifteenth century an image of conjugality apart from the larger family to Italian merchants who were less familiar with it at home, so, too, northern marriage or betrothal portraiture influenced Lotto, who had been in touch with Albrecht Dürer in 1505 and 1506 and who remained interested in German art throughout his life.

---

the queen of Cyprus, laws directed against such extravagance suggest that the practice of ceremonial gift-giving in the chamber of the new mother was common at all levels of the aristocracy and citizen class. The provenance of the painting and its title are uncertain.

19 For evidence of the continued use of *cassoni* for storing clothes, see Titian's *Venus of Urbino* (1538), in which servants fish the goddess' clothes from the *cassoni*. On the birth salvers, see Anne Jacobson-Schutte, "Trionfo delle donne: tematiche di rovescimento dei ruoli nella Firenze rinascimentale," *Quaderni storici*, XLIV (1980), 474–496. An unusual *cassone* illustrated by Giovanni di Paolo also contains scenes in which women triumph over men. Schubring, *Cassoni*, Table CI, 442. Unfortunately we do not know its history. On the topos, see Natalie Zemon Davis, "Women on Top: Symbolic Inversion and Political Disorder in Early Modern Europe," in Barbara Babcock (ed), *The Reversible World* (Ithaca, 1978).

Yet Lotto, closer to the source of humanism, also appropriated classical example in the construction of the picture. The cupid who hovers over the couple in an explicit reference to love was clearly suggested by a German portrait type, but it also suggests the Juno Pronuba or Jugalis who joined Roman couples in marriage and to whom the yoke with which he binds the couple surely alludes. Yet Lotto's emphasis on the ring that the groom places on the third finger of his wife's left hand, and which replaces the typical *dextrarum junctio* of classical art, suggests also an indebtedness to ecclesiastical influence and symbolism propagated through artistic renditions of the marriage of the Virgin popularized by Giotto's fresco in neighboring Padua. If the gift of the ring suggests an authority of the husband, one which the lower, slightly angled position of the bride might confirm, the yoke affirms the equality of the union as their harmonious faces suggest the consent that the church required.[20]

Lotto produced several double portraits that convey the harmony of the conjugal union and celebrate the marriage bond. The painting of a man and his wife seated on either side of a table covered with a rug gives us a glimpse of the artist's purposes (Fig. 4). In the drawing that represents an early sketch of the subject, the couple do not confront the spectator directly. Instead Lotto set them diagonally in a more natural (and intimate) pose. What encouraged him to destroy their natural intimacy for the larger portrait was a desire to emphasize the clearly emblematic elements that he (or his patrons) must have considered important: the dog, a symbol of marital fidelity, that the wife holds in her left arm; the prudent, saving squirrel to which the husband points with his right hand; and a slip of paper that he holds in the left. Its inscription, *Homo numquam,* which has puzzled those who sought to interpret the work, may refer to Cicero's insistence in a famous defense that the "man . . . [who] has never been among men" could not know of or participate in society's corruption— an argument for the moral superiority of the domestic nest and its intimate bonds and homely virtues. Are we then to see in these

20 Pope-Hennessy, *Portrait in the Renaissance*, 226–227; Mariette van Hall, "Messer Marsiglio and His Bride," *Connoisseur*, CXCII (1976), 292–297. As van Hall points out, some German portraiture also employed the ring, but it too would have had an ecclesiastical source.

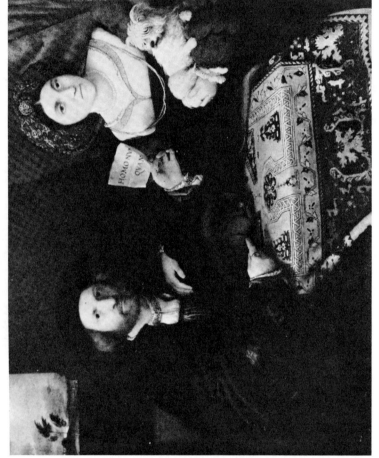

Fig. 4 Lorenzo Lotto, Family Portrait, c 1523.

SOURCE: Reprinted by courtesy of The Hermitage, Leningrad.

double marriage portraits signs of a strengthening of the conjugal bond and development of domesticity that Goldthwaite sees reflected in the architecture of contemporary palaces?[21]

The clearly emblematic nature of these portraits should reveal the dangers of such an approach. As emblems they remind us that they are valued precisely because what they represent is not a single fact or account of the lives of those who chose them, but rather because they are complex, ambivalent, and even ambiguous in their meanings. There is probably little question of the meaning of the dog's fidelity or the squirrel's husbandry; what is in question is the precise connection between those qualities and the character of the individual who displays the emblem in his or her portrait. And beyond that, each of these emblems implies certain stories of fidelity or husbandry or domestic devotion that the emblem itself does not tell; and hence the spectator, like Nastagio's beloved or the Florentine bride, are encouraged to imagine or recall stories appropriate to these emblems.[22]

But if memory should fail or if the spectator should not recall the significance of these emblems, conjugal portraits of the early modern period could make the reminder more explicit by translating the untold story of the emblem into the didactic language of moral axioms. Thus a family portrait that obviously descends from Lotto's *Engagement Portrait* substitutes for his uniting cupid a child who is, at least symbolically, the fruit of that union and whose didactic mandate shapes the union and the nature of the portrait. Like the husband in Lotto's double portrait, the child holds an instructive note that lets the father say, "I would rather, son, that you be heir to good morals than to riches"; and the mother, that her son "fear God and observe his commandments." The portrait, which thus suggests the same kind of conjugal intimacy as does the portrait from which it derives, is transformed by its clearly didactic purpose: the message of implanting correct attitudes in a child. But its purpose is more complex, for through its moral message it hopes also to convey not only to their children

---

21 Cicero, *Oratorio pro Sex. Roscio Amerino*, XXVII, 76, where Cicero uses as a defense against accusations of his client's corruption his retirement from the civic world. For a comparison of portrait and sketch, see Pope-Hennessy, *Portrait in the Renaissance*, 231–233.
22 On the emblematic meaning of these portraits, see Arthur Henkel and Albrecht Schöne, *Emblemata* (Stuttgart, 1967), coll. 490–494, 556–557; Guy de Tervarent, *Attributs et symboles dans l'art profane 1450–1600* (Geneva, 1958), I, 94–95, 154.

but also to later spectators the integrity and moral uprightness of the sitters.[23]

Such emblematic portraiture, which was extremely popular in the first half of the sixteenth century, thus poses interpretive problems for historians, as it may have presented them even to its original beholders. Correggio's presumed portrait of Ginevra Rangone permits us to consider some of the rich ambiguities that the canvas holds in suspension. Its beautiful subject is portrayed wearing the scapular of a Franciscan tertiary and holding a bowl the contents of which are identified in the Homeric inscription as nepenthe, a drug used to quench the sitter's sorrow. The symbolic ivy on the tree trunk suggests a continuing devotion that death has not shattered. Those emblems persuaded Finzi to reject an earlier identification of the sitter as the poet Veronica Gambara, who might have deserved the laurel that Correggio awarded her and whose husband's death in 1518 may have driven her to nepenthe. She was not, however, a Franciscan tertiary and was, furthermore, not beautiful. He advanced instead the likely identification of Ginevra, who managed to match beauty with Franciscan devotions and wide literary interest with conjugal rectitude. The widow of Giangaleazzo Correggio, to whom she had been a model wife, she was beloved not only by her husband but by her father-in-law. To both this status and this character the emblems clearly testify. Yet she is not dressed in the full mourning that a widow of her stature would properly have worn for a year after her husband's death in 1517; her dress is indeed remarkably décolleté. It is likely, therefore, that the portrait was completed sometime after 1518. By the following year, however, Ginevra had remarried. What, then, does this clearly emblematic portrait relate? Was it painted less to commemorate her devoted widowhood than to transform the inevitable treachery of a still young and talented widow, who abandoned her husband's memory for another's bed, into an image more acceptable to his lineage?[24]

23 The derivative portrait is attributed to Andrea Previtali. See *I Pittori bergamaschi dal XIII al XIX secolo. Il Cinquecento* (Bergamo, 1984), I, 162, Fig. 3.

24 Roberto Longhi, "La Fasi del Corregio giovane e l'esigenza del suo viaggio romano," *Paragone,* IX (1958), 34–53; R. Finzi, "Il ritratto di gentildonna del Correggio all'Ermitage di Leningrado," in *Nuove lettere emiliane,* I (1962), 5–8; Pope-Hennessy, *Portrait in the Renaissance,* 219–221. Stella Mary Norton has also pointed out that the sitter's décolleté would have been as unusual for a Franciscan tertiary as it would have been for a widow: Cecil Gould, *The Paintings of Correggio* (London, 1976), 211.

The history of art and culture of this period is notoriously filled with examples of the *momento mori* (itself popular as a device in the double portrait), a reminder of what is obviously feared or inevitable. But it may also be filled with examples of what might be called the *absit omen*, a representation that is meant to avert a dreaded or feared condition or to transform a state of affairs perceived as painful, unacceptable, or dangerous into its desired opposite. The concept of *absit omen* provides a useful guide through a tangle of family art and portraiture of the late sixteenth and seventeenth centuries, when the family relations that the portraits seem to suggest are at variance with those suggested by other forms of evidence. It may help especially to explain a touching desire of fathers to have their daughters memorialized in paint.

Pictorial representation may always have served to preserve and strengthen the bond between the lineage and its women—the ties between fathers and daughters, and especially between brothers and sisters. For even after they had left it as young brides (or nuns), these women remained present on the walls of family chapels to witness its baptisms, marriages, and funerals. The daughters of Stefano Porro, count palatine and counsellor of Gian Galeazzo Visconti, Duke of Milan, were thus cast formally as members of the lineage in two fourteenth-century frescoes recording the family's generosity and asking for intercession in its favor. And narrative cycles that decorated the chapels of the Florentine patriciate in the following century portrayed its unmarried daughters as characters in the Biblical stories that they told.[25]

Their pictorial identification with the lineage may be a sign not of the strength of the links that bound them to it but of their weakness. It masks, for example, a steady erosion of their right to an equal share in the family estate and to a place in the funeral group that mourned the passing of members of the lineage. Their presence may be as ghostly as the posthumous male relatives that Titian added to the family group in the Pesaro altarpiece to create lineal unity and depth. Their affectionate familial relations may be as manufactured as the tender warmth that Ghirlandaio portrayed between a child and his grandfather, whom the artist had first sketched as the old man lay on his bier. Yet their presence

---

25 *Storia di Milano* (Milan, 1957), VI 69–70, for Porro. A good example of the chapel narratives are Ghirlandaio's frescoes in Santa Maria Novella for the Tornabuoni.

may have served a purpose by keeping alive their memory and insisting on their familial role. It may have helped to ease their return as widows with reduced prospects to a house now peopled with their married brothers and nephews, who so often tried to avoid the obligation to house them that fathers insisted on it in their wills.[26]

The exclusion of daughters grew significantly more extensive in the sixteenth century as the concept of lineage dominated its individual members, casting off younger sons as it had already begun to cut out daughters through the use of primogeniture and entail. That narrowing of inheritance inevitably restricted marriage, encouraging the courtesan society that northern visitors marvelled at in Venice and Rome and filling populous convents with nuns whose obvious lack of vocation became an object of literary and artistic satire.[27]

The sloughing off of younger sons and the incarceration of daughters in nunneries threatened the bonds of the conjugal family as it reduced the lineage itself. Portraiture quickly recorded lineal reduction within the noble and patrician class. Van Dyck's Genoese portraits, for example, never reveal the populous families that its patriciate was still clearly able to produce. When Giovanni Francesco Lomellini commissioned the artist to paint his family, he seems to have felt that two children, a boy and a girl, were sufficient to convey his lineal notions, although he and his wife

26 Hughes, "From Brideprice to Dowry," 292–296. For funerary exclusion, see in Florence, for example, C. Guasti and A. Gherardi (eds.), *I capitoli del comune di Firenze* (Florence, 1893), II, 105–106; for Lucca, G. Tommasi, "Sommario della storia di Lucca dal MIV al MDCC," *Archivio storico italiano,* X (1847), 89–92. On the Gherlandaio portrait, see Pope-Hennessy, *Portrait in the Renaissance,* 56–57. On fathers' concern for widowed daughters, see Hughes, "Domestic Ideals and Social Behavior: Evidence from Medieval Genoa," in Charles Rosenberg (ed.), *The Family in History* (Philadelphia, 1975), 139–140.
27 For a general sketch of lineal narrowing and entailment in Europe, see J. P. Cooper, "Patterns of Inheritance and Settlement by Great Landowners from the Fifteenth to the Eighteenth Centuries," in Jack Goody et al. (ed.), *Family and Inheritance* (Cambridge, 1976), 192–312. For a sketch of the demographic consequences of such practices within the Florentine aristocracy, see R. Burr Litchfield, "Demographic Characteristics of Florentine Patrician Family Sixteenth to Nineteenth Centuries," *Journal of Economic History,* XXIX (1969), 191–205. Within that group, dowries increased threefold in the sixteenth century, a rise that helps to explain why 44% of daughters who survived infancy in the following century were committed to convents. On the life of nuns and courtesans in Venice, see Pompeo Molmenti, *La storia di Venezia nella vita privata* (Bergamo, 1929; 7th ed.), III, 373–400, esp. 384–387 for artistic representations of visitations at the *parlatorio* of the nunnery.

would produce at least four children. The artist's series of portraits of the Brignole-Sale family similarly show only one son of a family that had more. His so-called Dama d'Oro appears with two children, suggesting that this limited number represents the restricted group allowed the lineal privilege of marriage and significant rights to its resources. Only in Venice, where palaces continued to embrace the unmarried members of the lineage, did portraits of the seventeenth and even the eighteenth century regularly record the large lineal group of an earlier age.[28]

Sacrifice of children to the lineage suggests the kind of parental authority so well articulated in Manzoni's characterization of the relations of the nun of Monza with her father. Contemporaries also understood the cold malignity of fathers, who, knowing that daughters must consent to enter the convent, moved them relentlessly toward that goal. Prandoni, in his *De parentum in pueros disciplina,* castigated fathers who turned their daughters to the convent by deliberately depriving them of love and affection until, like the nun of Monza, they bowed to their will and voluntarily took the veil. But he also recognized another kind of persuasion, when fathers spoke gently to their daughters, saying,

> Surely you are my life, my love. O, little daughter, it is my heartfelt wish that you follow your conscience. I would willingly see you outside the nunnery, placed instead in matrimony. But consider, daughter, how much shame and unhappiness a wife must bear. There is the husband who, serving in the army, wounded in war, gives up the flesh for the spirit. Another, given to gambling and wine, cares nothing for his wife and children. A third irresponsible wretch digs deep into his own estate and that of his wife. Another, corrupted by lechery, infects himself and sometimes even his wife. Only a few women to whom Heaven has been kind find a husband who is faithful. In contrast, what happiness and joy it is to have brothers in common (Ps. 132), who lack nothing, possess all, and

---

28 Erik Larsen (ed.), *L'Opera completa di Anton van Dyck* (Milan, 1980), I, pl. lvii. When, however, Vincenzo Malo of Cambrai established himself in Genoa and painted a family in a way clearly reminiscent of van Dyck's *Lomellini Portrait,* he allowed room for more children and relatives. See Jan K. Ostrowski, *Van Dyck et la peinture génoise du XVII⁰ siècle* (Cracow, 1981), 29–31. Did van Dyck suggest to his patrons a more limited family group on the canvas? On the demographic patterns of the Venetian nobility, see James C. Davis, *A Venetian Family and Its Fortune, 1500–1900* (Philadelphia, 1975), 93–95.

lead a happy life while awaiting the most blessed and perpetual felicity of their celestial groom.[29]

Perhaps we should read the popularity of the mystic marriage of St. Catherine of Alexandria in light of the intensification of the conventual containment of patrician daughters in the sixteenth century and the new subtleties employed by fathers to gain their consent. A daughter of Stefano Porro had taken the role of St. Catherine to marry the infant Christ in a fourteenth-century fresco designed for the walls of the family chapel. We do not know whether she became a nun or whether the role merely suggests that Catherine was her name saint. But the popularity of the scene increased as female monastic incarceration became a standard tool of lineal survival. As patrician daughters slipped into her clothes, the Alexandrian saint (who had first married Christ in the four-teenth century) became ever more fashionable and her relationship with the infant Christ ever more tender. Many Catherines were actual portraits and Catherine was the most popular saint for aristocratic role-playing. The memorialization of daughters in the role of the virgin martyr may have been the final persuasion that fathers offered their daughters to submit to lineal needs.[30]

In the later seventeenth century, as fathers were being called to task for sacrificing their daughters at the convent door, the popularity of the mystic marriage began to dwindle. Daughters were still sent to nunneries, but a new awareness of the extent of their sacrifice seems to have encouraged families to find pictorial means of effacing the act from the lineal record. Anonymous portraits of four daughters of Giuseppe M. Arconati of Milan, painted in the last half of the seventeenth century when between

29 Pietro Antonio Prandoni, *De parentum in pueros disciplina* (1649), 251–252. The char-acter of Gertrude, the unfortunate nun of Monza who appears in *I promessi sposi,* was most fully delineated by Manzoni in the first version of his novel, known as *Fermo e Lucia*: Alessandro Manzoni (ed. Alberto Chiari and Fausto Ghisalberti), *Tutte le opere* (n.p., 1964; 3rd ed.), II, pt. 3. 160–207. The character is loosely derived from the life of Marianna de Leyva (*suor* Virginia Maria). See Italo de Feo, *Manzoni* (n.p., 1977), 292–299.
30 I consider the social use made of Catherine of Alexandria in some detail in a forth-coming article entitled "Dressing for Sainthood: Catherine of Alexandria and Italian Sumptuary Restriction." For a seventeenth-century example of a mystical marriage that has the feel of a portrait, see that painted by the Genoese artist Gioacchino Assereto (1600–1649), reproduced in *Mostra dei pittori genovesi a Genova nel '600 e nel '700* (Genoa, 1969), 114–115.

one half and three quarters of female aristocrats were stowed in convents, show nubile women poised for entry into the domestic rounds of the married world. They are dressed in the height of fashion, displaying not only a rich but a modish costume (complete with muffs, jewels, and elaborate headgear), that declared the family's ability to throw itself into the sumptuary wars that probably threatened its impoverishment. Their social accomplishments and domestic graces are suggested almost emblematically by the musical instruments that they finger, a cup of tea brought in by a servant, a letter about to be read. The message conveyed seems clear: here are daughters dressed for society and trained in the arts of the drawing room. Yet tags added later to the portraits tell us that all four sisters became nuns. Their father chose to remember them differently and put them in the portrait gallery of lineal memory as daughters whom the lineage had cherished. The pictorial lie did not change their status or eliminate their sacrifice, but it may have influenced succeeding generations of Arconati to look in a more positive way on the daughters who begged for a role in lay society. Even as Giuseppe Arconati's daughters entered the convent, the celibacy rate for daughters of the Milanese aristocracy had begun to fall. Within a century, 80 percent would be allowed to take up the domestic rounds represented in the portraits of the four Arconati nuns for whom they were only a dream.[31]

Their portraits let Giuseppe Arconati keep his daughters at home without sacrificing family honor by keeping them unmarried under his roof. As Pierre Clergue, the heretical priest of Montaillou, explained in the fourteenth century, dotal systems made men dream of incest:

> It would be better for a brother to marry his sister rather than to receive a wife who is a stranger, and similarly, for a sister to marry her brother rather than to leave the paternal house, taking with her a large amount of money as dowry in order to marry a husband who is a stranger: under such a system, the paternal house is practically destroyed.

31 The portraits are reproduced in *Storia di Milano* (Milan, 1958), XI 555–558. On the celibacy rate within the Milanese aristocracy, see Dante E. Zanetti, *La demografia del patriziato milanese nei secoli XVII, XVIII, XIX* (Pavia, 1972), 82–85, 108–111.

However, the Church demanded marital exogamy, for which only the convent stood as an acceptable substitute.[32]

The Church's relentless insistence on exogamy helped to confine such visions to the world of dreams, where, however, they may have gained new intensity in the sixteenth and seventeenth centuries. Artistic renditions of the story of Lot and his daughters increased in popularity as dowries rose. First developed in northern art, the theme had come to engage Italian artists by the sixteenth century, but they were still occasionally ignorant enough of its details to assign Lot an excess of daughters. Within a century, however, Lot's incest had become one of the most familiar of Old Testament events and one of the most popular of Biblical themes depicted in Italian art. One can find many reasons for its popularity in the history of iconographic transmission and in the Renaissance obsession with the mismatching of young and old. Its appeal in a period when dowries continued to rise but forced monacation was being seriously criticized may also suggest that Italian fathers had begun to have incestuous dreams.[33]

What aristocrats refused to do was marry their daughters down, an option that had become less attractive as the law began to insist on a woman's complete dependence on her husband's status. As de Luca put it in his enormously popular *Il cavaliere e la donna*, "the honorific quality of the woman conforms juridically and depends, as has been said many times, on the quality of the husband, as if she were a kind of moon that received all its light and splendor from the sun, that is the husband." Contemporary sumptuary law insisted visually on that dependence by adjusting the color and design of wives' attire to their husbands', not their fathers', rank. That law also envisioned her staged and visual absorption into the conjugal household. In Genoa, where lineal identity was particularly strong, portraiture may have been used to record the wife's incorporation. That seems an attractive way to read three portraits that Van Dyck painted of Paola Adorno, the marchesa Brignole-Sale. One, clearly the first, is a full-length portrait that shows her standing in a dress of white cloth spun with gold thread—a cloth that the sumptuary law throughout northern Italy generally allowed to nubile daughters and to young brides. For the second, she has removed that dress of chaste but

---

32 Emmanuel Le Roy Ladurie, *Montaillou, village occitan de 1294 à 1324* (Paris, 1975), 63.
33 Andor Pigler, *Barockthemen* (Budapest, 1974), I, 42–51; Oskar Bätschmann, "Lot und seine Töchter im Louvre," *Städel-Jahrbuch*, VIII (1981), 159–185.

sumptuous seduction to put on the more somber costume of a married woman: a dress of red and gold brocade. Finally, she appears in the presence of her young son, as a wife who has served the lineage by giving it a male heir. She has adopted the black costume that signifies and records her own lineal death and which custom and sumptuary law generally required her to don within three years of a marriage.[34]

Yet portraiture does not provide an unambiguous record of the wife's submersion in her husband's lineage. Although her legal and economic position within the conjugal household declined in the course of the sixteenth and seventeenth centuries as she was denied rights in her husband's estate and was allowed fewer claims in those of her children, she emerged to dominate the family portraits. Despite Tridentine reformers stressing the moral role of the father within the household and over its children, it is often to their mothers that they seem most obviously attached. Certainly post-Tridentine portraiture, particularly in Carlo Borromeo's Lombard stronghold, frequently cast fathers with their sons. But in more fully realized family portraits or groups, the father was often cast aside. Paola Adorno is by no means exceptional in being portrayed with the couples' children, while her husband, in a pendant portrait, stands apart from his progeny. Furthermore, the devotion of children to mothers provides the focus and life of numerous family groups. Van Dyck's so-called Dama d'Oro is seated with her two children, one of whom awards her a rose, a gesture that Bernardino Licinio had already employed in a group portrait of his brother Arrigo's family.[35]

In the very centuries in which the woman's position declined both within her own lineage and within the conjugal household, her visual presence grew ever more imposing. As in northern art, where her rising prominence seems to coincide with the domestication that Ariès described (and deplored), her Italian ascendancy

34 Giovanni Battista de Luca, *Il cavaliere e la donna* (Rome, 1675), 501–502. Hughes, "Sumptuary Law and Social Relations in Renaissance Italy," in John Bossy (ed.), *Disputes and Settlements* (Cambridge, 1983), 97–98. Larsen, *L'Opera di van Dyck*, I, pl. xxv (Frick portrait in white and gold); pl. xxiii (National Gallery portrait in black); Mario Menotti, "Van Dyck a Genova," *Archivio storico dell'arte*, III (1897), 451 (Palazzo Rosso portrait in red and gold). For the details of the family, see Battilana, *Genealogie*, under Brignole-Sale. On visual lineal withdrawal, see Hughes, "Sumptuary Law," 93–94; *Riforma, e Prammatica sopra l'uso delle perle, gioie, vestire, e altro per la Citta e Contado di Firenze* (Florence, 1638).
35 For the Licinio portrait, see *I Pittori bergamaschi*, IV, 391.

may depend, at least in part, on conjugal enclosure and the refinement and elevation of a domesticity that wives came to embody and to extend.

It is not easy to measure the march of domestication, but we can certainly find attempts to combat some of its excesses in sumptuary laws that, from the sixteenth century, began to enlarge their scope beyond the individual extravagance of clothes to control embellishment of the domestic space. However, the laws do not suggest that domestic extravagance and elaboration, unlike sartorial excess, were particularly female vices. Yet there are hints in the paintings of the seventeenth and eighteenth centuries not only that the domestic world was a creation of women, but also that men may have viewed it as a threat to their former authority.

Dogs rather than people provide the most arresting evidence for the domestic argument that the pictures convey. The dogs that represented marital fidelity in Van Eyck's *Arnolfini Marriage* or in Lotto's double marriage portrait had become, by the seventeenth century, symbols of domestic bliss. They were particularly attached to women. Van Dyck's portrait of *Three Siblings with a Dog* conveys this attachment very well. The two boys, still children, but yet old enough to put on adult dress, carry the swords that indicate the public, aristocratic persona that each will bear outside the household into the larger community. Between them stands their sister, holding in her hand a little (adult) doll. It is on her that the lapdog playfully jumps. The bond forged with the little girl was extended throughout the century as small terriers and spaniels caught women of all ages and children of both sexes in their domestic embrace. Yet aristocrats were occasionally troubled by the thought that portraiture, by permanently identifying male heirs too closely with a domestic milieu, might threaten their later claim to public authority. Van Dyck's third portrait of the children of Charles I (1637) distinguished the future king not only by placing him at the center of the canvas and dressing him in male attire (in contrast to his brother James), but also by letting his hand rest on a great mastiff. Earlier portraits that showed the prince in infant skirts or with small spaniels trapped in a domestic world of female dresses and little dogs had displeased the king.[36]

36 Larsen, *L'Opera di van Dyck*, I, 75; Christopher Brown, *Van Dyck* (Oxford, 1982), 181–185.

Italians may also have viewed the domestication of the court with a certain ambivalence, suggested in Giuseppe Baldrighi's portrait of Parma's Bourbon rulers (Fig. 5). The artist had studied in Paris, where he was influenced by the playful domestic scenes that had become popular in the northern capital. When he was commissioned in about 1757 to execute the Parma portrait, he evidently wrote to his old master Boucher for ideas and may have been supplied with a sketch of one of those animated and colloquial domestic scenes that we use as a measure of the relaxed intimacy of family life in the eighteenth century. However, Baldrighi chose to transform the suggestion into what some have called a still life composed of people. Its life is provided not by Boucher's suggested intimacies, but rather by a contest, a playful dispute in which the little Marie Louise robs from her brother the sword that represents his future manhood and public authority. It is surely no coincidence that a dog comments on the contest: the dog of the hunt that is not free to jump and run but that must sit quietly, for it is elaborately collared and restrained with a silken ribbon. It is not that Baldrighi simply failed to live up to his master's conceptions, but rather that he chose to create a scene almost emblematic in its intentions—one that shows and quietly satirizes the domestication of the court and the dominance in that domestic sphere of its women. Does it also comment, in the context of Parma, on what the French had wrought?[37]

However artists might play with women and their foibles, they became a central and unifying feature of eighteenth-century family portraiture. Alessandro Longhi's 1760 portrait of the Pisani family portrays a multigenerational family typical of the Venetian aristocracy, which conserved the patrimony by permitting one brother to marry and by encouraging the others to live celibate at home (Fig. 6). The ordering focus of the portrait, however, is not the Pisani heir but rather his wife. Earlier Venetian painters, faced with families that allowed more extensive marriage to their sons and that were still ruled by a patriarch, had found balance and order difficult to achieve. Cesare Vecellio, for example, squeezed seventeen members of a three-generational family around a table in a sixteenth-century portrait that is almost with-

37 Eugenio Riccomini, *I fasti, i lumi, le grazie: pittori del settecento parmense* (n.p., n.d.), 110–111.

Fig. 5 Giuseppe Baldrighi, *Don Filippo di Barbone with his Family*, 1757.

SOURCE: Reprinted by courtesy of the Galleria Nazionale, Parma.

Fig. 6 Alessandro Longhi, *The Pisani Family*, 1760.

SOURCE: Reprinted by courtesy of the Marchese Bentivoglio, Venice.

out a social or artistic focus. He managed to accord the patriarch some room in front at the left, and he scattered the children in front of the adults. But the scene is crowded and imbalanced, its familial order uncertain. It is reminiscent of, and may even take as a model, contemporary German family portraits in which conjugal families—parents and children—sit at a long table with Christ at its center.[38]

In Italy, however, that kind of egalitarian intimacy was less possible for religious as well as familial reasons. Longhi's more successful composition depends not only on the increasing discipline of Venetian aristocrats to limit the marriages of their members, but also on a more familiar religious model. The influence of ecclesiastical art on secular portraiture can be detected as early as marriage portraits that take up the theme and iconography of the marriage of the Virgin. Her celestial presence in the midst of other saints grew even more powerful in the Counter Reformation, as she abandoned earthly pursuits to rise immaculate to heaven. Her powerful iconographic position was bound to influence the representation of secular families in which a single mother was also portrayed. In the Longhi portrait, the wife, surrounded by her children, becomes the virginal focus of a painting in which the men, like shepherds or magi, bow, visit, and adore, while nymphs and cherubs replace the saints and angels. Does her centrality indicate the wife's domestic victory or does it largely reflect demands of its religious model?

Such stylistic habits and concerns, along with the emblematic nature and didactic purposes of so much family portraiture, should encourage us to approach with caution the family history that it seems to tell. The problem extends beyond composition and style into the nature of artistic and cultural models, which were often in conflict with family designs. Thus the lineal and dotal systems that shaped the Italian family and served to exclude its wives and limit its daughters came of age in a world that had begun to center its religious fervor on the Virgin and to embrace the cultural ideals of chivalry and courtly love. Such ideals often

38 See, for example, one clearly Protestant family portrait by Ludger Tom Ring the Younger (1522–1584) in which a central Christ is flanked by the donor and his family: New York, Metropolitan Museum. The Vecellio portrait is reproduced in *Architettura e Utopia nella Venezia del Cinquecento* (Milan, 1980), 231.

challenged the patrilineal ideology and patriarchal structure that shaped the Italian bourgeois household, and it should come as no surprise that an early example of domestic decoration employed a courtly theme only to emphasize its threatening nature.

The full decoration of the Davizzi palace, apparently occasioned by the marriage in Florence in 1350 of Paolo di Gherardo degli Davizzi with Lisa degli Alberti, concentrated in one of its rooms on scenes from a French romance that had lately gained popularity in Tuscany. The romance and the frescoes that faithfully and vividly retell it recount illicit passions that upset both domestic and civil relations at the court of Burgundy: the passion of a knight and vassal of the Duke of Burgundy for the beautiful Donna del Verzù, who resisted her family's attempts to place her in marriage so that she might continue their affair, and the desire of the Duchess of Burgundy for that knight, who rejected her advances. The unraveling of their desires leads eventually not only to the death of all the lovers but also to a weakening of the political fabric as the duke, publicly betrayed by his wife, loses stature and a trusted vassal.[39]

Although the dominant position of women in courtly romance may have reflected their real position of wealth and power in French courts, it hardly mirrored their role in urban households, where the refusal of the Donna del Verzù to bow to the authority of her family and marry would have been viewed as an unacceptable independence that ultimately led to the duchess' more flagrant crime. The elevated social position of the Alberti coupled with Lisa degli Alberti's extravagant dowry, which seems to have improved Davizzi fortunes significantly, may have encouraged its recipients, in decorating their walls for her entry, to think also of the possible effects on a household of powerful, independent, and willful women. Yet the decoration of their house with scenes from the romance of the "Donna del Verzù" ensured not only that future generations of Davizzi would daily see the destructiveness of uncontained desire and contemplate the ability of wives and daughters to thwart familial order and design, but also that the characters of a courtly romance would continue

39 On the history of the decoration see Paul F. Watson, *The Garden of Love in Tuscan Art of the Early Renaissance* (Philadelphia, 1979), 43–51. An Italian text of the romance is printed in Natalino Sapegna (ed.), *Poeti minori del Trecento* (Milan, 1962), 824–842.

to entertain and to seduce the urban patriciate of Renaissance Florence.[40]

The cultural centrality of women in both secular romance and religious lyric, which the poets of the *dolce stil nuovo* shaped in an authoritative and authentically Italian way, was bound to influence social expectation as well as artistic representation within the Italian city. Such a cultural model helps to explain why, if by the seventeenth century a woman's status was always reflective, her moon might still shine brighter than the sun. But its decorative use in the Davizzi palace also suggests how complex and almost infinitely reflexive the relationship between social behavior and cultural models might be, threatening to trap its modern interpreters in a deceptive hall of mirrors. In the end, the significance of familial representation may lie less in what it can tell us about a particular family or moment of decisive change in family configurations and more in the messages, ideas, and often outright lies that families passed on to future generations about the bonds, affections, and familial attitudes of their ancestors. For pictures surely supply, as we know family diaries sought to do, not only a history but also an ethos of the family, a controlling myth that shaped its later growth.

40 Georges Duby, "Youth in Aristocratic Society," in *idem* (trans. Cynthia Postan), *The Chivalrous Society* (Berkeley, 1977), 112–22.

Christoph L. Frommel

Papal Policy: The Planning of Rome during the Renaissance

The investigation of patronage and town planning has become increasingly important for our understanding of the history of architecture and in particular for the history of Roman Renaissance architecture. The projects of individual popes have been thoroughly analyzed, but no attempt has been made to look at papal building policy during the Renaissance as a whole, to find out its principal motives, or to distinguish between continuous and discontinuous forces. This article suggests that much of the unique beauty of Renaissance Rome is the result of the particular character of papal government.[1]

The center of the old city of Rome differs from that of other Italian towns in that it has two centers of gravity: the Vatican and the Capitol. Until 100 years ago both were situated on the periphery of the city. The Capitol, which since the Middle Ages had been the seat of the communal administration, only attained its present representative character during the sixteenth and seventeenth centuries and earlier was anything but impressive. Even before its recent isolation from the rest of the city was achieved by archaeologists and patriots seeking to preserve its character, it did not play a role comparable to that of the urban centers of Venice, Florence, Siena, or other smaller towns. The Vatican, at

Christoph L. Frommel is Director of the Bibliotheca Hertziana in Rome. He is a co-author of *Raffaello architetto* (Milan, 1984).

An earlier version of the article was presented at the Congress of the Istituto Gramsci in 1983 and a revised version appeared in Italian in C. De Seta (ed.), *Le città capitali* (Rome, 1985), 95–110. The author thanks Julian Gardner for assistance with the English text of this article.

1 On Roman Renaissance urbanism in general, see Gustavo Giovannoni, "Roma dal Rinascimento al 1870," in Ferdinando Castagnoli et al., *Topografia e urbanistica di Roma* (Rome, 1958), 343–420, 499–517; Torgil Magnuson, *Studies in Roman Quattrocento Architecture* (Rome, 1958), 3–211; Frommel, *Der römische Palastbau der Hochrenaissance* (Tübingen, 1973), I, 11–24; Luigi Spezzaferro, "Place Farnèse: urbanisme et politique," in Ecole française de Rome (eds.), *Le Palais Farnèse* (Rome, 1981), I, 1, 85–123; Manfredo Tafuri, "Roma instaurata. Strategie urbane e politiche pontificie nella Roma del primo cinquecento," in Frommel et al., *Raffaello architetto* (Milan, 1984), 59–106.

the opposite end of the city, dominates the area. Suffice it to compare the scale of its square with that of the Campidoglio.

This dual structure of the city reflects its uncommon urban history: whereas in Venice, Mantua, or Urbino the communal and the spiritual centers of the town are more or less identical, and in Florence, Siena, or Milan one needs just a few minutes to move from one to the other, in Rome such a walk would take about half an hour. And if the Roman cathedral of St. John Lateran—a church which has been completely on the periphery since the early Renaissance—is included as a third point of gravity, the circle becomes even larger.

This uncommon urban structure, together with a series of atypical urban phenomena, is the result of a development which started long before the exile of the popes to Avignon. But it became permanent only after their return at the beginning of the Renaissance. This article concentrates on the period between Nicholas V, whose main architectural adviser was Leon Battista Alberti, and Pius IV, who commissioned Michelangelo to execute the Piazza del Campidoglio in 1560.

Before Nicholas V started his vast Vatican building schemes soon after his election in 1447, he must have debated whether the Vatican should really be the papal residence—and not the Lateran palace, the traditional seat of the Roman bishop. But there was probably no real dispute. The Lateran was a distance from the town and partly in ruins, whereas the medieval, fortified residence on Vatican hill and old St. Peter's were still intact. St. Peter's had become the far more important of the two basilicas. As if to stress the bipolarity of the city, Nicholas commissioned, in the first year of his reign, the modernization of both the Capitol and the Vatican palace.[2]

A huge northern wing, which overlooked the splendid gardens and served as the private apartment of the popes, was added to the Vatican palace early in Nicholas' reign. Its rooms were richly decorated with mosiac floors, stained glass windows, and frescoes, later to be replaced by those of Pinturicchio and Raphael. The stern and sober exterior, with its tower, scarp, and crenella-

2 Carroll William Westfall, *In This Most Perfect Paradise* (London, 1974), 94–101, 129–165.

tion, still followed the pattern of a medieval fortress. This stark exterior, contrasting with the lavish interior, was to remain a characteristic of papal buildings for at least another sixty years. The popes, recently returned from a traumatic exile, did not feel entirely safe. Danger threatened not only from outside, but also from the different warring factions within the city. The northern wing of the Vatican palace was unexciting both because of its fortress-like character and because its architect, the justly unknown Antonio da Firenze, was a good engineer, but not a great artist.[3]

Only in 1451, when the huge peperino tower and part of the Vatican fortifications had already been executed, did the far more modern Bernardino Rossellino arrive from Florence and immediately start rebuilding St. Peter's. The project was apparently his, but a year later work was interrupted on the advice of the great Alberti. Alberti, who had been *scriptor brevium* (papal writer) since the pontificate of Eugene IV and was on friendly terms with both popes, was then finishing his great treatise, "De re aedificatoria," which he dedicated to Nicholas V in 1452. Thus Nicholas' famous building program, which we know of only from Giannozzo Manetti, his posthumous biographer, and which is imbued with Albertian ideas, was formulated only between 1452 and Nicholas' death in 1455. Many popes, like Nicholas, only succeeded in establishing a coherent building policy after having been in power for some time.[4]

This building program, which has been reconstructed, interpreted, and repeatedly discussed, is important not only for the beginning of Roman town planning, but also for the city's subsequent development. Nicholas V believed, as did Alberti, that architecture had a highly political impact. "Not for ambition," Nicholas said on his deathbed, "nor pomp, nor vainglory, nor fame, nor the eternal perpetuation of my name, but for the greater authority of the Roman church and the greater dignity of the Apostolic See . . . we conceived such buildings in mind and

---

3 Eugène Müntz, *Les arts a la cour des papes* (Paris, 1878), I, 111–112; Magnuson, *Roman Quattrocento,* 91–92.

4 See Westfall, *Perfect Paradise,* 167, for a different opinion. But Michael Canensius, in a biography of Nicholas, does not mention any of the particularly Albertian aspects of Nicholas' building program: *Ad beat. D.N. Nicolaum V Pont. Max.,* Cod. Lat. Vat. 3697, Biblioteca Vaticana.

spirit." He may have become aware of this lack of buildings which attested to the dignity of the Roman church when, during the Holy Year of 1450, thousands of pilgrims found the architecture of Rome much inferior to that of central and northern Italian towns. In 1452, however, the emperor Frederick III may well have been greatly impressed by the beginnings of Nicholas' new buildings, which were far more monumental than anything then existing in Vienna.[5]

The more relevant aspect for Roman urbanism of this building program was not so much the papal palace, with its marble theater, its huge library and stables, the atria, or the dining and assembly halls, but the idea of connecting the square in front of Castel Sant'Angelo with St. Peter's Square by three straight and wide modern streets. Each of them was to be flanked by houses with shops on the ground floors and apartments above, the hierarchically most important central street being reserved for the highest class of merchants and artisans, the right one for the intermediate, and the left one for the lowest class. This rational system of regular streets, found already in newly planned medieval towns such as Scarperia, was realized neither under Nicholas nor thereafter.[6]

For centuries every sort of systematic, long-range plan for Rome came to naught. The primary reason was the high degree of egocentrism behind subsequent papal building activity—an egocentrism which would have been impossible in a democratic commune or even in states with a continuous dynasty. The popes were elected and frequently came from unimportant families; often they were aged and had only a few years more to live. Thus they had no time to lose if they wanted to do something for their own glory and for the future of their own lineage. Many of them, being humanists, were often, at least during the Renaissance, better trained to be patrons than the average prince or community leader; they were also more eager to emulate the traditional approach to art and architecture. Had they been guided, at least in part, by Nicholas' sense of altruistic responsibility and his sound long-range building program, the layout of Renaissance Rome would have become more coherent and more similar to that of

---

5   Westfall, *Perfect Paradise,* 33.
6   Magnuson, *Roman Quattrocento,* 55–97.

Florence or Siena. But there would also have been fewer outstanding architectural monuments.

Nicholas' successor, Calixtus III, did not start any building of interest. But the first important postmedieval private palace of Rome, the still existing Palazzo Sforza Cesarini, was begun by his favorite nephew, Rodrigo Borgia, who later became Alexander VI. Rodrigo had been named cardinal when he was twenty-six years old and vice-chancellor, the most important position after the pope, when he was twenty-eight. His palace, situated prominently on Via dei Banchi Vecchi, one of the main streets in the center of the city, was the first of a long series of palaces built by papal relatives which imbued Rome with much of its splendor. Its exterior tower and crenellation followed, as had Nicholas' Vatican wing, the pattern of castles and fortresses; the large courtyard, with its porticoes and garden, provided the owner with the comforts of the new age.[7]

Pius II Piccolomini, Calixtus' successor, was another great humanist and had actively collaborated in Nicholas' attempt to reestablish the Roman papacy. He was also in close contact with Alberti, who accompanied him when he made a long trip to Mantua after his election. This trip had two important results for the history of architecture: the foundation of the town of Pienza, and Alberti's first entirely new building, San Sebastiano in Mantua. It would have been much more logical had Pius continued Nicholas' building program for Rome, and it would have been equally logical had Pius appointed Alberti to execute what may have been partly his program. Instead Alberti left Rome for Mantua to serve Lodovico Gonzaga from 1459 to 1463 and from 1470 to 1471, and Rossellino instead was commissioned to build Pienza.[8]

This development was more a series of unplanned coincidences and spontaneous decisions than the result of a conscious change in building policy. It is unlikely that Pius II knew whether or what he would build in Pienza when he left Rome in 1458 to

7 Ludwig von Pastor, *Geschichte der Päpste seit dem Ausgang des Mittelalters* (Freiburg, 1925; rev. ed.), I, 759–767; Magnuson, *Roman Quattrocento*, 230–239.

8 Pastor, *Geschichte der Päpste* (1894; rev. ed.), II, 14–34; Girolamo Mancini, *Vita di Leon Battista Alberti* (Florence, 1911), 382–393; Guido Guidetti, "Leon Battista Alberti direttore della Fabbrica di San Sebastiano," in *Il Sant'Andrea di Mantova e Leon Battista Alberti* (Mantua, 1974), 237–241.

organize a crusade against the Turks. But when he arrived at his native Corsignano and witnessed its misery, he saw in it the opportunity both to eternalize his memory and to realize an architectural utopia impossible in Rome with all its existing buildings and traditions. Unlike Nicholas V, his primary incentive was not to relieve the misery of the population, acquire material profit, or encourage religious devotion, but rather to enhance his own glory as was the intention of other great patrons of the period. A similarly egocentric approach is evident in the papal building policy of the next century, whether in Rome or elsewhere.[9]

Immediately upon his return from Mantua, in the autumn of 1460, Pius commissioned the renewal of St. Peter's Square. Its main facade was to be an eleven-bay, two-storied Loggia of Benediction in white marble, with antique columns in front of its pillars and huge classic-styled stairs (Fig. 1). As architect he chose a hitherto unknown and since forgotten humanist and papal financial officer, Francesco del Borgo, whose ideas turned out to be closer to Alberti's than those of any other contemporary.[10]

Francesco was the first directly to imitate the massive structure of Roman exteriors, such as the Tabularium or the Coliseum. Thus he became the founder of Roman Renaissance architecture as opposed to the more abstract Tuscan Renaissance of Filippo Brunelleschi, Michelozzo, or Rossellino. The classical character of Pius II's Loggia of Benediction and its prominent urbanistic role as the main façade looking into the most important square of Christianity marks a decisive change in approach toward antiquity when compared to Pope Nicholas' more fortress-like project. His more advanced notions may also explain why he did not continue Nicholas' heavy and inelegant project for St. Peter's. Instead he began religious buildings, such as the chapels for the head of St. Andrew which had arrived during his pontificate from the east and which was meant to symbolize a reunification with the Christian past. There can be no doubt that his building policy was increasingly inspired by religious motives.

A similar lack of continuity in papal building policy was evident after Pius' death in 1464, when another great patron, Paul

---

9 Enea Silvio Piccolomini (ed. Luigi Totaro), *I Commentarii*, lib. II, cap. 20 (Milan, 1984), I, 314.
10 Frommel, "Francesco del Borgo: Architekt Pius' II. und Pauls II.: Pt. I," in *Römisches Jahrbuch für Kunstgeschichte*, XX (1983), 107–154.

Fig. 1   Reconstruction of Pope Pius II's Loggia of Benediction, St. Peter's Square, Rome.

II Barbo, succeeded him. Although the next holy year of 1475 was approaching, Paul II left both Pius' and Nicholas' buildings unfinished and concentrated instead on a completely different project: the transformation of the palace that he had occupied as a cardinal near San Marco into a second papal residence (Fig. 2). His architect was the same Francesco del Borgo who had begun the Loggia of Benediction. Again the fortress-like exterior of the palace had little to do with the humanistic articulation of the Palazzi Rucellai or Piccolomini; all Renaissance splendor was concentrated in the interior with its classically styled courtyard, vestibule, hanging garden, staircases, and monumental halls. Paul's motives were rather obvious: like Pius he did not want to be the anonymous follower of his predecessor but longed for personal glory, as had Pius at Pienza. Venetian born, he wanted to confer a new importance on San Marco, the patron saint of his former titular church; and building was a passion in itself. His intention, ultimately realized, was to enjoy a comfortable life which, in the

Fig. 2 Palazzo Venezia, Rome. Reconstruction Project of 1465.

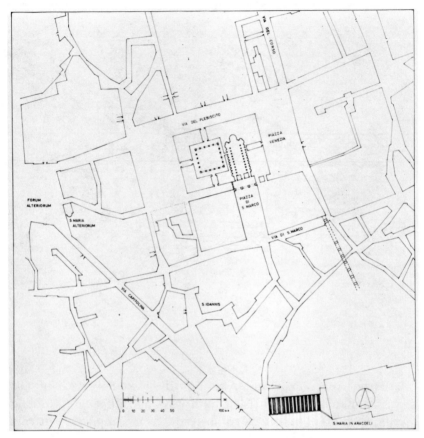

SOURCE: Drawing by Emanuela von Branca in *Römisches Jahrbuch für Kunstgeschichte*, XXI (1984), 125, Fig. 23.

dark Vatican, much gloomier than a modern palace, was more difficult.[11]

For the further development of Roman urbanism by far the most important goal was Paul's wish to establish the papal residence "*in centro urbis*" near the Forum and the Capitol. Paul tried to establish curial offices and install wealthy merchants around the two new squares which were laid out in front of San Marco

11 *Ibid.*, Pt. II, in *Römisches Jahrbuch*, XXI (1984), 71–164.

and the palace. He reopened the antique Via Flaminia, which had been partly blocked by medieval buildings, to accommodate the carnival, formerly held at the Testaccio. The Corso, as it was named, created a direct connection between the palace and the northern Porta del Popolo, so that Frederick III, on his second visit to Rome, or Borso d'Este, the Duke of Ferrara, could ride along a direct route to the new papal palace even before visiting the Vatican.[12]

Like the first building activities of Nicholas and Pius, those of Paul also, after some years, reached a critical juncture. Paul felt himself threatened by a group of humanists associated with Pomponio Leto, who were wrongly suspected of conspiracy. Paul believed that members of Leto's circle had hidden themselves in the unfinished parts of his new palace, which thus proved to be highly insecure. After Francesco's death that same year, 1468, the pope returned to the safety of the Vatican and concentrated increasingly on its renewal. The approach of the holy year of 1475 seems to have induced him to take up again Pius' Loggia of Benediction project and Nicholas' choir of St. Peter's. He even returned to Nicholas' idea of making Caesar's obelisk the center of the new St. Peter's Square.

No sooner was Paul succeeded by Sixtus IV della Rovere (1471–1484), a Franciscan, than papal building policy once again changed completely. Sixtus was less hedonistic and a much more pragmatic and functional patron. Instead of spending his money on a few costly monuments, he tried—the first of all post-medieval popes to do so—to create a sound urban system of roads and bridges, hospitals, churches, and chapels—the last mostly dedicated to the Virgin. He replaced the old Vatican Capella Magna with the spacious but again fortress-like Capella Sistina and began, next to the atrium of St. Peter's, a huge building to house the most important offices of the curia.[13]

12 *Idem,* "Chi era l'architetto di Palazzo Venezia?" in Silvana Nacchioni and Bianca Tavassi La Greca (eds.), *Studi in onore di Giulio Carlo Argan* (Rome, 1984), II, 44.

13 James S. Ackerman, "Rome in the Renaissance: The City and the Myth," in Paul A. Ramsey (ed.), *Papers of the Thirteenth Annual Conference of the Center for Medieval and Early Renaissance Studies* (New York, 1982), 7–11; Tilman Buddensieg, "Die Statuenstiftung Sixtus' IV. im Jahre 1471," in *Römisches Jahrbuch für Kunstgeschichte,* XX (1983), 54–72; Maria Luisa Madonna and Anna Maria Cerioni, "Momenti della politica edilizia e urbanistica dello Stato Pontificio nel '400. L'exemplum della Piazza del Comune a Viterbo," in Roberto Cannata and Claudio Strinati (eds.), *Il Quattrocento a Viterbo* (Rome, 1983), 23–89.

But Sixtus would not have been the follower of Calixtus, Pius, and Paul had he concentrated exclusively on the needs of the church and the holy year. He apparently supported the enormous building activity of his many kinsmen who began to construct huge palaces in such different places of the city as San Pietro in Vincoli, Santi Apostoli, Sant'Apollinare, and Piazza Scossacavalli. Other cardinals, such as Guillaume d'Estouteville, the rich chamberlain, built Sant'Agostino and its adjacent palace. Each of these palaces had its own square and was connected as directly as possible to the older street system. Their effect on Roman urbanism was, on a smaller scale, similar to what had happened around Palazzo Venezia: the new palaces and churches became radiating centers of urban renewal. Sometimes there was the danger that different street systems conflicted, as happened with the Palazzo Farnese, where the axial access, the Via dei Baullari, did not harmonize with the older street system around the Cancelleria. The authority of the responsible urban planners, the *maestri di strada* and their architects, was not as strong as the egocentrism of papal kinsmen.[14]

If, under Sixtus, churches and public institutions were still equally important, further development favored the private palaces. It is symptomatic that Sixtus' nephew and new chamberlain, the young Raffaele Riario, could destroy the famous early Christian basilica of San Lorenzo in Damaso and incorporate its successor invisibly in the large body of his palace. Nearly every Renaissance pope concentrated just on his secular residences and thought only subsequently of ecclesiastical building.

Riaro, in close contact since his early youth with the great humanists of his time, was the first Roman patron to eschew a fortress-like exterior for his new palace. This was not so much a question of function as of appearance, since the Cancelleria, his residence, was equally safe and was built with fortified corner-rooms. Its exterior surpassed even the standards of the Palazzi Rucellai and Piccolomini. It was, however, a long time before

---

14 Günther Urban, "Die Kirchenbaukunst des Quattrocento zu Rom," in *Römisches Jahrbuch für Kunstgeschichte,* IX/X (1961/62), 274–276. Sixtus' two famous bulls were meant to stimulate the building of sumptuous palaces, and showed the strong influence of nepotism. The bull of 1475 allowed prelates to leave a palace or country house near Rome to relatives even if it had been built with income from the church; the second bull, of 1480, enabled builders of sumptuous palaces to incorporate adjacent land or houses: Müntz, *Les arts* (1882), III, 180–187. Spezzaferro, "Place Farnèse," 115–123.

others followed his new pattern. This conservative phase resulted partly from the lack of first-rate architects and partly from Sixtus IV's interest in quantity rather than in the quality of architecture. Only at the end of his pontificate did the arrival in Rome of Baccio Pontelli herald a change in style. Pontelli was a young Florentine who had been trained in Urbino and may have designed not only the castles of Ostia and Grottaferrata but also the Cancelleria, the belvedere of Innocent VIII, Santa Aurea in Ostia, and San Pietro in Montorio—all of them representing a more refined and classical style.[15]

Sixtus' successor, Innocent VIII Cibo, was not a great builder, but his Belvedere, on the northern slope of the Vatican hill, was the first real Roman villa. It was no accident that it was more or less contemporary with the Cancelleria. Although apparently part of the Vatican fortification, it opened onto the landscape as did its famous prototypes in Florence and Urbino. But, as in the case of the Urban palace, it was many years before the open, outward-looking villa in Rome became an aim of the architecture of the great masters.[16]

This delay was partly a consequence of the personality and policy of Rodrigo Borgia, Innocent's successor on the papal throne from 1494 to 1503. As Alexander VI he did not dare to build open palaces or villas. He tried primarily to guarantee his own and his family's security by strengthening the fortifications of Castel Sant' Angelo, adding the strong Torre Borgia to the Vatican apartment, and by building such impressive fortresses as that at Civita Castellana. The latter was by far the most important building project of his pontificate. Again, the stern exteriors of these buildings were balanced by the splendor of their interiors—be it the beautiful courtyard at Civita Castellana, Pinturicchio's frescoes of almost oriental splendor in the Appartamento Borgia, or the gilded ceiling of Santa Maria Maggiore.[17]

Alexander's preparations for the important jubilee of 1500 were astonishingly modest. He did not finish either Pius' Loggia

---

15   Armando Schiavo, *Il palazzo della Cancelleria* (Rome, 1963), 37–62; Frommel, "Raffaele Riario e la Cancelleria," unpub. ms. (1985); idem, *Palazzi Romani del Rinascimento*, forthcoming; idem, "Chi era l'architetto?" 51.

16   Dioclecio Redig de Campos, *I palazzi Vaticani* (Bologna, 1967), 71–78; David R. Coffin, *The Villa in the Life of Renaissance Rome* (Princeton, 1979), 240–279.

17   Redig de Campos, *I palazzi Vaticani*, 81–85; Frommel, "Raffael und Antonio de Sangallo der Jüngere," in *Raffaello a Roma* (Rome, 1986), 262–266.

of Benediction or the Via Alessandrina, one of the two new streets between Castel Sant' Angelo and St. Peter's Square which had already been planned by Nicholas V. Only in February 1499, ten months before the arrival of the pilgrims, did he decide to open this straight, wide street which—characteristically—led directly to the portal of the palace—and not to that of St. Peter's. All houses in the way were demolished without regard to their owners, who were obliged within two months to build new houses at least 15.63 meters high along the street. If they did not obey, the ground was to be sold by the Camera Apostolica to willing builders.[18]

Via Alessandrina was, not by accident, the first artificially straight street since the days of ancient Rome. Nicholas V had planned such streets but never realized them, and not even Sixtus IV had dared to undertake the necessary demolitions. But Alexander's ruthless example was followed by many of his successors and thus with him opened the authoritarian age of Roman urbanism. One of its most powerful representatives was Julius II (1503–1513), who succeeded Alexander after the short interlude of Pius III. Giuliano della Rovere, Pope Julius II, was the nephew and protégé of Sixtus IV and already, as a cardinal, a patron of such important architects as Baccio Pontelli and Giuliano da Sangallo. Immediately after his election he appointed Donato Bramante his first architect—Bramante, the most talented architect of his generation, who had come voluntarily to Rome after the fall of Milan but had not received any large commission from Alexander VI. Following the pattern of earlier Renaissance popes, Julius did not touch the unfinished Via Alessandrina—which was only completed by Leo X—and soon moved out of the residence of his hated predecessor.[19]

Julius did try, however, to transform the nepotism and dynastic imperialism of the Borgias into a papal policy with the goal

18 Frommel, "Francesco del Borgo," I, 123; Marcello Fagiolo, "Arche-tipologia della piazza di S. Pietro," in *idem* and Gianfranco Spagnesi (eds.), *Immagini del Barocco: Bernini e la cultura del Seicento* (Rome, 1982), 117–132; Madonna, "Una operazione urbanistica di Alessandro VI: La via Alessandrina in Borgo," in Maurizio Calvesi (ed.), *Le arti a Roma sotto Alessandro VI* (Rome, 1981), 4–9.

19 Pastor, *Geschichte der Päpste* (1924; rev. ed.), III, 896–953; Frommel, "Capella Iulia: Die Grabkapelle Papst Julius' II. in Neu-St. Peter," in *Zeitschrift für Kunstgeschichte*, XL (1977), 26–62; Loren Partridge and Randolph Starn, *A Renaissance Likeness: Art and Culture in Raphael's Julius II* (Berkeley, 1980), 37–41; Frommel, "Il Palazzo Vaticano sotto Giulio II e Leone X. Strutture e funzioni," in *Raffaello in Vaticano* (Milan, 1984), 123.

of reunifying Italy under the papal flag. Again his first commission was a secular building, the famous Cortile del Belvedere. Julius probably had first insisted on a viaduct between the old palace and Innocent VIII's villa, and it was certainly Bramante's idea to transform the whole intermediate area into an enormous villa (Fig. 3). It was unrivaled in size by any Renaissance building and thus became the adequate expression of the pope's imperial ambitions. His ambition was also clearly expressed in the unjustly ignored foundation medal, the inscription of which compared the project with Nero's Domus Transitoria.[20]

The survival of his name on earth and the reception of his soul in heaven was the subject of Julius' great funeral monument, begun by Michelangelo early in 1505. Only when he considered placing the monument in the choir of St. Peter's, started by Nicholas V but never finished, did Bramante and others persuade Julius to rebuild the whole of St. Peter's. This project required so much money and artistic energy that the Cortile del Belvedere was neglected and work on the tomb completely abandoned—another characteristic case of irrational and spontaneous papal building policy. Only a year after the foundation of the new St. Peter's did Bramante design a coherent building program for the Vatican—a program which comprised the Stanze, the Loggie, and the Sistine Chapel, but which required awkward changes in the fragmentary Cortile del Belvedere. After a hectic start, this project was also abandoned during the last three years of Julius' reign.[21]

Julius' contributions to Roman urbanism were similarly lacking in coherence. They started, understandably, only after the large Vatican projects were realized but in a no less arbitrary manner. In October 1508, the pope planned "infinite changes," one of them being a huge palace for the different Roman lawcourts which was to be built on a new square opposite Rodrigo Borgia's palace, the Cancelleria Vecchia. Houses, shops, and a church worth 40,000 ducats were to be destroyed without compensation in the construction of this project. The plan was Bramante's famous Palazzo dei Tribunali, the first real office building since ancient Rome. This attempt to centralize administration and the

20 *Idem,* "Capella Iulia," 60–61; Ackerman, *The Cortile del Belvedere* (Vatican, 1954); Arnaldo Bruschi, *Bramante architetto* (Bari, 1969), 291–434, 865–882; Frommel, "Lavori architettonici di Raffaello in Vaticano," in *idem* et al., *Raffaello architetto,* 357.
21 Frommel, "Capella Iulia," 26–27; *idem,* "Il Palazzo Vaticano," 122–132.

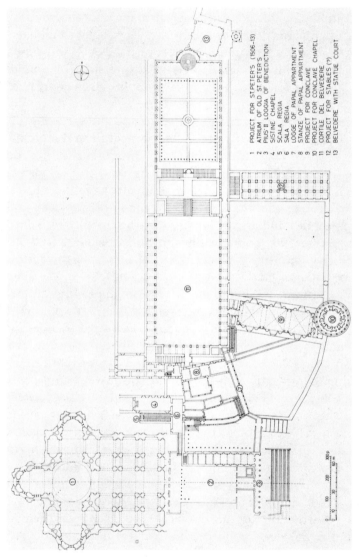

Fig. 3 Reconstruction of Bramante's Project of 1506/7 for the Vatican.

1 PROJECT FOR ST.PETER'S (1506-13)
2 ATRIUM OF OLD ST.PETER'S
3 PIUS II LOGGIA OF BENEDICTION
4 SISTINE CHAPEL
5 SCALA REGIA
6 SALA REGIA
7 LOGGE OF PAPAL APPARTMENT
8 STANZE OF PAPAL APPARTMENT
9 PROJECT FOR CONCLAVE
10 PROJECT FOR CONCLAVE CHAPEL
11 CORTILE DEL BELVEDERE
12 PROJECT FOR STABLES (?)
13 BELVEDERE WITH STATUE COURT

SOURCE: Drawing by Georg Kohlmaier in *Raffaello in Vaticano* (Milan, 1984), 123.

different lawcourts was hardly acceptable to the old republicans who jealously guarded the few privileges left to them. This may have been one of the reasons why Julius abandoned the project after two or three years. Only in 1694 was it taken up in the Curia Innocenziana on Monte Citorio.[22]

But Julius II would not have been a product of his time had he planned this urban renewal without any egocentric intention. The old palazzo of the detested Rodrigo Borgia had become the residence of his nephew, Cardinal Sisto della Rovere. The new square between the two palaces, had the project been realized, would have become a Forum Iulium. Once more the memory of the Borgias would have been replaced by the imperial splendor of Julius and his family. Julius wanted also to rebuild Nero's Pons Triumphalis as his uncle Sixtus had rebuilt the bridge of Marcus Aurelius, both worthy successors of the Roman pontifices Maximi. For the transformation of Via Giulia into one of Rome's most prestigious streets potential patrons of churches and palaces were sought. One of the smaller side streets was filled with simple but standardized row-houses—a system which has made Via Giulia, even without Forum Iulium, a great urban success even today.

On the other side of the Tiber, Bramante traced a nearly parallel street, the Via della Lungara, which connected the Vatican with Trastevere and the main harbor. Although it was not protected by walls, it attracted wealthy and sophisticated patrons such as Agostino Chigi, Raffaele Riario, Alberto Pio da Carpi, Filippo Adimari, and Baldassarre Turini who built suburban palaces and villas along the new street. People felt safer under the great Julius and longed for a *"vita in villa"* even in their permanent urban residences. Many of the new buildings of both Via della Lungara and Via Giulia overlooked the river (Farnesina, Palazzo dei Tribunali, Palazzo Farnese, San Eligio, and San Giovanni dei Fiorentini, among others), which thus became part of the urban system and was used by the pope himself when he went by boat to Ostia or to the Magliana (Fig. 4).[23]

22 Spezzaferro, "La politica urbanistica dei Papi e le origini di via Giulia," in Luigi Salerno, Spezzaferro, and Tafuri, *Via Giulia* (Rome, 1973), 58–64, 314–322.

23 Frommel, *Die Farnesina und Pereuzzis architektonisches Frühwerk* (Berlin, 1961), 163–170; Emanuel Rodocanachi, *La première Renaissance: Rome au temps de Jules II et de Léon X* (Paris, 1912), 93.

Fig. 4 Town Planning of Rome under Pope Julius II.

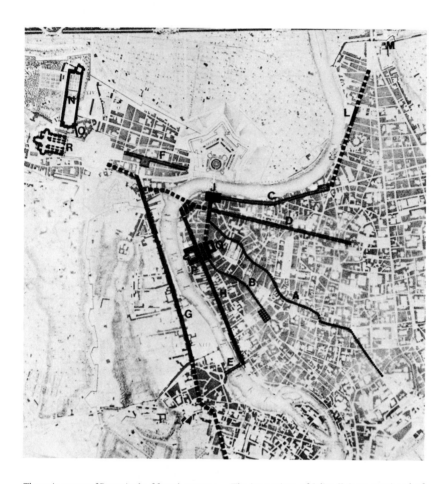

The main streets of Rome in the fifteenth century
A Via Papale
B Via Florea and Campo di Fiori

The innovations of Sixtus IV (1471–1484)
C Via Sistina
D Via Recta
E Ponte Sisto

The innovations of Alexander VI (1492–1503)
F Via Alessandrina

The innovations of Julius II (1503–1513) and of Bramante
The executed innovations
G Via della Lungara
H Via Giulia
I Piazza and Canale di Ponte
L Via di Ripetta
M Apse of Santa Maria del Popolo
N Cortile del Belvedere
O Logge Vaticane

The planned but unrealized innovations
P Palazzo dei Tribunali
Q Enlargement of the old Cancelleria
R St. Peter

SOURCE: Map by Manfredo Tafuri in Frommel et al., *Raffaello Architetto* (Milan, 1984), 69.

Little wonder then that Julius' successor, the young Leo X, changed building policy again, if only to show that he was a Medici. Leo was a great diplomat and connoisseur, but not as powerful a leader and patron as Julius had been. But only under Leo did Roman Renaissance architecture reach its first climax. Julius had burdened Bramante almost exclusively with all important commissions. Most of Julius' building activity was concentrated on the Vatican area and only a few outstanding buildings were not designed by Bramante. By 1513/14, after Julius' death, Bramante's assistants and pupils had become independent; each of them, not only Raphael and Antonio da Sangallo, but also Giuliano da Sangallo, Baldassare Peruzzi, Andrea Sansovino, and, from about 1518 onward, Jacopo Sansovino and young Giulio Romano also took part in new building activities. Cardinals as well as prelates, patricians, lawyers, doctors, rich artists, and, above all, young Roman patricians, who by now had become conscious of their past, began to build small but highly sophisticated *palazzetti*. Associations comprising inhabitants of single towns or countries, such as the Florentines, the French, the Spanish, and the Sienese; guilds, such as the goldsmiths, the bakers, and the carpenters; and devotional confraternities all started to build their own churches and oratories. In a few years Rome began to acquire an urban character which it had previously lacked. If we look at the first realistic views of Renaissance Rome, be it that of the Codex Escurialiensis of about 1500 or those of the 1530s, antique ruins and medieval campaniles as well as towers of noble families and new building fragments rise in isolation above a sea of small and miserable houses, most of them not more than four or five meters high. Only during the eighteenth and nineteenth centuries did Rome acquire the coherent texture that we admire today. But Leo X and his talented architects doubtless appreciated their contemporary problem and tried to solve it.[24]

Much less successful were Leo's own projects. His first initiative in 1513 was to double the dimension of the already monumental Julian project for the new St. Peter's and to use much more travertine and marble than his economical predecessor had proposed. Thus the costs rose so enormously that at the end of

24 Hermann Egger, *Römische Veduten* (Vienna, 1931), II, pl. 104, 105, 106, 107; Richard Krautheimer, *Roma Alessandrina: The Remapping of Rome under Alexander VII* (Poughkeepsie, N.Y., 1982).

Leo's pontificate work had hardly proceeded and many doubted whether it would ever be finished. Leo's tendency to enrich and thus appropriate the projects of his predecessor succeeded only on a smaller scale, as in the Vatican Loggie which Raphael transformed into a luxurious *"Gesamtkunstwerk."* In order to give Via Giulia a new center of gravity and a new meaning, Leo replaced Julius' Palazzo dei Tribunali with the pantheon-like church of San Giovanni dei Fiorentini at its northern end. Raphael himself, although not a Florentine, wanted to build his new palace opposite this new church, and Antonio da Sangallo the Younger his next to it, the only one of these projects to be realized. The southern end of Via Giulia acquired a new focus with the palace of Cardinal Alessandro Farnese, an old friend and recent relative of Leo. From its inception in 1514 it was meant to be the seat of the rising Farnese dynasty, with two apartments for Alessandro's two sons, and probably also two facades: the present one oriented toward Via Arenula and another toward the new Via Giulia. Its architect, Sangallo, was largely inspired by Bramante's abortive project for the Palazzo dei Tribunali, which Sangallo himself had helped to prepare.[25]

Even more illuminating for Leo's building policy was the new Via Ripetta (Fig. 5). It was the fourth straight street ruthlessly cut through the old Roman city since 1499. Its northern part had already been started under Julius, probably in order to provide a worthy access to his favorite church of Santa Maria del Popolo. It was certainly a happy accident that the fifteenth-century Roman residence of the Medici, the actual Palazzo Madama and Senate, was situated very close to the southern extension of Via Ripetta. Since Palazzo Madama was flanked on one side by the Roman university, the old Sapienza, and Palazzo Lante, the new house of Leo's sister-in-law, and on the other by the French national church, Luigi dei Francesi, Leo's architects had the opportunity to counterbalance Piazza del Popolo and its della Rovere church with an even more important and glorious Medicean center.[26]

25 Frommel, "Lavori architettonici," 368; Tafuri, "Roma instaurata," 94–98; Frommel, *Der römische Palastbau,* II, 265, 318; *idem,* "Raffael und Antonio da Sangallo," 264–266; *idem,* "Sangallo et Michel-ange (1513–1550)," in *Le Palais Farnèse,* I, 1, 128–129.
26 Tafuri, "Roma instaurata," 82–88.

Fig. 5 Reconstruction Project of 1516/17 for Via Ripetta, Rome.

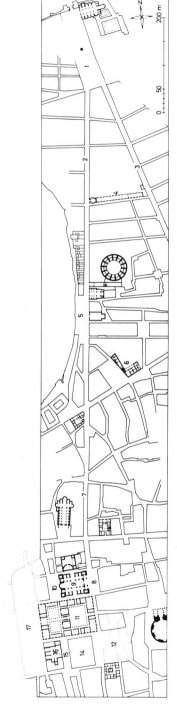

1 PIAZZA DEL POPOLO
2 VIA RIPETTA (LEONINA)
3 VIA DEL CORSO
4 OSPEDALE S GIACOMO
5 PORTA DI RIPETTA

6 PALAZZO SIGISMONDO CHIGI (THEN BORGHESE)
7 VIA DELLA SCROFA (LEONINA)
8 PIAZZA SAPONARA (S LUIGI)
9 A DA SANGALLO THE Y'S PROJECT FOR S LUIGI
10 PIAZZA S LUIGI

11 A DA SANGALLO THE Y'S FOR PAL. MEDICI-MADAMA
12 PIAZZA S. EUSTACHIO
13 PALAZZO MEDICI-LANTE
14 SAPIENZA
15 PIAZZA S GIACOMO D SPAGNOLI

16 S GIACOMO
17 PIAZZA NAVONA

SOURCE: Drawing by Helmut Peuker, Bibliotheca Hertziana, Rome.

This ambitious project also had a political impact since it coincided with Leo's attempts to establish close relations with Francis I and the house of France. Leo subsidized the renewal of the Sapienza; his kinsmen, Giuliano de'Medici and Lorenzo de'Medici, commissioned Sangallo the Younger completely to rebuild Palazzo Madama; Cardinal Giulio de'Medici in 1518 laid the first stone of San Luigi dei Francesi and the French sculptor and architect Jean de Chenevières began in the square of front of San Luigi a round monument which was adorned with the emblems and the virtues of the French king. The new Medici palace was to have two courtyards and its main façade was to overlook Piazza Navona, thus vaguely alluding to Constantine the Great's palace in Constantinople. Five different squares were to separate these splendid new buildings from each other. The other end of the road led into Piazza del Popolo, which Raphael wanted to transform into a long rectangle with an antique obelisk in the center. A series of important buildings such as the Ospedale di San Giacomo in Augusta, remodelled by Leo in 1516, different private palaces, and the monumental Orsini garden on Augustus' Mausoleum made the new Via Leonina another pinnacle of Roman Renaissance urbanism, all stressing Medici patronage.[27]

Leo's main aim, the establishment of a new urban center around the Medici palace, never came to anything after his brother Giuliano's death in 1516. Instead Cardinal Giulio, the most talented of all the Medici, undertook to immortalize Medicean patronage in Rome and started, largely assisted by his cousin Leo, the grand Villa Madama. Situated on the slope of Monte Mario just above Ponte Milvio, it became the first modern building to be seen by visitors coming from the north. It provided the ideal opportunity for both Raphael and his architecturally trained patron to realize the zenith in Renaissance architecture, a synthesis of a Medicean and an antique villa, with reconstructions of a Roman theater and Roman bath, a swimming pool, a hippodrome, and all sorts of loggias, grottoes, and architectural gardens. The surviving fragment of Villa Madama has become the most impressive Medici monument south of Florence.

27 Frommel, *Der römische Palastbau*, I, 18–19.

This short golden age of architecture ended with Leo's death, although multifarious building activities of a high standard went on even after the sack of Rome. Leo's Dutch successor, Hadrian VI, was, in the view of Leo's artists, rightly regarded an "enemy of the arts." But, strangely enough, when, after only two years, Giulio de' Medici became pope Clement VII, he did not resume his cousin's patronage. The political situation was critical and the pope had to concentrate on serious matters. Nevertheless, there was no plausible reason why he should not have finished Villa Madama; many subsequent counterreformation popes found ways to build their own huge villas. But Clement VII left its exterior even more fragmentary and poorer than we see it today. He did not progress much with St. Peter's or the Vatican buildings; nor did he start any other Roman building of importance. Instead he spent most of his money on Michelangelo's various projects for the Florentine Medici church of San Lorenzo, with its tomb chapel and the adjacent library, as well as on the pilgrim church of Loreto. Maybe the sudden extinction of the secular line of his house induced him to look for its survival in stone near to its place of origin rather than in Rome, where a successor would have been tempted to overshadow the Medici achievement.[28]

The most spectacular urban achievements of Clement's pontificate were the *tridente* (a triple fork of streets) of Piazza del Popolo and the curved facade of Banco San Spirito, both inventions of his favorite Roman architect, Sangallo the Younger. The *tridente*, the logical extension of Raphael's earlier little *bidente*, was a typically modern Roman invention, forming as it did a radiating center of urban areas which could not be organized according to the older and simpler right-angle grid system. It was repeated many times in later Roman urban development, not just schematically, but with the visual center of an obelisk or a fountain as had already been envisaged by Raphael and Sangallo the Younger. In the case of the Piazza del Popolo, however, the *tridente* ruined Raphael's project of a rectangular square and made it dif-

28 André Chastel, *Il sacco di Roma* (Turin, 1983), 121–122; Ackerman, *The Architecture of Michelangelo* (London, 1964), II, 22–42; Kathleen Weil Garris, *The Santa Casa di Loreto* (New York, 1977), I, 57–89.

ficult for subsequent planners to give the piazza a new and coherent shape.[29]

The increasing tendency of Rome's architects to conceive of the city's urban planning in visual terms was even more obvious in the concave façade of the former Zecca, the Banco San Spirito. It was perhaps the first façade completely independent from the building behind it—a sort of triumphal arch for Clement VII and for the pilgrims who would mark the forthcoming holy year of 1525. As such it was to be the visual apex for anyone coming from Ponte Sant' Angelo and moving to Via del Governo Vecchio, the old Via Papalis, or Via dei Banchi Vecchi. The façade was built by Clement's cunning chamberlain, Francesco Armellini, with taxes raised from his neighbors. Since Armellini owned the older house behind the façade, we can be sure that he did not improve it simply out of veneration for his master.[30]

If the further decline of Clement's Roman building activities after 1527 is often said to be a consequence of the sacking of Rome, his successor, Paul III Farnese (1534–1549), proved how rapidly the situation could change for the better. Paul, who was eight years older than Clement, had also lived for some time in the circle of Lorenzo il Magnifico, and his two favorite architects were also Sangallo the Younger and Michelangelo. Until his election he had exclusively employed Sangallo, whom he had already discovered in 1513 and who had built not only the family palace but many other important buildings throughout the Farnese territory around Lake Bolsena. Whereas Clement's patronage was mainly oriented toward his native Florence and favored commemorative rather than dynastic projects, Paul was a conscious Roman. Immediately after his election he buttressed his power as pope, as lord of Rome, and as head of the Farnese dynasty in a manner comparable only to Julius II to whom Paul, as Cardinal Alessandro Farnese, had been quite close. His new approach was most evident in his first building, the Torre Paolina, which he built in 1535 on the site of the antique Capitoline arch, next to Santa Maria in Aracoeli. This fortified villa served as airy adjunct and belvedere of the Palazzo Venezia, which Paul III used as his

29 Frommel, *Der römische Palastbau*, I, 22.
30 *Ibid.*, II, 35.

summer residence, the first pope to do so since the time of its builder, Paul II. It was connected by a viaduct, although a much simpler one than the Via Julia between the Vatican palace and its belvedere. Paul's next step in appropriating the Capitol was to transfer the statue of Marcus Aurelius from the Lateran in 1538. The inscriptions on its new pedestal made it clear that this emperor had been Rome's wise lord and that the pope was his legitimate successor. The outline of Michelangelo's monumental project for the *area capitolina* may already have been conceived by this date.[31]

At about the same time as the Torre Capitolina was being built, Paul commissioned the replanning of St. Peter's. Probably at Paul's request all projects envisaged a centralized plan which Julius II had given up for religious as well as functional reasons. Since the time of Nicholas V, and even since Julius II, attitudes had changed; the formal aspect of architecture had become much more important and St. Peter's was regarded more and more as an architectural monument. The aesthetic effect, which was meant to be increased by its centralization, became nearly as important as its functional one. This formalistic tendency was even increased when Paul authorized Michelangelo to destroy a good deal of what had been built before, including some of the functionally important secondary rooms, and to reshape the exterior into a unified sculptural body.[32]

In 1537 Paul founded a Farnese duchy for his son Pierluigi Farnese and commissioned Sangallo to build Castro, its new capital. The result was, before its destruction, perhaps less impressive than Rossellino's Pienza. Politically, however, it became the embryo of a new European dynasty, and the fulfillment of Alessandro Farnese's lifelong dreams.[33]

31   Giovannoni, *Antonio da Sangallo il Giovane* (Rome, 1959), I, 150–169, 210–214; Frommel, "Raffael und Antonio da Sangallo," 269; Jacob Hess, "Die päpstliche Villa bei Araceli: Ein Beitrag zur Geschichte der kapitolinischen Bauten," in *Miscellanea Bibliothecae Hertzianae* (Munich, 1961), 239–254; Ackerman, *Michelangelo*, II, 50–51; Frommel, *Michelangelo und Tommaso dei Cavalieri* (Amsterdam, 1979), 80.
32   Ackerman, *Michelangelo*, II, 85–95; Frommel, "Die Peterskirche unter Papst Julius II im Licht neuer Dokumente," *Römisches Jahrbuch für Kunstgeschichte*, XVI (1976), 89; idem, "Capella Iulia," 51–60.
33   Hildegard Giess, "Die Stadt Castro und die Pläne von Antonio da Sangallo dem Jüngeren, II," in *Römisches Jahrbuch für Kunstgeschichte*, XIX (1981), 85–140.

The other symbol of Paul's dynastic ambition, the Roman Palazzo Farnese, was continued in its original dimensions only after 1540. Sangallo transformed its interior into a *"palazzo non più da Cardinale, ma da Pontefice"* (no longer a cardinal's palace, but a pope's). For the same reason a huge regular piazza was laid out in front of it, as large as the palace itself and bigger than any such piazza before. Its main axis was extended to the Via Papalis and, according to Michelangelo's plan of 1546, it would have continued across the garden and a new bridge, up to the Farnese vineyard in Trastevere. Most of it was paid for by the Apostolic Chamber, although neither Castro nor the Palazzo Farnese were meant to be papal property. This new emphasis on a longitudinal axis even in the more private sphere of the Farnese gardens is another illuminating symptom of formalization in Roman urbanism. This axis was not important for improving the traffic flow, as had been the aim of the Via Alessandrina, the Via Giulia, and the Via Ripetta; it was meant to impress people (Fig. 6).[34]

This high degree of formalization was even more evident in Michelangelo's monumental project for the Capitol, which he may already have designed for Paul, but which was executed only after 1560. For Michelangelo it was no longer sufficient to counterbalance existing buildings with new ones, as had been the case in all earlier Roman squares; to distinguish the different functions and significance of two lateral palaces as Rossellino had done in Pienza; or to envelop preexisting structures with surrounding porticoes as in Vigevano or Ascoli Piceno. Michelangelo reshaped the two existing buildings and, primarily for reasons of symmetry, added a third which was to house the Sala del Consiglio. Thus he created, more impressively than had anyone before, the image of hierarchically organized power. A new street, the actual Via Capitolina, led axially to the ramp. Already climbing up this ramp one feels grandeur and elevation. Once on the square the eyes progressively are led to the dominant Palazzo dei Senatori. In its central loggia planned by Michelangelo, the senator, as the pope's vicar, was to appear to the obedient crowd.[35]

---

34 Frommel, "Sangallo et Michel-Ange," 145–174; Giorgio Vasari (ed. Gaetano Milanesi), *Le vite de' piu eccellenti pittori scultori ed architettori* (Florence, 1880), V, 469–470; Frommel, *Palazzi Romani del Rinascimento.*

35 Harmen Thies, *Michelangelo: Das Kapitol* (Munich, 1982), 216–236.

Fig. 6 Michelangelo's Reconstruction Project around Palazzo Farnese.

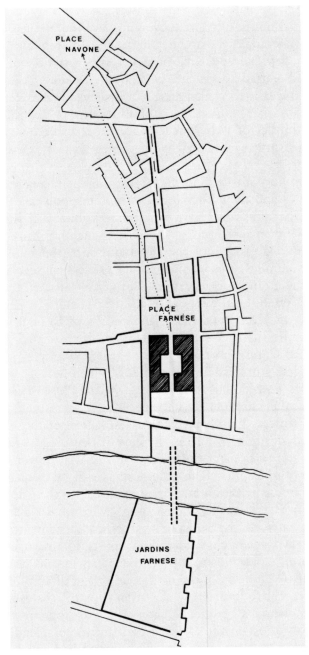

SOURCE: Map by Luigi Spezzaferro in *Le Palais Farnèse* (Rome, 1981), I, 1, 120, Fig. 10.

Each individual element of Michelangelo's project stressed the hierarchical nature of papal power, as was made explicit by the imperial figure of Marcus Aurelius and the inscription on its pedestal. It marked the architectural defeat of republican autonomy, the final consequence of papal appropriation of the city which had started so much more cautiously under Nicholas V. By the time that Michelangelo's Capitol was realized, the Holy See had lost its significance as a European power and as the potential unifier of Italy, but it had gained absolute power over its capital. Roman bipolarity had become primarily a formal phenomenon.

Thus, notwithstanding the contrasting characters of Renaissance popes and their discontinuous building policies, there was a continuity and even a sort of regular evolution in Roman urbanism. Roman urbanism of the Renaissance not only reflected the continuous process of the city's appropriation by the popes and their families, but also a gradual process of secularization, beautification, and formalization. But above all it was a gradual process of embuing the city with an imperial aura.

If the motives, tendencies, and results of Roman urbanism during the Renaissance seem to be rather obvious, their transformation into art remains mysterious. The best example, again, was Michelangelo's project for the Capitol, which he conceived only a few years after having risked his life for the Florentine republic, which was then conquered by the pope and his kinsmen. At about the same time as he glorified the assassination of the Florentine duke Alessandro de' Medici in the bust of Brutus, he had to obey the pope and to transfer the symbol of imperial power from the Lateran to the Capitol. The grandiose axis of his project for the Palazzo Farnese or the authoritarian hierarchy of the Capitol were certainly not invented by the old pope who, for so many years, had been satisfied by Sangallo's rather conservative structures; they were Michelangelo's individual answer to a particular papal commission. Consciously or not, Michelangelo thus became one of the artistic pioneers of the forthcoming age of absolutism.

During the following two centuries Roman urbanism reached its climax. Rome's baroque squares and radiating street systems overshadow most of the earlier achievements in splendor, monumentality, and coherence. The urbanism of Renaissance Rome, so overwhelming in its final result, reflects not only the classic-style grandeur of the popes, but also their egocentric spontaneity, their will to overshadow their predecessor at any cost, to print their own mark on the city, and to eternalize the glory of their family. But most of these monumental squares, from Piazza Navona and St. Peter's Square to Piazza Sant' Ignazio and Piazza di Spagna, now have a religious focus. The patron himself is no longer glorified, save as the patron as faithful subject of the church.

Randolph Starn

Reinventing Heroes in Renaissance Italy
Renaissance Italy saw one of the great bursts of heroic image-making in the history of public art. The patriotic icon, the portrait cycle of culture heroes, and the equestrian monument all emerged in their characteristic post-classical Western forms in this context. More exactly, they emerged with what can be understood as the reinvention of the male figure as a primary host, talisman, and exemplar of strategic social and political interests. This process of recovery and appropriation cuts across the usual classification of works of art by different media and genres; it also suggests connections and continuities where historians, if they refer to art at all, tend to see discrete situations and particular cases.[1]

The Italian city-states came relatively late to their uneasy independence, with few incontrovertible heroes of their own. Sanctity, chivalry, and scholastic learning defined the highest values long after the textbook triumphs of the new civic culture, and the authority of popes, emperors, and kings was admitted to be superior. By these standards these civic communes of the twelfth and thirteenth centuries, and even later regimes, with their highly developed republican or princely institutions, remained technically provisional, notoriously open to political change, and without clearly defined standing either among themselves or in their relations with outside powers. Burckhardt took this "illegitimacy" to be a driving force in the development of Italian Renaissance culture—in those areas where the Italians were lacking, they

Randolph Starn is Professor of History at the University of California, Berkeley. He is the author of *Contrary Commonwealth: The Theme of Exile in Medieval and Renaissance Italy* (Berkeley, 1982).

This article was written in conjunction with work in progress (and in collaboration with Loren Partridge) on audience halls in medieval and Renaissance Italy. For valuable suggestions the author thanks Thomas Laqueur, and members of his graduate seminar at Berkeley, in particular William Connell, Helen Ettlinger, and Carol Staswick.

1 For classic analyses of the "hero function," see Vladimir I. Propp (trans. Laurence Scott), *Morphology of the Folktale,* (Austin, 1968; 2nd ed.), 51–58; F. R. Raglan, *The Hero* (London, 1936), 3–16.

made or revived artistic and literary forms that put a dazzling layer of cultural finish over chronic shortcomings. Current research emphasizes the continuities, constraints, and strategies of social control underlying what Burckhardt saw as yet another demonstration of Renaissance individualism. But the notion of a persistent need for legitimating identity is an apt characterization for the appropriation of heroic figures, a kind of symbolic bodysnatching, which became a major theme of Renaissance art in Italy.[2]

This process can be understood as a matter of meeting the competition. Through the great ideological lenses of the Middle Ages, social structures were perceived either as a single body or as a series of corporate groups. In descending hierarchical order, priests were custodians of Christ's body; secular rulers of the body politic temporarily resident in them; and nobles, with martial duties, property, and epic lore embodied in blood and lineage. This bio-political schema of the *corpus Christianum* relegated towns to the physical trunk, the sustaining but inferior and dependent zone of the third estate. They were endowed with head, spirit, and arms only by virtue of their submission to the higher estates.[3]

The communal governments of the Italian city-states originated between the eleventh and thirteenth centuries as more or less voluntary associations in which private interests and public functions were combined or, in the language of medieval sociability, "incorporated." In the eyes of the traditionally superior authorities, the communes were unruly assemblies, without a proper head or a fit nobility. Even to their own citizens they seemed at times shapeless legal fictions comprising discrete institutions and rivalling other, more powerful, allegiances embodied in the family, neighborhood, guild, business company, or religious confraternity.[4]

2 Jakob Burckhardt (trans. S. G. C. Middlemore), *The Civilization of the Renaissance in Italy* (New York, 1958), I, 9–11. The best single guide to more recent views is the Einaudi *Storia d'Italia* (Turin, 1972), I, II. For the major views on the symbolic uses of the body, see Jonathan Benthall and Ted Polhemus (eds.), *The Body as a Medium of Expression* (New York, 1975). For use of bodily metaphors in the Renaissance, see Leonard Barkan, *Nature's Work of Art: The Human Body as Image of the World* (New Haven, 1975).
3 Ernst Kantorowicz, *The King's Two Bodies: A Study in Medieval Political Theology* (Princeton, 1957); Georges Duby (trans. Arthur Goldhammer), *The Three Orders: Feudal Society Imagined* (Chicago, 1981).
4 Lauro Martines, *Power and Imagination: City-States in Renaissance Italy* (New York,

How, then, could the city-states have heroes of their own making in a world where authority was thought to be a kind of incarnation? How could they not have them? We have been obliged to give up much of the grand vision of the Italian communes as republics bearing the torch of liberty during the dark ages of priests and kings. Two generations of historians have shown that these communities were jointly controlled by a mixed elite; that they bought, sold, and negotiated their independence more often than they won it; and that they were generally patriarchal and conservative. Although they occasionally fought for recognition or in self-defense, these were not institutions to mount extreme revolutionary challenges to established symbols of authority. Yet realist interpretations often show inadvertently that social conflicts alone do not make or legitimate a government. One result of analyzing social interests in all their concreteness and particularity is the demonstration that symbols are needed to bridge the gaps. In this sense, the stock of heroic figures in civic iconography is a measure of new aspirations and not simply a defensive response.[5]

When Dante has Pia de' Tolomei proclaim "Siena made me," we are close both to a heroic personification of communal life and to the problem of producing it. Dante's Pia projects the community as a figurative subject capable of "making" citizens. But Siena remains an abstraction. If the community had been adequately pictured, the result would likely have been androgynous and disjointed, an anatomical grotesque rather than a heroic figure. The republican commune was in one sense a shapeless legal fiction; it was also the collectivity within and near the city walls. In yet another sense, it was a congeries of factions, institutions, and perceptions which were too peculiarly shaped to be represented as an organic whole; to personify authority in a single figure was to threaten a republican ethos which called for political decentralization and collective decision-making. Moreover, the distinctive urban activities based on business, voluntary associa-

1979), 7–71. For important studies of a particular case, the first emphasizing civic identity and the other politics, see Richard C. Trexler, *Public Life in Renaissance Florence* (New York, 1980); John Najemy, *Corporatism and Consensus in Florentine Electoral Politics, 1280–1400* (Chapel Hill, 1982).

5 For the realist interpretation, see Sergio Bertelli, *Il potere oligarchico nello stato-città medievale* (Florence, 1979). For the ritualist interpretation, see Trexler, *Public Life*.

tion, and the written word were held to be inorganic because they could be called into being and changed at will Money and the mechanisms of finance were particularly suspect since they were so obviously artificial and so frequently disruptive of traditional relationships. In these pre-capitalist conceptions of economics, money was a mere sign, unable to reproduce itself organically like human generations and traditions. Such ideas were not conducive to powerful new analogies between the body and the conduct of social and political life—in important respects, the communal experience was not suited to generating heroic imagery. The most celebrated scenes of communal life, the frescoes of "good and bad government" by Ambrogio Lorenzetti in the Palazzo Pubblico at Siena (1338–1340), are notable for the heterogeneous assemblage of anecdotal scenes and didactic symbols.[6]

The problem was not so much to imagine heroes as to represent them in appropriate forms. Every town had its legendary or actual worthies; people remembered the feats of Guelph and Ghibelline champions, prodigies of sanctity, virtue, and learning, ancestors dignified more than they deserved, and so forth. The quickening recovery of classical sources expanded the range of literary and iconographical possibilities beyond the already considerable resources of chivalric culture. With the erosion of communal institutions and the conversions of the party boss, ambitious noble, or upstart oligarch into princes, cults of personality and dynasty and the cultivation of the rhetoric and iconography of heroism were often inseparable. None of this may be at issue. But the city-states had to borrow and transform models for representing heroes—in particular for the body heroic—from rival sources of authority. In the following pages we shall look at three such transformations.

Let us start, as civic imagery often did, with the figure of the civic saint. As the devotional image, shrine, and relic have come into the domains of cultural anthropology and social history, we have learned to appreciate how the civic authorities claimed and

6 Dante Alighieri, *Divina Commedia, Purgatorio,* V, 134, in Manfredi Porena and Mario Pazzaglia (eds.), *Opere* (Bologna, 1966), 385. For the perennial methodological differences between historians of art and historians of society, see Michael Baxandall's discussion of the Lorenzetti frescoes in "Art, Society, and the Bouguer Principle," *Representations,* 12 (1985), 32–43.

used the bodies of the saints. Civic saints guarded boundaries or extended them, overcoming rival cults. They interceded for the towns they protected; they modeled the proper ties of mutual service and dependence that were supposed to bind patrons and their clients. These were concrete, human functions, performed by once-living human beings who acted as Christian heroes. It would have been as difficult to imagine their good works disembodied as it would be to picture a bodiless Hercules.[7]

There were few Italian towns of importance which did not claim legendary founders and re-founders. In these tales, heroes and saints succeed one another, overlap and exchange places, always claiming or affirming a transfer of authority. An archetypal race of founders might include not only Aeneas but a whole diaspora of Trojan worthies and a pioneering early Christian saint or a later reforming one. The Venetians, for example, had their founding set of Trojan warrior-heroes and their St. Mark, whose most serious competition as a domineering civic patron was Rome's St. Peter. The story of the body of St. Mark, stolen from Alexandria to fulfill the prophecy given to him in a storm in the lagoon (which he surely never saw), is a classic of its kind, made exotic by the eastern connection and by the tenacious literalness of the Venetians in matters of state. No one really knows whether a *translatio* of the body or of some relic of the saint actually occurred in the 820s, but the various interpretations of historians point clearly enough to tactics of arrogation. St. Mark made claims on the spiritual authority of the rival patriarchates of Aquileia and Grado, challenged the influence of the Franks, stood above the local autonomies of other towns and islands around the lagoon, and gave the doge a claim to apostolic sanction like that of the pope from St. Peter. An anecdote told by Burckhardt underscores the interchangeability of saints and heroes with grisly humor: not knowing how to reward a soldier who had saved them from defeat, the citizens of a certain town supposedly decided to kill him and worship him as a saint.[8]

7 Peter Brown, *The Cult of the Saints* (Chicago, 1981), 86–105; Heinrich Peyer, *Stadt und Stadtpatron in mittelaltlichen Italien* (Zurich, 1955); Alba Maria Orselli, *L'idea e il culto del santo patrono cittadino della letteratura latina cristiana* (Bologna, 1965).
8 For St. Mark, see Edward Muir, *Civic Ritual in Renaissance Venice* (Princeton, 1981), 67–69, 78–92. For the recurrence of myths of origins in Venetian art, see Patricia Fortini Brown, "Painting and History in Renaissance Venice," *Art History*, VII (1984), 263–294. Burckhardt, *Civilization*, 12.

The most celebrated hero in all of Renaissance art provides one of the best illustrations of the absorption or, more exactly, reincorporation of sacred figures in a civic frame. In 1504, Michelangelo's *David* was transferred from the cathedral workshop to its place beside the main portal of the Palazzo Vecchio at the civic center of public life in Florence. Behind the actual event lay lines of artistic descent and political interest that go directly to the early fifteenth century and can easily be extended much farther back to trace a remarkable confluence of precedents and programs in Michelangelo's work.[9]

The story of the *David* is one of the best-known stories in the art-historical literature. Along the most direct line of descent, the statue is the culmination of a longstanding sculptural program for a series of prophet figures on the buttresses of the cathedral of Florence. The idea may have originated early in the fourteenth century, perhaps with Giotto di Bondone; in any case, a large terracotta Joshua by Donatello had been placed on the north side of the cathedral around 1412, and Agostino di Duccio, commissioned in 1464 to continue the program with a marble David, actually began to carve the famous block which was left in a rough state until it was given by the cathedral works to Michelangelo in 1501. This line of prophets intersects at the cathedral with a line of Hercules figures. One, a colossal figure in terracotta, was possibly set up on the south side around 1464. A famous relief of Hercules from the 1390s ornamented the north portal of the cathedral; this figure has been associated in turn with the allegorical Fortitude-Hercules by Nicola Pisano at Pisa (c. 1260) and the Hercules on an early Florentine seal. There are also related traditions—notably the line of Florentine Davids from Donatello to Andrea del Verrocchio and the ancient colossi known from literary descriptions and surviving examples in Rome.

When art historians assert that Michelangelo's *David* reflects the influence of Donatello's *St. George,* which scholars have also regarded as a "crypto-David," it is difficult to see where the genetic pool of sculptural motifs and historical sources is supposed to end. The same is true of the iconographical possibilities that such composite associations bring to mind, from the fortitude of

9 Charles Seymour, Jr., *Michelangelo's David: A Search for Identity* (Pittsburgh, 1967); N. Randolph Parks, "The Placement of Michelangelo's *David*: A Review of the Documents," *Art Bulletin*, LVI (1975), 560–570.

Fig. 1   Michelangelo, *David,* 1501–1504.

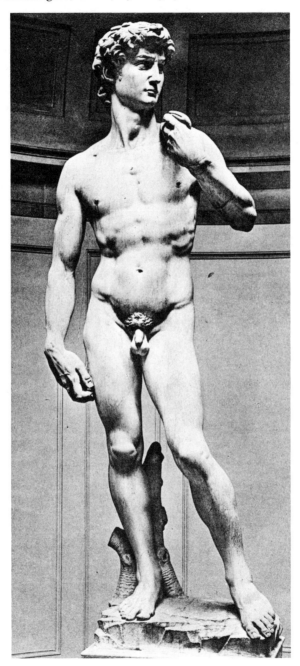

SOURCE: Accademia, Florence.

Hercules, to the justice of David, to the suggestions of divinity and salvation that forerunners of Christ signify in standard Christian exegesis. And beyond or, more exactly, beneath the learned interpretations of the art historians, the people of Florence would surely have seen in Michelangelo's work something of the carnivalesque giants, the sexual swagger, and the unfulfilled corporality of popular politics and popular culture.[10]

The figure of Michelangelo's *David* was a manifestation of accumulated charges of heroic form and significance. The patriotic icon took on sacred imagery and conflated and inflated symbolic codes. Since the figure embodied so much symbolic power, drawn from such varied sources, it was easily adaptable to different contexts as the political milieu changed. The *David* was commissioned from Michelangelo at a time of particular danger for the Florentine republic that had been restored in 1494. Moving it from the cathedral workshop was virtually a translation of an icon to the civic center. Once located, after much discussion, outside the Palazzo Vecchio, it symbolically threatened the enemies and rallied the friends of the regime. Yet after their victories over the republic in the 1530s, the Medici dukes left the statue where the republicans had placed it—one more tribute to the uncanny ability of the family to capture the symbols of the republic. Michelangelo's work was paired with a hulking (princely) Hercules crushing a cowering (republican) Cacus in the much-maligned sculptural group by Baccio Bandinelli. Finally, Giorgio Vasari chose to perceive the *David* as emblematic of the palace, the occupant of which was his patron, Cosimo de' Medici.[11]

We find analogous patterns of displacement and substitution in a second kind of hero-image—the portrait cycle of "illustrious men," which was a major genre in Italian painting after the later fourteenth century. Here it is the so-called Nine Worthies whose position was challenged. These chivalric heroes-in-chief made their appearance as a well-defined group in literature and art early in the fourteenth century. They were represented as champions of the "three laws": Joshua, David, and Judas Maccabeus of the Old Testament; Hector, Alexander, and Julius Caesar of pagan

10 Horst W. Janson, *The Sculpture of Donatello* (Princeton, 1963; 2nd ed.), 28.
11 See Seymour, *Michelangelo's David*, 58–59; Virginia L. Bush, "Bandinelli's *Hercules and Cacus* and Florentine Traditions," in Henry A. Millon (ed.), *Studies in Italian Art and Architecture* (Cambridge, Mass., 1980), 163–206.

law; Arthur, Charlemagne, and Godfrey de Bouillon of the new dispensation. While organizing scattered traditions in a transcendant pattern, the scheme of the Nine Worthies, by dividing history into three ages of model knights, also codified the position of the chivalric hero. In the borderland between legend and history, he was first and foremost a warrior-chieftain. His virtues— prowess, loyalty, largesse, *courtoisie*—manifested themselves in deeds, his gestures were formulaic, and his formalities were those of all true knights. In this way the mission of chivalry, like the formal motifs of chivalric culture in song, literature, and art, or the ideal feudal tenure, could be regarded as a legacy passed on through time. Poets—for reasons of patronage or conviction— vied to name the tenth worthy, who was supposed to belong to and fulfill the same tradition as the first.[12]

This medieval conviction that the exemplary person could be replicated was also fundamental in the Renaissance. Almost by definition, Renaissance culture was committed to revivals and reproductions, not simply of ideas, but of those revered figures who embodied them. Collections of written biographies and images of *viri illustres* or *uomini famosi* were the outcome. Such works have an authentic Renaissance founder in Petrarch; and a proper culmination in Paolo Giovio's sixteenth-century portrait gallery. There is no better rationale for this genre than one of the first, a preface by Petrarch's literary executor dedicating his master's collection of Roman biographies, together with his own additions, to Francesco da Carrara, lord of Padua. A painted cycle based largely on adaptations from the biographies was evidently complete in the Carrara palace at the time of its dedication in 1379:

> As an ardent lover of the virtues, you have extended hospitality to these *viri illustres*, not only in your heart and mind, but also very magnificently in the most beautiful part of your palace. According to the custom of the ancients you have honored them with gold and purple, and with images and inscriptions you have set them up for admiration. . . . [You] have given them outward expression

---

12 See Horst Schroeder, *Der Topos der Nine Worthies in Literatur und Bildener Kunst* (Göttingen, 1971); Eugene Vance, "Roland and the Poetics of Memory," in Josué Harari (ed.), *Textual Strategies: Perspectives in Post-Structuralist Criticism* (Ithaca, 1979), 374–409; Howard Bloch, *Etymologies and Genealogies: A Literary Anthropology of the French Middle Ages* (Chicago, 1983), 64–108.

in the form of most excellent pictures, so that you may always keep in sight these men whom you are eager to love because of the greatness of their deeds.[13]

This passage might have been written of a cycle of Worthies, a possibility that makes the differences in program all the more striking. Although Petrarch's early plans for the project included biblical heroes, his *illustri* were eventually limited to Roman military men, statesmen, and emperors—presumably on his principle that the only good history was Roman history. This break with the medieval rule of continuity eliminated figures from the Bible and Christian history. By implication, the ancients were neither linked to the present by unbroken descent nor subject to the foreordained design of Providence. But although Petrarch's scheme was in this sense more restrictive than the chivalric counterpart, it was also more expansive. Petrarch went beyond kings and emperors to include republican heroes; he admired qualities of statesmanship as well as martial skills. Most important, he made virtue his criterion of achievement—not only the conventional list of good deeds classified under the rubrics of cardinal and theological virtues, but the self-disciplined, well-schooled, and carefully externalized deportment of the ancients who had once been living classics.[14]

There were few, if any, rooms of *uomini famosi* on strictly Petrarchan lines after the Padua cycle was almost completely destroyed by fire in the fifteenth century. However, no subsequent Nine Worthy cycles are known in Italy, with the exception of one (1418–1430) by a French painter in the castle of Manta near Saluzzo in Piedmont. Instead there was a population explosion of second and third generations of famous men and famous women painted in communal structures, in private palaces and villas, and in the great halls or studies of princes. There were as many as 300 in the Palazzo Orsini in Rome (completed 1432), and as few as the six famous Florentines painted with three legendary hero-

13 Theodor E. Mommsen, "Petrarch and the Decoration of the Sala Virorum Illustrium," *Art Bulletin*, XXXIV (1952), 95–116; Christiane L. Joost-Gaugier, "The Early Beginnings of the Notion of 'Uomini Famosi' and the 'De Viris Illustribus' in Greco-Roman Literary Tradition," *Artibus et Historiae*, 6 (1982), 97–115. Dedication to Francesco da Carrara quoted in Mommsen, "Petrarch and the Decoration," 96.
14 See, e.g., Mommsen, "Petrarch's Conception of the Dark Ages," *Speculum*, XVII (1952), 226–240.

ines by Andrea del Castagno (between 1447 and 1451) in the Villa Carducci at Legnaia near Florence. "Good Romans" were still preferred and the majority were still statesmen and soldiers; yet space was also given to poets, scholars, and other civic luminaries. In Florence, for example, Dante, Petrarch, and Giovanni Boccaccio appeared in at least four separate painted cycles; Filippo Brunelleschi and Giotto were among the famous Florentines whose busts (1447, 1490) were mounted along the inside walls of the cathedral (Fig. 2). Heroism was still embodied in exemplary figures, but they multiplied outside a special caste or calling. In principle, at least, it was sufficient to win renown in the republic of virtue and talent. A hero need never have lifted a sword or performed the *beau geste*. We are close here to the library frieze or museum corridor with their lineup of culture heroes or even to the modern media stars whose bodies are billboards for the latest claim to fame.[15]

The third genre we need to consider was the quintessential heroic type—the equestrian monument. Perhaps we have not really been able to believe in heroes since the triumph of the internal combustion engine. The main lines of the history of this genre clearly establish the crucial place of Renaissance Italy. From the Lombard horse-and-rider tombs of the fourteenth century to Francesco Mochi's Baroque monuments, which give the Piazza dei Cavalli in Piacenza its name, virtually all of the possibilities of this genre were explored in Italy. Leonardo da Vinci alone nearly exhausted the repertory, and Donatello's *Gattamelata* (1447–1453) and Verrocchio's *Colleoni* (1479–1496) are practically emblematic of the Renaissance. The great exemplars were monuments to mercenary soldiers whose technical skills and ceremonial presence were both essential to the city-states and, with the professionalization of warfare, impossible for citizens to provide on their own. The equestrian figure was a means of recuperating political authority and prestige through the body heroic—or better, through two bodies, horse and rider.[16]

A recent controversy has plunged art historians inadvertently into these issues. The fresco traditionally known as *Guidoriccio da*

15 Mommsen, "Petrarch and the Decoration," 115; Joost-Gaugier, "The Early Beginnings," 112.
16 See Janson, "The Equestrian Monument from Cangrande della Scala to Peter the Great," in *idem, Sixteen Studies* (New York, 1973), 157–188.

Fig. 2 Andrea del Castagno, *Francesco Petrarca*, c. 1450.

SOURCE: Uffizi Gallery, Florence.

Fogliano at the Siege of Montemassi, dated c. 1330, in the great council hall of the Palazzo Pubblico at Siena, has long been considered the prime incunabulum of Renaissance equestrian portraits and a masterpiece by Simone Martini (Fig. 3). One of the few points of agreement at present is that this fresco is not the only survivor of a whole series of painted castles which served as records and trophies of the conquest of feudal strongholds by the hired captains of Siena. Another fresco showing another castle and two large enigmatic figures has been discovered beneath the first as a result of a heated imbroglio. It has been argued that the so-called *Guidoriccio* is neither by Simone nor a contemporary tribute by the republic of Siena—that, indeed, the painting may well be a pastiche of some later century. The whole controversy illustrates the characteristically touchy relationship between community and *condottiere*.[17]

Suspicion, celebration, mutual dependence, and contempt—the discordant strains in such relationships—run through the evidence. A surviving record of payments in May 1330 to "Maestro Simone dipentore" for painting the castles of Montemassi and Sassoforte does not mention a figure of Guidoriccio, although he was the Sienese commander at Montemassi (1328); neither does any other early source, including descriptions of the palace. We do know, however, that Guidoriccio left town in 1333, disgraced and in debt after being dismissed as captain-general—and that he returned in the same capacity between 1348 and his death in 1352. One of the arguments against the traditional identification of the mounted figure as Guidoriccio is that it would not have survived his disgrace. One of the reasons given to account for the over-painting of the newly recovered fresco is that one of *its* figures is Guidoriccio, complete with signs of scarred plaster suggesting that the portrait was intentionally defaced. None of this conjecture would be plausible but for the intense cross-currents that revolved around the *condottiere* in practically every city-state.

The crucial question is: how can civilians—that complicated category that dates only from the clear separation of civil and military functions in the post-medieval world—supervise professional military men, with their technological expertise and com-

17 For full bibliography and a concise summary of the Guidoriccio issues, see Alice Sedgwick Wohl, "In Siena, an Old Masterpiece Challenged, a New One Discovered," *News from RILA*, 2 (1984), 1–4.

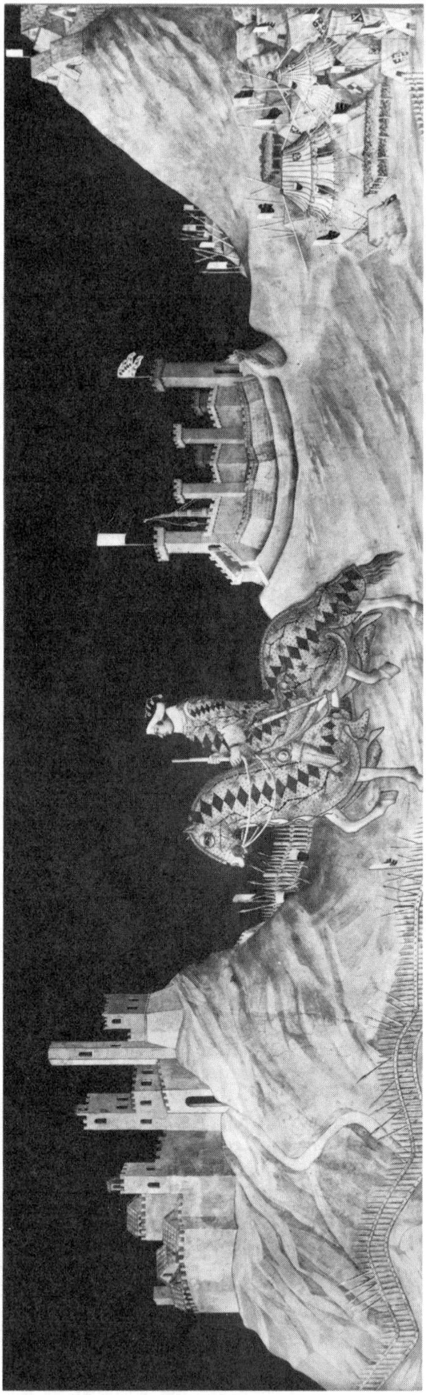

Fig. 3   Simone Martini(?), *Guidoriccio da Fogliano at the Siege of Montemassi(?)*, c. 1330(?).

SOURCE: Palazzo Pubblico, Siena.

mand of force? Renaissance answers tended, despite Niccolò Machiavelli's plans for a citizen's militia, toward a division of labor which left the professional to face the dangers and the homefront to finance the campaign, inspect the troops, and mobilize the propaganda. In the intimate animosities of this relationship, each side was anxious to be rid of the other but was unable to let it go. The *condottiere* was a free agent, yet, for his term of service, a dependent; mistrusted as a hireling but the champion of communal expansion and the bulwark of security; feared as a strongman but admired for the same reason as a strutting cynosure of communal pride and as a high-priced investment. Nevertheless, for all the uncertainties in the affair of Guidoriccio, it is clear enough that the effigy of the captain could be disposed of as the real person could not, that the soldier could withdraw but that, besides the pursestrings, the commune controlled the means whereby he would either be remembered or forgotten, celebrated or consigned to oblivion.[18]

The Florentines, inconsistent and obsessive, generally waited years—then perfunctorily painted a few *condottieri*. But the Venetians were masters of this political art, which they exercised in combination with regular contracts, concessions of territory and titles to their soldiers, and a watchful civilian administration. The major equestrian monuments by Donatello and Verrocchio were put up in Venetian territory. The first and most influential of these, Donatello's *Gattamelata,* was as much a monument of the soldier overtaken by the state as it was a monument to the baker's son from Umbria who had acquired wealth and a castle after nine years' service under the Serenissima. The statue stands in Padua on the edge of the square of the Santo, the Franciscan pilgrimage church of Sant' Antonio (Fig. 4). It has never been proven that there was official funding—we know that a state funeral was held, complete with the fashionable humanist euology—but even in the unlikely event that the heirs paid the entire cost, such a project must have had the express approval of the highest authorities, given the cautious policies of the Venetians toward *condottieri* and

18 See Charles C. Bayley, *War and Society in Renaissance Florence: The* De Militia *of Leonardo Bruni* (Toronto, 1961); Michael Mallett, *Mercenaries and their Masters: Warfare in Renaissance Italy* (Totowa, N.J., 1974); Starn and Partridge, "Representing War in the Renaissance: The Shield of Paolo Uccello," *Representations,* 5 (1984), 32–65.

Fig. 4 Donatello, *Gattamelata*, 1447–1453.

SOURCE: Piazza del Santo, Padua.

subject cities such as Padua. But even if we cannot be certain of the written record, we can see how the play of formal details and symbolic associations claims Donatello's *Gattamelata* for the state.[19]

19 For Venice, see Mallett and John R. Hale, *The Military Organization of a Renaissance State: Venice c. 1400 to 1617* (Cambridge, 1984). For Donatello, see Janson, *Sculpture of Donatello*, 151–161; Sunnie Evers, "The Equestrian Monument as the Commemoration of the Individual and as a Statement of Political Propaganda in Florence and Venice in the Fifteenth Century," unpub. ms. (Univ. of Calif., 1978); Cristelle Baskins, "Mediating Virtue: The Image of the *Condottiere* and Donatello's *Gattamelata* in Padua, 1447–59," unpub. ms. (Univ. of Calif., 1983).

The great models of the free-standing equestrian monument were permeated with the aura of empire and the mystique of Rome—most notably, in Italy, the *Marcus Aurelius* in Rome and the so-called *Regisole* in the cathedral square in Pavia. Medieval and Renaissance equestrian monuments in Italy were always commemorative; in medieval times they were tomb sculptures and hence located in or near the burial church. The artistic repertory of horse-and-rider types was most fully elaborated in battle scenes, which until Donatello's time meant that battles were still represented (and actually fought) with an emphasis on encounters of men-at-arms in knightly trappings (however pseudo-chivalric they may have seemed).

This background charges the borrowed associations at work in the *Gattamelata* with significance. The earliest known description of the monument refers to it as "a triumphant Caesar"; other fifteenth-century sources complain that it is too antique for a contemporary commander and even more pretentious than the Romans would have allowed. This perception corresponds to what we can see for ourselves. *Gattamelata* obviously has its Roman prototypes and can rightly be compared to them in terms of form—but surely not of form alone. The aura of imperial domination associated with the classical models must have worked to transform this monument into a perceived emblem of Venetian empire, conspicuously so when placed in the pilgrimage square of Venice's chief subject-city.

Drawing upon another line of associations, this monument, with funeral motifs such as the doors in the base deriving from mausoleum doors on Roman sarcophagi, is a cenotaph which has migrated from the usual burial context to the square outside the church. In effect, the body of the individual who left money and heirs to provide the tomb and other observances has been resurrected in effigy in an open, public space, one of the most sacred in all Italy. The symbolic reflection, absorption, and supervision of the potency of the shrine and the church can hardly be missed and could not have been more consistent with the official cult of the republic of St. Mark.

Finally, the sculptural details portray Gattamelata as a late-medieval warrior—for example, the structure of the "antique" armor, which experts maintain actually corresponds to contemporary pieces; and the fantastic cats' heads on the saddle, helmet, and pedestal which were the armorial transcription of his name in good medieval fashion. Epitaphs written for or about the monument refer, with less than perfect candor, to the "loyalty" or "faithfulness" of the man, that most admired chivalric virtue. Yet these knightly attributes became aspects of the monument and instruments of the fictive body of the state that occupied the figurative body of the hero.

Some ten years ago the art historian Janson claimed that, from a "post-heroic" age, our best response to monuments for long-dead heroes is nostalgia for the "Faith of our Fathers." But such monuments are not so much projections of faith as products of hard work, unsentimental interests, and what it is tempting to call in this context "interdisciplinary activism." In Renaissance Italy, it was well understood that heroes were not born but made—or, rather, re-made. Renaissance Italians were unwilling simply to accept received disciplines insofar as heroes were concerned; by transforming the imagery that they had inherited, they reappropriated the figure of the hero to display the claims of their own power, ideology, and art.[20]

20 Janson, *The Rise and Fall of the Public Monument* (New Orleans, 1976), 1, 52; Lawrence Alloway, "Public Sculpture for the Post-Heroic Age," *Art in America* (Oct., 1979), 9.

J. R. Hale

The Soldier in Germanic Graphic Art of the

Renaissance The individualized soldier, the infantryman, made a late first appearance in the arts. Although wars could not have been fought without him, in ancient and medieval art he remained a notational cypher. He could not pay his way into the visual record, as could the centurion or the knight; but he was also absent because, unlike serving women, jugglers, friars, peasants, and huntsmen, he was not wanted there.

Around 1500, in Switzerland and southern Germany, this conspiracy of silence was broken. In drawings and prints, glass painting and sculpture, the soldier emerged as a type, often strongly individualized; as a stereotype, familiar and real enough to bear a considerable weight of moral and allegorical resonance; and as a member of an occupational group whose appearance, way of life, and relationships with comrades, civilians, and women were of avid if perturbing interest. By the end of the 1530s, artists had enabled us to know the soldier through visual evidence as we cannot know the practitioners of any other pursuit.[1]

This focus on the reality of military service was all the more remarkable because warfare's previous representative figure—the knight—was never just a man-at-arms; whether on tombs or in stained glass or in illumination, he was also chieftain, landlord, or chivalrous hero when represented as an individual, and an

John R. Hale is Professor of Italian History at University College, London. He is the author of *War and Society in the Renaissance* (London, 1985).

This essay, written while the author was a member of the Institute for Advanced Study, Princeton, represents work in progress for a book to be entitled *Warfare and the Arts in the Renaissance*.

1 The only relevant general work is Georg Liebe, *Der Soldat in der deutschen Vergangenheit* (Leipzig, 1899), reprinted as *Soldat und Waffenhandwerk* (Cologne, 1972). The only monograph that isolates the military component in an artist's work is Christiane Andersson, *Dirnen, Krieger, Narren: Ausgewählte Zeichnungen von Urs Graf* (Basel, 1978). The following notes indicate where reproductions of the drawings and prints mentioned in the text may be found.

anonymous member of the armed and landed second estate when represented as part of a cavalry troop. While the image of the soldier was being developed, that of the knight persisted. But it remained either that of an individual commemorated for responsibilities additional to his military role, or that of an ideal of selfless service to God. Thanks to the confluence of the ideas of Desiderius Erasmus' *Enchiridion* (Antwerp, 1503) and Maximilian I's view of himself as Europe's premier Christian Knight, Hans Burgkmair could record the emperor and St. George as mirror images of one another. It was again Erasmus who prompted Albrecht Dürer to set his knight pacing past the devil and death, secure in the passport of his faith. And, Protestantized, that image of the wayfaring-warfaring soul was taken up in increasingly allegorized forms: the Christian Knight's ascent of the ladder to heaven hampered by ropes tugged by poverty, sickness, lust, and death.[2]

Freed of any challenge from the cavalryman as a figure to be domesticated and seen in genre terms, the portrayal of the infantryman—the Swiss Reisläufer and the German Landsknecht—was unimpededly humanized, all the more freely because in nationalistic Swiss and urban German eyes, the knight was either a foreign or local oppressor. This surge of interest in the soldier was almost entirely limited to Switzerland and Germany, but even there it did not last. It petered out in Switzerland in the 1520s: in Germany its momentum slowed from the 1530s, although it continued, sometimes impressively, into the 1570s. This breadth of interest in the ordinary soldier, what he looked like, how he lived, and what he could be made to stand for, hardly recurs until the nineteenth century, in spite of the renewal of interest in military genre in seventeenth-century Dutch painting and in the contemporary graphic work of Jacques Callot and Franz Ulrich Franck. In none of the succeeding centuries did the common soldier's life attract the attention of a cluster of artists of the caliber of Dürer, Albrecht Altdorfer, Hans Baldung, Wolf Huber, Urs Graf, and, at their best, Niklaus Manuel Deutsch, Hans Schäufelein, Aldegraver, and the brothers Hans Sebald Beham and Barthel Beham. What we have is an exceptional moment: one in which both

2 Max Geisberg (revised by Walter L. Strauss), *The German Single-Leaf Woodcut, 1500–1550* (New York, 1974), II, 438–439; Erwin Panofsky, *The Life and Work of Albrecht Dürer* (Princeton, 1955), Fig. 207; Helene Henze, *Die Allegorie bei Hans Sachs* (Tübingen, 1972), pl. 6.

popular demand and the creative interest of artists turned to evoking the appearance and experience of the practitioners of a trade.

Typologically, portrayal of the soldier as a self-sufficient subject for art can be divided into three distinct categories: single figures; groups; and series which illustrated a wide range of military non-commissioned ranks, arms, and supporting functions.[3]

The single-figure representations concentrated on three subjects. One—announced in a powerful drawing and a much milder engraving by Dürer, both of which have been dated c 1502—was the standard-bearer, the soldier responsible for displaying and guarding from capture the flag that was an essential focus in combat to troops who had become scattered, and to commanders who had to send orders to the captains of companies. As the standard was also the focus of regional or unit pride—on the march or in camp, as well as in battle—its bearer provided not only the pictorial advantage of his swirl of cloth, but also an emotional charge. Seldom shown wearing armor, he was expected to die with the standard wrapped around him so that it would not be borne away as a trophy by the enemy. Taken up by Altdorfer in a succession of engravings from 1506, in a drawing by Hans Süss of Kulmbach in 1510, in woodcuts by Schäufelein from c 1512, and in engravings by Hans Sebald Beham from 1519, the standard-bearer figure reached a peak of strutting intensity in drawings and woodcuts by Graf (Fig. 1). Thereafter his image hardened or dulled, as though the weight of what he stood for had diminished interest in who he was and in what he did.[4]

The second single figures were those of the fifer (the fife was really a transverse flute) and the drummer. Although it is uncertain how far these instruments were used to transmit orders in battle (they are very seldom shown there) as well as to provide diversion on the march or in camp, they are, in groups, almost habitually associated with the standard-bearer. Altdorfer in 1510 introduced

3　I refer in this article to both the Swiss Reisläufer and the German Landsknecht simply as "soldier." They can often be distinguished by the Swiss St. George's or the German St. Andrew's crosses cut into their doublets, sleeves, or hose.

4　Strauss, *The Complete Drawings of Albrecht Dürer* (New York, 1974), II, 625; idem, *The Illustrated Bartsch* (New York, 1978), X, 195; Franz Winzinger, *Albrecht Altdorfer: Graphik* (Munich, 1963), *passim*; Friedrich Winkler, *Hans von Kulmbach* (Kulmbach, 1959), Fig. 27; Geisberg, *Single-Leaf*, III, 1045; F. W. H. Hollstein, *German Engravings, Etchings and Woodcuts ca. 1400–1700* (Amsterdam, n.d.), III, 115–118; Andersson, *Dirnen*, Fig. 20.

Fig. 2   Cranach the Elder, *Landsknecht*, woodcut.

Fig. 1   Urs Graf, *Standard-bearer*, drawing.

SOURCE: Max Geisberg, *The German Single-Leaf Woodcut, 1500–1550* (New York, 1974). II, 596.

SOURCE: Christiane Andersson, *Dirnen, Krieger, Narren: Ausgewählte Zeichnungen von Urs Graf* (Basel, 1978), Fig. 20.

them as separate genre subjects, but as such they were only intermittently brought to life in comparison with the establishment of the single figure of the common soldier: swordsman, pikeman, halberdier, or arquebusier.[5]

Anticipated in some studies for figures in paintings, the infantryman, the third single-figure representation, may have first appeared in his own right as the *Knave of Pinks* in the Master PW's engraved playing card series, conjecturally dated c 1500. But as the same figure appears reversed and considerably naturalized in Dürer's mysterious (and surely mistitled) *Knight on Horseback and Landsknecht* woodcut of c 1497, it may pre-date the latter. Hans Funk used two halberdiers as supporters in a painted heraldic window in c 1501. Dürer's first treatment of a common soldier as a single figure was in a drawing of 1502, and drawings by Baldung in 1505 and others by Süss from about that date, woodcuts by Lucas Cranach in perhaps the same year (Fig. 2), and an engraving by Altdorfer in 1506, taken together with a group of drawings and a woodcut by Schäufelein in 1506/7, establish both the interest of artists and their anticipation of an interested audience. As pursued in drawings by Huber and Altdorfer and an engraving by Graf of 1513, whose casual mastery took the subject for granted and firmly established how the basic image of the Landsknecht/Reisläufer was to be rendered thereafter, those years—1502 to 1513—virtually guaranteed that the soldier-image would be set in company and would supply the imaginative current for the visual description of the soldier's life, character, and power of suggestiveness that I explore below.[6]

The group genre had appeared in 1489 with Dürer's uneasy drawing of *Three Armed Men Conversing*. Dürer's group is an unlikely one. The halberd and feathered javelin are pure fantasy. No footman carried a battleaxe. But the intentness of communication across the composition, and the tentative greeting to the onlooker offered by the central figure, makes this a work prophetic of much that was to follow. Some years later a gauche but

---

5 Winzinger, *Altdorfer: Graphik,* Fig. 110.

6 Ernst Schleuter, *Der Meister PW* (Leipzig, 1935), pl. vii, Fig. 3; Geisberg, *Single-Leaf,* II, 596, 657, III, 1054; *Niklaus Manuel Deutsch,* catalogue (Bern, 1979), pl. 154; Strauss, *Drawings,* II, 627; *Hans Baldung Grien in Kunstmuseum Basel,* catalogue (Basel, 1978), pl. 20. Winkler, *Hans von Kulmbach,* Fig. 1; idem, *Die Zeichnungen Hans Süss von Kulmbach und Hans Leonhard Schäufeleins* (Berlin, 1942), Figs. 6, 20, 52, 53; Winzinger, *Altdorfer: Graphik,* Fig. 100; Hollstein, *German Engravings,* XI, 17.

lively engraving by the Master MZ brought together the single figures whose fortunes we have noted: standard bearer, drummer, fifer, and halberdier (Fig. 3). Dürer's drawing and two engravings of c 1500 by the Master PW, each showing two footsoldiers in conversation, may have influenced Süss' early drawings of similar groups: a pair of soldiers, and a group of three, all engrossed in what they are talking about.[7]

Once more it was Altdorfer who took the lead in assuming that there was an audience for an almost journalistic interest in the soldier. An engraving of c 1505/6 shows three soldiers in relaxed conversation. His sketchy engraving of c 1508 of a standard-bearer in conversation with a bitter-faced woman of the camp (wearing a matching feathered headdress) anticipated, if it did not influence, works produced in or around 1515: Georg Lemberger's pleasantly casual drawing of a soldier, a female camp-follower, and a dog; the drawing by the anonymous Master of the Landsknechte showing a halberdier stopping to examine something on the ground, watched by a mounted pikeman; another drawing, by the artist known only as the Master of the Historia Friderici et Maximiliani, which demonstrates how naturally, through technique and mood, the soldier figure could be absorbed into a landscape; a lively, relaxed conversation piece woodcut by Huber; and Schäufelein's comparable *Three Arquebusiers*.[8]

The *Three Arquebusiers,* by introducing firearms, points us to the category of the military series. At intervals from the mid-1520s, Hans Sebald Beham produced ten single woodcuts illustrating different ranks and arms. Before his series was finished, both Niklas Stoer and Erhard Schoen, in the 1530s, produced versions of their own comprising respectively twelve and twenty-three sheets, covering ranks (captain, lieutenant, and sergeant), arms (pikeman, halberdier, swordsman, arquebusier, and gunner), occupations (quartermaster, mustermaster, provost, and *Brandt-*

---

7 Strauss, *Drawings,* I, 37; Alan Shestack, *Fifteenth-Century Engravings of Northern Europe,* catalogue (Washington, D.C., 1967), no. 151; Schleuter, *Der Meister PW,* pl. 11, Figs. 5, 6; Winkler, *Die Zeichnungen,* Fig. 3. Many of the print makers of this period were known only by the monograms that they used as signatures, e.g. Master PW, Master MZ.

8 Karl Oettinger, *Altdorfer-Studien* (Nuremberg, 1959), Fig. 7; Winzinger, *Altdorfer: Graphik,* Fig. 106; *idem, Wolf Huber: Das Gesamtwerk* (Munich, 1979), 2 v., cat nos. 215, 220; Otto Benesch, *Collected Writings* (London, 1972), III, Fig. 66; Geisberg, *Single-Leaf,* III, 832, 1050.

Fig. 3 Master MZ, *Four Soldiers,* engraving.

SOURCE: Alan Shestack, *Fifteenth-Century Engravings of Northern Europe* (Washington, D.C., 1967), catalogue no. 151.

Fig. 4 Albrecht Dürer, *Recruiting Scene* (?), engraving.

SOURCE: Walter L. Strauss, *The Intaglio Prints of Albrecht Dürer* (New York, 1981), 33.

meister—the official charged with the burning of farms and villages if they harbored enemy soldiers or refused to give up animals and foodstocks), and non-combatants (wife, soldier-servant, and seamstress). Many of the woodcuts, in all series, had brief verses in which the protagonist explained his duty or spoke in his ('Claus Wintergrin') or her ('Little Ursula, the soldier's sweetheart') own voice, thus becoming, through re-issues of these series up to the 1560s, folk representatives of the military life.[9]

A generation before draftsmen of the highest quality began to find it interesting, in drawings, and profitable, in prints, to portray the lives of these soldiers and of the non-combatants who accompanied them, an interest in the military here-and-now had been expressed, albeit clumsily, in the miniatures illustrating patriotic chronicles, like Bendicht Tschachtlan's *Berner Chronik* of 1470, or Diebold Schilling's *Berner Chronik* of 1474 to 1483. These series illustrated not only battles and sieges but also camp sermons and camp recreations, the payment of troops, the treatment of the wounded, and the burial of the dead. Such scenes suggest something of the atmosphere from which less naive artists drew impetus for their essays in military genre, which, although broadening into other typological categories—trains of soldiers on the march, camp scenes, and military panoramas—enable us to follow the military career of the common soldier from enlistment to death or demobilization.[10]

Against the background of this extending interest, we can read Dürer's 1495 engraving, *Five Landsknechts and an Oriental on Horseback,* as a recruiting scene (Fig. 4). Two civilian agents discuss terms with a small party of free-lance soldiers: two pikemen, a halberdier, and a stradiot, one of those semi-orientalized Balkan light horsemen whose steadiest employer was Venice but who also filtered, gypsy-like, into other European armies. No other occupational group, apart from merchants, was shown by artists so frequently in circumstances involving money as were soldiers. They were shown gambling for and squandering it: Graf summed

9 *Ibid.,* I, 251–260, 354–355, III, 1144–1164, 1166–1171, IV, 1316–1328.

10 H. Bloesch, L. Forrer, and P. Hilber (eds.), *Tschachtlan Berner Chronik, 1470,* facsimile (Zurich, 1933); Diebold Schilling (ed. Bloesch and Hilber), *Berner Chronik,* facsimile (Bern, 1943–1945), 4 v. See also Robert Durrer and Hilber (eds.), *Luzerner Bilder-Chronik, 1513* (Lucerne, 1932); Bloesch, Hilber, F. Liebherr, and E. Wyler (eds.), *Spiezer Bilder-Chronik, 1485* (Bern, 1939). Walter Muschg, *Die schweitzer Bilderchroniken des 15/16: Jahrhunderts* (Zurich, n.d.).

up this aspect of the military character—so fascinatingly different from the mores expected of civilians—by giving a standard-bearer a flag with the insignia of a wine bottle, dice, and a pack of cards. They, especially the Reisläufer, were famous for bargaining about the settlement of arrears of pay on the very eve of battle. And this, in spite of its being described as a council of war, is what they are doing in a drawing of 1515 by the same artist. In two later drawings Graf commented on the fecklessness that brought soldiers home empty-handed at the end of a campaign. In one drawing, a young Reisläufer tries to explain to his pregnant wife why his purse is so light. In the other, a veteran Landsknecht strides grimly on with "Al mein Gelt verspilt" inscribed on the two-handed sword that he carries over his shoulder.[11]

Battle was the death-risk upon which the soldier's wage was postulated and against which his manner of life was judged. It was also the moment in a soldier's life that artists, faced with the problem of making compositional sense of conflict between large numbers, normally treated by putting pattern and symbolic personal combat above the record of shared personal experience. It is an index of the strength of the Germanic interest in the genre aspects of the soldier's life that a more realistic way of recording conflict emerged.

As far as actual experience is concerned, battles are shapeless and limited, as Erasmus recognized in his dialogue between the Carthusian and the Soldier, to what the individual did and saw. Only after the event can they be mulled into a shape that necessarily distances them from what was felt and done.[12]

In their attempts to make experiential rather than aesthetic sense of active warfare, artists differed in their approach. Master PW superimposed genre details that denoted the incursion of combat into normality on a schematized bird's-eye topographical engraving view of the Swiss countryside during the Swabian War. A skirmish of shocking veracity and small patrols suggestive of larger forces to come: these coexist with glimpses of ordinary life. A woman on horseback with a feathered headdress converses

11 Strauss, *The Complete Engravings, Etchings, and Drypoints of Albrecht Dürer* (New York, 1972), no. 6; Hollstein, *German Engravings*, XI, 26; Jean-René Bory, *La Suisse à la rencontre de l'Europe* . . . *L'épopée du service étranger* (Lausanne, 1978), Fig. 170; Andersson, *Dirnen*, Figs. 35, 31.
12 Erasmus (trans. Nathan Bailey), *Familiar Colloquies* (Glasgow, 1877), 136–140.

with a foot soldier; a peasant woman walks along, bundle on head, supporting herself with a stick; and a deer stretches its neck to sniff the bottom of another. A similar sense of war's confusion is shown in Baldung's drawing, the so-called *Great Battle of the Lake of Constance*. There is no "great battle" shown here, but the landscape is "occupied" by soldiers drifting towards the combat that the artist has decided not to encounter himself.[13]

When the actual clash of arms was portrayed during this early sixteenth-century period of experiment, it focused on close-ups where weapons, clothing, and facial expressions could be clearly visualized, as in Jörg Breu's *Episode from the Venetian War* of c 1516 or Burgkmair's *Weisskunig* woodcut from the same period, *The Battle before the Castle*. Armed conflict is democratized in these scenes: soldiers are not shown as depersonalized masses, or automata obeying a military master's will, but as men hacking and thrusting at one another as they were paid to do. And this spirit informs Holbein the Younger's superb sketch (of c 1530) for a large battle painting to be placed in the Great Council Chamber in the town hall of Basel. Here, indeed, high art is in control: the composition moves toward the spectator in an oblique V, and from it rise pike-staffs like rays of energy (Fig. 5). But the genre tradition holds as in no other European public commission of the period. It is a record of hand-strokes and poignant hesitations. Within the intellectualized shaping of battle-as-art is the intensity of battle as a life-or-death brawl.[14]

When common soldiers died in action they were shoveled into mass graves. Apart from a primitive but touching miniature of the drowned victims of the battle of Murten in Schilling's *Amtliche Berner Chronik* of 1484, even the most genre-prone of artists drew back from recording that scene, inevitable as it was after every battle. But there was, in the Germanic lands (and nowhere else) a pictorial concern for the wounded. Wounds were then difficult to cure. Knowledge of this harsh fact seems to inform a drawing by an imitator of Altdorfer of an injured hal-

---

13 Liebe, *Soldat*, Fig. 12. There is no "readable" reproduction of Master PW's superb and large (6 plates) work. The best complete copy is in the print room of the Basel Kunstmuseum. Benesch, *Writings*, III, Fig. 402.

14 Ludwig Baldass, *Der Künstlerkreis Kaiser Maximilians* (Vienna, 1923), pl. 29, 41; *Deutsche Kunst der Dürer-zeit*, catalogue (Dresden, 1971), Fig. 99; Heinrich Alfred Schmid, *Hans Holbein der Jüngere* (Basel, 1945), pl. 58.

Fig. 5   Hans Holbein, *Battle,* drawing.

SOURCE: Heinrich Alfred Schmid, *Hans Holbein der Jüngere* (Basel, 1945), pl. 58.

Fig. 6   Albrecht Altdorfer, *Baggage Train* (detail), woodcut.

SOURCE: Franz Winzinger, *Albrecht Altdorfer: Graphik* (Munich, 1963).

berdier who ruefully props his back against a tree and waits beside his dead companion.[15]

Soldiers joined up less for the wage, which was barely a subsistence one, than for the chance of booty and for a life which, although subject to savage punishments for breaches of military law, was free from many of the moral and behavioral constraints within civilian society. These outsiders were joined by something like equal numbers of non-combatant camp-followers: wagoners, sutlers, armorers, pioneers, soldier-servants, and foragers; together with wives, mistresses, and prostitutes who doubled as cooks, laundresses, seamstresses, and nurses. Armies, averaging 8,000 to 12,000 men and as many non-combatants, were as populous as towns. Their migrations, as these vast crowds trailed across the countryside at a foot-pace, and their tented settlements aroused curiosity, part fearful, part admiring or envious, that ensured an audience for representations of marches and encampments. Both became specific aspects of military genre.

The march or military train theme was announced in a drawing of 1475 to 1485 by the *Hausbuch* Master packed with genre detail. But it was Altdorfer who, in a six-block processional woodcut measuring 2.34 meters in length (c 1517/18), established the genre with a brilliant luxuriance of detail. There are a few soldiers, but the work is devoted to depicting the baggage-train of camp-followers. There are wagons piled with chests, tubs, and cauldrons; sumpter horses; and a goat laden with pots and pans led by a woman whose knapsack bristles with spoons. Dogs abound. Children are urged along. A man carries spare shoes strung along poles balanced across his shoulders. Men, women, and animals all move at the slow trudge of the laden along a stony road past trees and a distant town (Fig. 6).[16]

Altdorfer's work was done in connection with the vast cooperative plan for the *Triumphzug* of Maximilian I, but the interest in the appearance of armies on the march long outlasted the stimulus given by the Emperor and his cultural advisors. Soon after 1530 came Hans Sebald Beham's attractive four-block *Baggage Train,* with its boy-servants carrying their masters' weapons,

15 Muschg, *Bilderchroniken,* pl. 60; Winzinger, *Albrecht Altdorfer: Zeichnungen* (Munich, 1952), Fig. 119 (authorship not assured).
16 Johannes Waldburg-Wolfegg, *Das Mittelalterliche Hausbuch* (Munich, 1957), Figs. 37–38; Winzinger, *Altdorfer: Graphik,* Figs. 76–81.

and its women, some of whom have scarves over their mouths against the dust while others escort a mounted man with his arm in a sling and a bandage around his thigh. Wagons bring up the rear. From the same period came Schoen's eight-block *Soldiers on the March* and Stoer's six-block treatment of the same theme. Both omit the baggage-train and devote themselves—in elaboration of the single-soldiers series—to showing detachments of men bearing different arms, sword, pike, arquebus, and halberd, all urged along by drum and fife.[17]

After anticipations in illuminations and drawings (the *Hausbuch* Master again), a number of prints illustrated military leisure pursuits, and Hans Wandereisen's woodcut, *Encampment,* usefully brought them all together: a form of bowls, putting the weight, listening to military music, dicing, drinking, eating, and wenching. Much later, in the 1550s and 1560s, came the illustrations by Jost Amman and others of the military treatises by Reinhard Graf von Solms and Leonhart Fronsperger, which show, as well the more formally military side of camp activities, the swearing in of new recruits, the ratification of promotions, and the taking of attendance—in the ring formation characteristic of Landsknecht assemblies—at executions, and at the even more gruesome penalty of running the gauntlet. Such illustrations reflect the unusual degree to which Landsknecht company morale was sustained by a sharing, or at least a witnessing of decisions by all ranks. But meanwhile a far more extraordinary genre was being developed, which deserves—but will not receive here—extended treatment in its own right: the military panorama.[18]

The first mature manifestation of the military panorama was in a work which is hardly less than astonishing: Hans Sebald Beham's six-block 360-degree view of the *Siege of Vienna,* designed in 1529 and published in Nuremberg during the following year. Depicted, as the inscription insists, from the top of the tower of St. Stephen's in the center, the walls graphically explode outwards and are void of all but location-giving churches, contingents of the garrison (labelled with the names of their commanders), and the disembowelling of a traitor within a ring of soldiers.

---

17 *Ibid.,* 74–78; *idem, Die Miniaturen zum Triumphzug Kaiser Maximilians I* (Vienna-Graz, 1972–1973), 2 v; Geisberg, *Single-Leaf,* I, 246–250, III, 1173–1180, IV, 1329.

18 Waldburg-Wolfegg, *Hausbuch,* Figs. 40–41; Geisberg, *Single-Leaf,* IV, 1442; Fronspergier, *Kriegssbuch* (Wiesbaden, 1976).

Cleared of houses, the inside of the perimeter wall shows the placing of defensive artillery and the perambulation of sentinels. Farther out, in a concentric zone of countryside reaching to the horizon, are Turkish vessels on the Danube; skirmishes; troop formations of both sides; peasant men and women in flight, their children spitted on pikes embedded in the ground; a supply train of camels and grazing horses; dead bodies; villages in flames; and the encampments of the besiegers. There is no major engagement in the field; no crucial assault on the walls. What is envisioned here is a major city and the whole of its surrounding countryside as far as the eye can see given up to the presence of the military and their violent, but at the same time domestic way of life.[19]

Beham had been a student and associate of Dürer, and it is possible that behind the confidence that he brought to *Vienna* lay works like the latter's hasty but meticulous bird's-eye drawing of 1519, *The Siege of Hohenaspern* (which he had witnessed), with its careful depiction of the siege batteries and the besiegers' tented camp, in which soldiers talk and lounge about while pioneers dig pits for latrines. Almost certainly Beham's deft landscape notations for fields, slopes, and trees, and for the flames of burning villages, come from such works as Dürer's *Landscape with Cannon* etching (1518) and his *Siege of a Fortress* woodcut (1527). From Dürer, too, may have come the formulas for the minute but animated and surprisingly differentiated men and beasts which animate *Vienna* and many of its successors. Among these successors were Schoen's *Siege of Münster* (c 1535), with its distinction between the stark no-man's land outside the wall, and the cooking, chatting, and dicing of the base-camp; and Lucas Cranach the Younger's 1542 eight-block panorama of *The Siege of Wolfenbüttel*, which lavishes far more care on the domestic details of encampment life than on the bombardments and skirmishes of the siege itself.[20]

One such landscape, Hans Mielich's *Encampment of Charles V at Ingolstadt*, published in 1549, merits a fuller description. Composed of sixteen blocks, over three meters in length, it contains far more legible visual information than any other work of com-

19 Geisberg, *Single-Leaf,* I, 261–267.
20 Strauss, *Drawings,* III, 1775; *idem, Engravings,* no. 86; Willi Kurth, *The Complete Woodcuts of Albrecht Dürer* (New York, 1963), Figs. 344, 345. Geisberg, *Single-Leaf,* IV, 1210–1213, II, 640–649.

parable size. Like Beham's *Vienna,* this woodcut was planned from a church tower, that of the Frauenkirch, though the perspective was subsequently modified. The artist has portrayed himself there in the lower sixth block; smartly dressed, he holds an inkpot in his left hand and has lifted his right from the paper as he looks out before adding another detail to the paper spread out on the parapet (Fig. 7). We look down with him at the inside of the city wall, across to the army among their tents or exercising in parade formation, and away to the low horizon beyond. Basic formulas are used for men, animals, wagons, tents, market stalls, horse troughs, blocks of troops, and landscape features, but as each is done with care and freshness, and with an apparent and intent interest, the representations of humans and horses have a remarkable variety of costume, gesture, and gait. Labels indicate where the horses were watered, and which ground was allocated to the artillery and the pioneers. Men stroll and quarrel. The steam rises from cooking pots. Women wash clothes in the river

Fig. 7 Hans Mielich, *Encampment at Ingolstadt* (detail), woodcut.

SOURCE: Max Geisberg, *The German Single-Leaf Woodcut, 1500–1500* (New York, 1974), III, 907.

(and use it for less salubrious purposes). Peasant carts rumble in with supplies.[21]

This interest in how soldiers, and the alternative society that they formed, lived in their temporary townships was whetted by their edgy relationship to the civilians upon whom they relied for supplies and, on occasion, for lodging, but on whom they might turn with contempt and savagery. This dangerous volatility of the soldier's mood was summed up in two planetary woodcuts of 1531 by Georg Pencz. Under the genial sign of the sun, citizens watch delightedly while soldiers exercise: wrestling, fencing, racing to break the tape, and throwing the weight against a mark. But when Mars is in the ascendant they are shown killing peasants and abducting their women. The breaking into farms and stealing crops and livestock from browbeaten peasants—illustrated in a woodcut of 1539—was so common that it was referred to in a rueful colloquialism as "gardening."[22]

Soldiers' cruelty to civilians was not a specifically Germanic theme. Pencz's (and the *Hausbuch* Master's) *Mars* had been anticipated in an Italian engraving of 1464/5, and *Boerenverdriet* was to become a familiar pictorial subject in the Netherlands during the Forty Years' War. But no non-Germanic image so grasped the pitting of outsider society against insider society as did a woodcut in Johannes Stumpf's *Schwytzer Cronica,* which shows a village casually looted by soldiers *and* their predatory female camp-followers, nor produced a figure so appallingly telling as Graf's 1514 drawing, *An Armless Girl with a Wooden Leg* (Fig. 8). Given the soldier-artist's preoccupation with the squalors and misery of the military life, as well as with its swagger, it is legitimate to re-title this pathetic figure *A Casualty of War.* These disfigurements—and an eye appears to be injured and a breast maimed—are not the result of birth defects or the pox. The soldiers have first been in her, and then at her. And, it is suggested, she has been left an outcast from her own lakeside home.[23]

The written record bears ample witness to sexual atrocity. Artists did not, in published works, dwell on it. But in keeping

21   *Ibid.,* III, 892–909.
22   Winzinger, *Triumphzug,* pl. 9, 5; Geisberg, *Single-Leaf,* III, 948–949.
23   Waldburg-Wolfegg, *Hausbuch,* Fig. 15; Arthur M. Hind, *Early Italian Engraving* (London, 1970), pl. 119; Bory, *La Suisse,* Fig. 242; Andersson, *Dirnen,* Fig. 24.

Fig. 9 Niklaus Manuel, *The Beggared Soldier*, drawing.

SOURCE: *Niklaus Manuel Deutsch* (Bern, 1979), catalogue, Fig. 117.

Fig. 8 Urs Graf, *Armless Girl*, drawing.

SOURCE: Christiane Andersson, *Dirnen, Krieger, Narren: Ausgewählte Zeichnungen von Urs Graf* (Basel, 1978), Fig. 24.

with the interest shown in the soldier's life and character, his sexual habits were explored with some thoroughness.

The theme of the soldier's farewell to a wife or sweetheart entered German art from the mood of late chivalry and the pictorial tradition of the *Liebespaar*. In *The Knight and his Lady* of 1467/8 by the engraver ES, the knight, in his delicate Gothic armor, recoils from the helmet that the sad-faced lady holds out to him and takes up a fold of her skirt instead. Dürer's engraving of 1497 subtly democratizes the motif. A finely dressed young woman on a caparisoned horse rests her hand on the shoulder of a young halberdier as he sets off for the wars, and he touches her arm. Although it recurs in memorials, like the 1525 painted glass portrait of Johannes Schulbriger, a Swiss mercenary captain, leaving his wife to enter French service, it was not a motif that squared with the popular image of the ordinary soldier's relationship with women.[24]

The soldier was, after all, commonly—although not universally—portrayed as cocksure and aggressive, with swaggering stride and a codpiece more suggestively jutting than those attached to armor or shown in civilian costume. This suggestiveness was emphasized by its association with the hilts of swords slung in an impractically horizontal or inclined position. Soldiers were (as members of other occupational groups were not) frequently shown fully clothed while associated with (as on opposite sides of a dagger sheath design by Aldegraver) or while fondling naked women: Mars and Venus were brought down to the more readily believable level of negotiations between rankers and their camp tarts. Among the sketches in the *Musterbüchlein* of Niklaus Manuel, a soldier-artist, is a drawing which suggests the merely sensual feeling of soldiers for women: a clothed Reisläufer watches two naked women, one playing a lute, the other pouring wine into a glass. Still more purely allegorical is his depiction of what might be termed the three camp-follower goddesses: nudes holding respectively the goblet of expectation, the bow of love, and a skull. But in other sketches, which reflect his own military career, he portrays the routine life of the female camp-follower, as she cooks or sits at the door or a wattle shelter. He shows couples embracing with real, domestic tenderness.[25]

24 Shestack, *Engravings*, Fig. 12; Strauss, *Engravings*, no. 18; Bory, *La Suisse*, Fig. 217.
25 Hollstein, *German Engravings*, I, 105, 116; C. von Mandach, Hans Koegler, and R.

Except in those march scenes or camp panoramas where women appear as a natural part of military society, the relationships between the sexes were difficult to maintain as a straight genre subject. In part this was because, of all genre scenes, those concerning sex tended toward allegory or moralization, or even glorification, as in the Master of the History's drawing of a mounted and splendidly dressed *Lagerdirne* leading a troop of footsoldiers. But it was also because prostitution—licensed in armies and taken (with some awkwardness) for granted elsewhere—was widely associated with syphilis, identified as a potentially killing venereal disease in Switzerland and southern Germany by 1500. The known presence of syphilis among soldiers in Naples in 1495 may have been the reason that Manuel juxtaposed the soldier with the prostitute in his Dance of Death series in the church of the Dominicans in Bern. It is still more likely that he had this threat in mind in the remarkable drawing in which death, wearing the tattered remains of a soldier's finery, embraces a girl with one arm while with the other he lifts her skirt to touch her genitals. That the exchange of deadly infection could be a mutual one is surely the meaning of the woodcut of 1524 by Graf in which two Landsknechts, their codpieces carefully emphasized by encircling short-sword hilts, stroll past a tree, in which squats Death with his hour glass, towards a knowingly smirking prostitute and her baleful-eyed dog.[26]

The pox introduced a new element in the changing fortunes of military service. At first glance Manuel's soldier appears to be simply an allegory of the riches or rags that military service could bring (Fig. 9). But a sexual connotation extends to the figures on the columns of the gateway in which he stands—a camp-girl holding out a wine flask and a posy of flowers across the arch to an eager-looking young soldier—and to the arrows piercing the protagonist's vocal cords, sword-hand, and thigh. The patches on his other, bare thigh suggest the venereal sores represented by Dürer as early as 1496. For him the wars are over; he can only invoke the pardon of the Virgin sitting above one column and

Spreng, *Niklaus Manuel Deutsch* (Basel, n.d.), 107 top left, 103 bottom, 102 second from bottom.
26 Oettinger, *Altdorfer-Studien*, Fig. 57; Conrad André Beerli, *Le peintre poète Nicolas Manuel* (Geneva, 1953), pl. xix, xii; Ernst and Johanna Lehner, *Devils, Demons, Death, and Damnation* (New York, 1971), 107.

the protection of St. Sebastian—the saint who miraculously recovered from his own arrow wounds—above the other. It was not until the 1540s that genre art could take military sex in its stride again, as in Manuel the Younger's buoyant solicitation scene, or (later again) exploit the humor of Wolfgang Strauch's Landsknecht who smirkingly watches his wife attack his *fille de joie*. It was a humor which had meanwhile been reserved for such non-military themes as the mismatch between the young girl and the old, rich suitor, and the conjugal battle over who was to wear the trousers.[27]

By 1519, when Thomas Wolff, a Basel printer, adopted a standard-bearer as his publisher's mark, the infantry soldier had, along the cultural axis of Basel-Nuremberg-Vienna, achieved a status as the basic representative of war that was entirely new, and that anticipated by four centuries at least the emergence of comparable stereotypes: the Tommy, the Poilu, and the G.I.

Although the figure of the standard-bearer continued to carry the main weight of cantonal or regional patriotic feeling, military genre concentrated on the figure of the representative arms-bearing soldier. Whether wielding a gun, sword, pike, or halberd, this soldier-figure was distinguished by the ratty puffs and slashes of his doublet, the ostentatious nonchalance of his mismatched hose, and the ostrich feathers which adorned his headdress. These plumes were borrowed from the knight's *panache*. Significantly, in Erhard Altdorfer's woodcuts of 1512 of Landsknechts watching a tournament, knights are shown in a melee of purely decorative confusion, whereas the soldier loungingly surveying them are treated with genre-like seriousness. This costume, which was also frequently worn in battle except by the front-rank *Doppelsöldner* who used protective armor, was, as chroniclers lamented, in flagrant defiance of civilian sumptuary legislation; it was also a badge of entry into a society with daring and vain, if slatternly, conventions of its own. So generally indicative was it of the ranker-soldier that its extravagance and seediness were already satirized by Hans Weiditz around 1521 and in 1523 in the dazzling *Plumed Riesläufer* caricature drawing by Graf. The effective ferocity be-

---

27 *Manuel*, catalogue (Bern, 1979), pl. 114, cat. no. 175; Strauss, *Illustrated Bartsch*, X, 477; Hollstein, *German Engravings*, VI, 201; Strauss, *The German Single-Leaf Woodcut, 1550–1600* (New York, 1975), III, 1074.

neath the feathers emerges, however, in Altdorfer's forest encounter betweeen a peasant-turned-Landsknecht and landlord-
knight.[28]

By 1519 the soldier had not only become identified through
his defiantly anti-social costume but also by his titillating addic-
tion to paid sex, gambling, and drink. His image as a feared,
fascinating outsider had probably been consolidated all the more
quickly by artists' associating him with the lore of the *Wilden
Leute,* those hairy outcasts whose unlegitimated matings, poach-
ing, and gestures of fearsome welcome in forest glades had already
grasped the imagination of draftsmen and sculptors.[29]

The soldier-image would not have established itself as a stereotype of richly symbolic resonance had it not been steadied by
the careful observation of individuals—as in Baldung's somberly
scrutinized *Head of a Landsknecht* (c 1505)—and by the now general
interest in the soldier's way of life. Given the obstreperous tendency of soldiers to crow over their outsider status, it is remarkable how thoughtfully, even respectfully, they were represented;
in contrast to the almost equally popular peasant genre, they were
seldom shown as hawking, spitting, or turning savage in their
cups. Unlike the peasant, the soldier had a justification for his
foibles and failings. He defended society even while he threatened
it. And he had staked his life, not just his livelihood, on his
occupation. His visual image was thus sturdy enough to bear a
wealth of non-realistic ruminations.[30]

Some artists continued to turn out straightforward genre
depictions of soldiers, for which there was so clearly a public
demand. The career of Jacob Binck, for instance, is peppered by
the emission of engravings of single soldiers, of a series of military
types, of soldiers in groups, of soldiers with their girls, as well
as by representations, of a routine nature, of soldiers being called
away by Death. Binck's life was, however, an unusually peripa-
tetic one. Much of it was spent in northern Germany or Scandi-
navia. Among artists who remained in the heartland, as it were,

28 Oettinger, *Altdorfer-Studien,* 90–92; Geisberg, *Single-Leaf,* IV, 1475; Andersson, *Dirnen,* Fig. 18; Winzinger, *Altdorfer: Zeichnungen,* Fig. 30.
29 Liebe, *Soldat,* Fig. 53. By c 1520 "Martin Wildmann" had become one of the folk-
names given to soldiers.
30 Carl Koch, *Die Zeichnungen Hans Baldung Grien* (Berlin, 1941), pl. 8.

of the new image of the soldier, only the drabbest were content to limit themselves to subjects or themes of the most straightforward "after nature" or model-endorsing type.[31]

Dürer's approach, although far too individualistic to be dubbed instructive, is, at least, indicative. Like others (including the idiosyncratic Baldung), he was called upon to design armor for the knightly class. His personal interest in the accouterments of the noble cavalryman is shown by the inscription "This was the armor at that time in Germany" on a drawing of 1495 that he was later to use in his *Knight, Death and the Devil*. But he was quick to see that the knight was no longer a valid representative of warfare. In his *Man of Sorrows Mocked* engraving (c 1511), it is a footsoldier who is the mocker. In his marginal illustrations to Maximilian I's *Book of Hours* (1515), it is the infantryman whose presence—so flexible had the soldier-image become—reproaches sloth, stands firm sentinel against the wiles of foxy hypocrisy, and reminds the devotee of what to be wary of when reading the passage associated with the outbreak of war: *Quando bellum ad eundem est.*[32]

For other artists the soldier constituted a warning. Daniel Hopfer, in one etching, showed a soldier—identified readily by dagger and thrown-back feathered headdress—grasping the breasts of a by-no-means readily available young woman. Above them dangles the apple of temptation. In the background, a couple engage in amorous dalliance while a dog gulps down their unfinished meal. To accept a soldier's advances equals, the artist seems to suggest, improvidence. It is an approach that we are more familiar with in Dutch genre painting of the seventeenth century.[33]

The soldier-outsider's threat to normal, gainful society was expressed with great symbolic power in a drawing of 1512 by Huber. A soldier, exhausted or wounded, sits on the ground, head bowed over splayed knees. Another stands beside him, gesturing with one hand while holding aloft a flaming fire-bowl in the other. His expression is one of defiant invocation. The association of fire with an oath was put in clandestine, anti-societal

---

31 Hollstein, *German Engravings*, IV, 73 ff.

32 Koch, *Baldung*, pl. 120–121; Strauss, *Drawings*, I, 357, 1519, 1525, 1531, 1547; Hollstein, *German Engravings*, VII, 105.

33 William R. Levin (ed.), *Images of Love and Death in Late Medieval and Renaissance Art*, catalogue (Ann Arbor, 1976), cat. no. 40.

terms in Baldung's orgiastic *Three Witches* drawing two years later, in which the most licentious of the three holds up a fire-bowl. Its association with war was made not only through Mars' firebrand but also specifically through a fire-bowl in an engraving by Aldegrever of 1529 of a soldier with a flaming fire-bowl in one hand and a bucket in the other: the soldier can both bring the flames of war, and quench them. It is not unlikely, then, that Huber's soldier's oath both renews that of loyalty to comrades-in-arms made on enlistment and is one of vengeance on the society represented by the fortified mill whence, it seems likely, his companion received his wound.[34]

In Switzerland, distrust of the soldiery became more marked after the Confederacy's withdrawal in the 1520s from seeking territory in Italy. Thereafter the Swiss fought without a patriotic cause. In a glass painting of 1532, Funk shows a sober, stay-at-home burgher reproaching a gorgeously clad mercenary for employing himself abroad and bringing back, as an affront to the old ideals of the Confederacy, wealth, possibly, but also dissolute, disloyal, and blasphemous manners. The last reproach was not a new one. Graf, in an engraving of 1516, had shown a standard-bearer, accompanied by his servant carrying a stolen goose, striding with averted face past a wayside shrine, and, in a drawing of 1518, a soldier accompanied by the Devil. Baldung in 1516 set a group of soldiers beside a wayside crucifix in a woodcut illustrating the commandment "Thou shalt not take the name of the Lord thy God in vain," and Weiditz in 1532 went so far as to show a Landsknecht, during a tavern brawl over gambling, retching over a crucifix hanging on the wall.[35]

The most remarkable example of distrust of the soldier's irreligion was, however, the powerfully enigmatic drawing of 1511 of the Crucifixion by an artist known only as J. S., whose style was close to that of Altdorfer and Huber (Fig. 10). Despite the familiar group of the mourning Marys on the left, and the pitying John (dressed as a contemporary artisan), the atmosphere

34 Winzinger, *Huber*, II, cat. no. 18; James Marrow and Shestack (eds.), *Hans Baldung Grien: Prints and Drawings*, catalogue (Chicago, 1981), Fig. 30; Hollstein, *German Engravings*, I, 74.

35 Bory, *La Suisse*, Fig. 50; Andersson, *Dirnen*, Fig. 21; Karl T. Parker, *Drawings of the Early German School* (London, 1926), 51; Marianne Bernhard, *Hans Baldung Grien: Handzeichnungen, Druckgraphik* (Munich, 1978), 394; Walter Scheidig, *Holzschnitte des Petrarcha-Meisters* (Berlin, 1955), 72.

Fig. 10 Master J. S., *Calvary*, drawing.

SOURCE: Franz Winzinger, *Albrecht Altdorfer: Zeichnungen* (Munich, 1952), Fig. 127.

is that of a military place of execution. The foremost two crosses are being adjusted into their sockets. The Good Centurion-figure looking up at Christ (as yet unbloodied) seems by his gesture less to acknowledge that this is verily the son of God than to signal to his mates that the cross is now suitably vertical. He, and they, are the soldier-figures to whom we have become accustomed. Behind the crosses are the symbols of the military provost's jurisdiction: a gallows with a corpse dangling from it; and the wheel upon which malefactors were raised after having had their limbs broken. These are guarded by a soldier who looks warily about him, hand on sword. Beside him another kneeling soldier plunges a sword down at a man lying on his back. Because of the role played by soldiers throughout the scenes of Christ's Passion, artists treated them with some equivocation, especially in Italy, where a revival of historicism collided with the humanistic belief in the superior virtue of the Roman legionary. But there had been no parallel of this complete transferral of the supreme moment of the Christian story into the brutal genre-world of the military. The situation became more complicated, however, with the advent of religious wars. In 1521 Baldung, on the title page of Ulrich von Hutten's *Gesprächbüchlein*, showed a force of Landsknechts thrusting back the forces of popery.[36]

Given the popularity of the Dance of Death series in northern art, it is not surprising that there were many independent designs associating soldiers with death. Whereas elsewhere he was represented as a knight, a man of land and authority, in Switzerland and southern Germany his place was taken by the Reisläufer or Landsknecht. Hans Holbein, it is true, clung to convention: in his *Dance of Death* it is Der Ritter who is called away, or, in a later version, run through with his own cavalryman's lance. But, far more commonly, and at least from an anonymous broadsheet of c 1500 and Baldung's drawing of 1503, he is shown as a common infantryman. In that latter drawing he is a halberdier, and Death, conversing with him, holds a grotesque version of his own weapon made of bones. He is a halberdier again in an anonymous woodcut of 1504 and in Dürer's *Death and a Landsknecht in a Cemetery* woodcut of 1510. In the most telling image, another

36 Winzinger, *Altdorfer: Zeichnungen*, pl. 127; Matthias Mende, *Hans Baldung Grien: Das graphische Werk* (Untschiedheim, 1978), Fig. 453.

Baldung drawing, this time of c 1505, Death himself is shown as a standard-bearer, holding the standard upside down and stretching it out so that the artist has made a dreadful, shroud-like reference to the flag and at the same time has generalized the association with death to war itself (Fig. 11). This is a remarkable instance of how allusively a genre image, once it had acquired the status of a stereotype, could be manipulated by an artist who wanted more from it than a reminder of things seen.[37]

Another example of this allusiveness, based on the figure of the army prostitute, is Graf's delicious parody of Dürer's portentous, so-called *Nemesis* (c 1520). This image of Fortuna, like Dürer's, stands on a cloud-borne globe, but, unlike his gravely nude profile figure, she faces us and with a twist of the hips has

Fig. 11   Hans Baldung, *Death as Standard-bearer*, drawing.

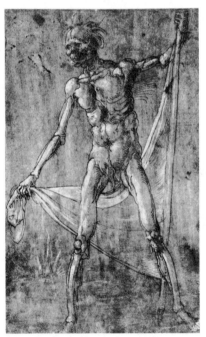

SOURCE: James Marrow and Alan Shestack (eds.), *Hans Baldung Grien: Prints and Drawings* (Chicago, 1981), catalogue, 96.

37   Franz Martin and Alfred Stix, *Die Einblattdrucke des XV. Jahrhundert in der Kupferstich-sammlung der Hofbibliothek zu Wien* (Vienna, 1920), I, pl. cxi; Koch, *Baldung*, pl. 15; Marrow and Shestack (eds.), *Baldung*, Fig. 29.

billowed her skirt up to reveal her thighs. Her sleeves are slit in the Reisläufer's St. George's cross and she wears a dagger. Like *Nemesis*, she holds a cup, but hers is of a grotesque size and doubles as a fire-bowl, sending up flames kicked awry by a little demon. She is a frivolous, but at the same time a serious image. Once more we are dealing with a figure which, without a genre base, could not have been so teasingly effective.

The purpose of this article has been to suggest the lively and varied interest expressed in contemporary soldiers in the art of a particular region. Some aspects of that interest, including much that was fantacized or disturbingly personal, may have been rejected by publishers and block-cutters or not offered to them. Leaving drawings aside (which perhaps we should not, given the number of finished and signed drawings produced, presumably, for sale or as gifts), the evidence of disseminated works—woodcuts, engravings, and etchings—prove the extent of public concern.

Some of this interest developed, in parallel, in the Netherlands. A little northern influence registered on the graphic arts in Italy. But essentially it was a Germanic phenomenon. Why was this so?

Although the answer cannot be simple, one cause suggests itself obviously. No patron of the graphic arts in the Renaissance was so lavish as Maximilian I. In most of his commissions it was understood by his secretaries and artists that he and his military deeds were to be represented as they were. He was not to be shown as a Roman hero, and his Landsknechts were not to masquerade as legionnaires. Among those working for him were Dürer, Burgkmair, Altdorfer, the Master of the History, Schäufelein, Cranach the Elder, Lemberger, and Baldung. This is not only an astonishing pool of talent but, apart from Süss and the Swiss Graf and Manuel, it also contains the very men who invented the soldier-figure and nourished early military genre. Nonetheless, the Landsknecht image was firmly established before work for Maximilian began, and the genre details in the prints and miniatures that he received were not there because he asked for them but because his artists were already conditioned to put them in.

If we consider, on the one hand, the visibility of soldiers to artists, and the extent to which campaigns-on-the-doorstep affected the market for works of art, then in our period the locus was overwhelmingly in Italy. On the other hand, the footsoldier in Switzerland had acquired some aura as a national liberator during the Swiss-Burgundian War and the Swabian War of Independence from the Empire. In Germany the Landsknechts had come to stand, if in a more contradictory way, for that Germanic character whereby Maxmilian's heterogeneous and ununified subjects distinguished themselves from other peoples. In the north there was a patriotic identification with soldiers that was far less strong in Italy, where there were also fewer urban artisanal recruits and thus fewer potential print-buyers. In addition, there was, in the south (apart from gunnery schools) little reflection of the para-military activities to which northern towns were accustomed: civic militias and widely publicized shooting competitions. And no Italian artist fought as a soldier as did Graf, Manuel, and Hans Leu the Younger (although Leu's work displays no interest in military life).

But an explanation that takes account of attitudes toward soldiers as determining the presence or absence of military genre loses much of its force when we consider the imbalance between social genre of all kinds north and south of the Alps. The rich exploration of peasant life, themes like the bath-house, the mismatched couple, the fountain of youth, and the Dance of Death—with its large cast of ways of life and occupations, however loaded with satirical or moral values they might have been—could not have been developed in the north without an empathic view of social reality shared by artists and the public for which they worked.

The Germanic image of the soldier and military genre were fully developed before the Reformation. It would be difficult to explain social genre in terms of a populist religiosity that distinguished north from south. More indicative, perhaps, is the northern preoccupation with the notion of folly, death's journalistic companion, who was so often shown as commenting on the manners of this world which provided so much fodder for his master.

The ground seems firmer if we approach the problem of the absent soldier from the Italian angle. Unlike Germany, which prior to Dürer's treatises was, as Panofsky put it, "a country averse to theorizing about art," there emerged in Italy an aesthetic theory, first clearly stated by Alberti, and kept alive by constant reference to the surviving works of classical antiquity, which centered on three ideas: that nature was a model to be improved upon; that art's function was to convey delight through grace, harmony, decorum, and a lucid ordering of parts; and that subject-matter could be graded from high to low. Among the low were soldiers. And when narrative or symbol (as in the guardian figures at the portal of Michelozzo's Medici bank in Milan) called for soldiers, the humanistic reverence for an age which among other perfections had produced a perfect form of soldiery ensured that they would be classical, or in some degree classicized, ones. Thanks both to the aesthetic appeal of the near-nude Antique cuirass, and the didactic exemplary force of the legionary, the Romanized "art soldier" almost routed the real one from the field of the artistic imagination. And most of the exceptions (Pordenone, Lotto, the Giorgionesque soldiers-in-a-pastoral among them) occurred in northern Italy where the influence of the German print was strongest.[38]

If we restrict our inquiry to the graphic arts, where comparison can be made most fairly, another component of the explanation emerges: in Italy, the book-independent, single-sheet woodcut did not—with the conspicuous exception of Titian—attract artists of the higher caliber. Engraving, after the venture into this form of Mantegna and Jacopo de' Barbari, came chiefly to be seen as a means of transmitting decorative or iconographic inventions or of broadcasting the studies or final compositions of painters. Prints did not, as in the north—and the same can be said of the finished, signed presentation drawing which was so much more common there in this period—fill the gap between the social activity of looking at the contemporary world and the creation of works that bore the responsibility of revising it according to the norms expected of high art—norms that did not inhibit stylistic or iconographic change but did restrict art's subject matter. The print, as a justifier of observation and a legitimizer of free invention (traits conspicuous in military genre), played a different role in north and south.

Yet important as market and media considerations may have been, they do not constitute a satisfactory explanation, even taken

38 Erwin Panofsky, *Albert Dürer* (London, 1948), I, 11; Cecil Grayson (ed. and trans.), *Leon Battista Alberti: On Painting and On Sculpture* (London, 1972).

together with the other factors that have been mentioned, if only briefly. Style—the Germanic permissiveness toward the exuberant outline of the soldier's plumed, slashed, and unsymmetrical costume and toward the organic confusion that was characteristic of marches, camps, and battles—has to be taken into account. So does, within the context of style, the northern acceptance of an expressiveness that gained force from a (never uncalculated) spontaneity of facial expression or gesture. But lurking in the background of all these factors is a consideration too complex and too controversial to be discussed in summary fashion: national temperament.

Richard L. Kagan

Philip II and the Art of the Cityscape   As mundane

as they may seem, city views occupied an important place in the
art and architecture of the Renaissance. The number and variety
of these views multiplied rapidly during the first half of the
sixteenth century, and, by 1550, the cityscape had developed into
an independent genre, claiming numerous artists for whom the
representation of cities was a particular speciality. Underlying this
development was a growing demand for urban panoramas of
various types. Cityscapes, along with maps, became a popular
form of wall decoration; popes, monarchs, nobles, and burghers
alike commissioned artists to adorn their residences with portraits
of cities, either alone or in series. An even larger market existed
for cheap, single sheet engravings of individual cities, and another
for city atlases, the most ambitious of which endeavored not only
to publish views of European cities, but also those of Africa, Asia,
and the New World. Yet, despite their number and appeal, city
views have attracted relatively little scholarly attention. In general,
they have been interpreted as a response to the growth of European cities and towns, as well as one facet of the growing interest
in geography sparked by the discovery of the Americas. They
have consequently been considered as a demonstration of European interest in mapping the world as faithfully and accurately as
possible.

   Yet city views had other uses. In some cases they served as
expressions of local patriotism and regional pride; in others, they
were used as demonstrations of suzerainty, both secular and spiritual. However, the personal and political uses of these views have
rarely been considered, and this is the principal concern underlying this article, which focuses on a series of commissions offered
by Philip II of Spain (1556–1598) to Anton Van den Wyngaerde
(c. 1512–1571), a Flemish artist who specialized in topographical
views.[1]

Richard L. Kagan is Professor of History at Johns Hopkins University. He is the editor
of *Spanish Cities of the Golden Age: The Views of Anton Van den Wyngaerde*, forthcoming.

1   For the artist's biography, I have principally relied on Egbert Haverkamp-Begemann,

Van den Wyngaerde was already well known for his faithful representations of various Dutch, Flemish, French, and Italian cities when, in 1557, he entered the service of Philip II, who was then residing in Brussels. The following year the artist journeyed to England where he prepared drawings of places that Philip had visited at the time of his marriage to Mary Tudor in 1555. Van den Wyngaerde was probably still in England in 1561 when Philip summoned him to Madrid. Shortly thereafter he was named *pintor de cámara*, a valued position that provided lodging at court in addition to a regular stipend. As a court artist Van den Wyngaerde's duties varied considerably, but he seems to have devoted most of his time to the art that he knew best: the topographical view.[2]

Van den Wyngaerde's earliest Spanish view, dated 1562, depicts the royal hunting lodge at Valsaín, near Segovia. Others representing Madrid, Toledo, and Segovia followed in quick succession, suggesting that initially the artist did not venture very far from the royal court. Beginning in 1563, however, Philip ordered him to embark on a series of protracted journeys for the purpose of executing topographical views of cities in various parts of the kingdom. His first trip took him to the kingdom of Aragon and in 1564 he went to La Mancha (Fig. 1). Later that year he was in Malaga and North Africa and in 1567 he undertook an extended trip through Andalucia and New Castile. His next excursion, a journey to Old Castile, took place in 1570. This particular trip definitely took place under royal protection. In a document dated August 8, 1570, Philip requested local Castilian officials to give all possible assistance to "our painter Antonio de las Viñas" who was travelling "upon our orders to paint the description of some of these most important towns."[3]

In the course of these travels Van den Wyngaerde was able to prepare views of no less than sixty-two important cities and towns, each of which was based upon sketches drawn from na-

---

"The Spanish Views of Anton van den Wyngaerde," *Master Drawings*, VII (1969), 375–399.

2 For references to salary payments paid to Van den Wyngaerde in 1565/66, see the Archivo General de Simancas: Casas y Sitios Reales, *legajo* 82, no. 95; *legajo* 275, pt. 2, fol. 54.

3 Cited in Haverkamp-Begemann, "Spanish Views," 378.

Fig. 1 Anton van den Wyngaerde, *View of Cuenca* (from the east), 1565.

SOURCE: Oesterreichische Nationalbibliothek, Cod. Min. 41, fol. 31.

ture, or, as the artist himself often noted in his drawings, *"facit ad vivum."* This collection forms an impressive record. With the exception of the prolific Joris Hoefnagle, no other sixteenth-century artist is known to have completed so many topographical views.[4]

Haverkamp-Begemann has proposed that the king may have intended the views to form the basis of a Spanish city atlas since Philip arranged, shortly after Van den Wyngaerde's death in 1571, to have the drawings sent to the Plantin press in Antwerp for engraving. Yet for some reason the atlas project was never completed. Instead Van den Wyngaerde's Spanish views were dispersed, possibly by the Plantin themselves. The majority of the drawings wound up at the Hapsburg court in Prague and eventually in the Austrian National Library in Vienna; the remainder found their way to England where they are now housed in the Ashmolean and the Victoria and Albert Museum. Although a number of the drawings have been published separately in the last hundred years, it is only now, roughly four centuries behind schedule, that the corpus of Van den Wyngaerde's Spanish views is being published as a complete collection.[5]

Although Van den Wyngaerde's drawings seem not to have been widely distributed, his artistry could be admired first hand by visitors to the court of Philip II. Contemporary reports indicate that the king had him decorate the walls and corridors of several palaces with paintings of maps and city views, some of which may have been large-scale versions of the drawings that the artist previously had made on his various trips across Spain and to other European countries. In a book published in 1582, Argote de Molina writes that El Pardo, the hunting lodge that Philip constructed near Madrid, contained a corridor in which could be seen, "painted on canvas, by the hand of Antonio de las Viñas, a noted Flemish painter, the principal islands and land of Zeeland,

---

4 Hoefnagle, however, is not known for the accuracy of his views. Most of his work was reproduced in Georg Braun and Franz Hogenburg, *Civitates Orbis Terrarum* (Antwerp, 1572–1617), 6 v. and later editions. For a checklist of Hoefnagle's Spanish views, see the fascimile edition of this work, edited by Raleigh A. Skelton (Cleveland, 1966), I, Appendix B.

5 See Kagan (ed.), *Spanish Cities of the Golden Age: The Views of Anton Van den Wyngaerde*, forthcoming.

with its towns, ports, rivers, banks, and dikes, as well as the sea, extending across to the great kingdom of England."[6]

In 1599 Cuelbis, a German visitor, reported that painted views of Amsterdam, Dordrecht, Ghent, Gravelines, and Lisbon, together with those of a number of Spanish cities, were hanging in the entrance hall to the Alcázar, the royal palace in Madrid. Cuelbis also states that the "*sala grande*" in this palace was decorated with views of a number of Spanish cities, including Antequera, Barcelona, Burgos, Córdoba, Granada, Lerida, Segovia, Seville, Toledo, Valencia, and Zaragoza. Although Cuelbis does not name any artist, it seems likely that these views, if not executed by Van den Wyngaerde himself, were at least copied from his other work. A 1686 inventory of the Alcázar specifies that many of these views were still on display, albeit in different parts of the palace, at the end of the seventeenth century. However, they were apparently destroyed, along with many other paintings in the Spanish royal collection, in a devastating fire of 1734.[7]

Philip's reasons for commissioning Van den Wyngaerde to paint the cities of Spain remain obscure. Were these cityscapes intended to demonstrate the extent of Philip's dominions and serve as a visual expression of his power and might? Or were they purely decorative: topographical views, devoid of any particular meaning, that simply reflected contemporary curiosity in geography and in maps? Such questions lead to a consideration of Philip's artistic and scientific concerns.

PHILIP II AND THE GEOGRAPHERS Philip II's attraction to the city view grew out of his interest in geography, a subject to which he was introduced by his father, the Emperor Charles V. Charles is known to have received instruction in geography, astrology, astronomy, and related subjects from some of the leading scholars

6 Gonzalo Argote de Molina, *Libro de montería* (Seville, 1582), ch. 47.
7 Biblioteca Nacional (Madrid): Ms. 18.472, Diego de Cuelbis, "Thesoro chorographico de las Espanas," fols. 39–42. Yves Bottineau, "L'Alcázar de Madrid et l'inventaire de 1686," *Bulletin Hispanique*, LX (1958), 456–481. Although the inventory does not offer any indication of the artist who produced these views, an entry for the views hanging in the "transito de las viviendas de las capellanes de la Encarnación," suggests that at least some were by the hand of Van den Wyngaerde: *ibid.*, 469. As in the case of the Alcázar, the views by Van den Wyngaerde that were displayed in the Pardo were destroyed by the fire that destroyed much of that palace in 1603.

of his day. He was in touch with Petrus Apianus, a noted mathematician, and Apianus's pupil, Gemma Frisius, a Ptolemeic geographer, as well as Gerard Mercator and Hieronymous Cock, famous cartographers. Geography was also a hobby of Philip's mother, Empress Isabella of Portugal. Daughter of Manoel I of Portugal, who was himself fascinated by the study of geography, the empress regularly commissioned maps and views of the New World, apparently for her own private enjoyment.[8]

Given such familial predilections, it is likely that Philip's exposure to geography began at an early age. His first formal introduction to the subject, however, seems to have occurred only in 1545 when his tutors drew up a list of books for his education that included the works of two influential ancient geographers, Claudius Ptolemy and Pomponius Mela. Philip's interest in geography may have been further whetted by a journey to Italy and the Low Countries in 1548 and by another to England and Flanders in 1555. Two years later, Frederico Bodoaro, the Venetian ambassador, reported from Brussels that "his Majesty loves learning and reads history; he also knows a great deal about geography and something of sculpture and painting.[9]

Philip's geographical concerns soon were expressed in a series of important commissions. The first of these went to Deventer, a Flemish cartographer, whom the king asked in 1558 for a series of detailed ground-plans of the cities of Flanders and of Holland, an ambitious project that required nearly two decades to complete. Following his return to Spain in 1559, Philip gave royal backing to a team of cartographers, headed by Pedro Esquivel, which was preparing a new map of the Iberian peninsula that was to be based upon the latest mathematical principles and surveying techniques. The efforts of the Esquivel group resulted in a remarkable set of maps, a copy of which still survives in the royal library at the Escorial.[10]

8   For a more extensive discussion of Philip's geographical concerns, see Kagan, *Spanish Cities*, ch. 2.
9   Louis P. Gachard, *Relations des ambassadeurs vénetiens sur Charles-Quint et Philippe II* (Brussels, 1856), 40.
10   See Bert Van 'T Hoff, *Jacob van Deventer* ('s-Gravenhage, 1953), 36; Jacques Deventer, *Atlas des villes de la Belgique aux xvie siècle* (Brussels, 1884–1929), 2 v. Biblioteca de El Escorial, Ms. K.I.1. For Philip's support of this project, see Felipe Picatoste y Rodríguez, *Apuntes para una biblioteca científica española del siglo xvi* (Madrid, 1891), 86–88.

Another of Philip's favorite geographical projects was the compilation of a detailed topographical description of every Spanish village and town on the basis of a standardized questionnaire. This collection was intended to replace Pedro de Medina's inadequate *Libro de las grandezas de España* (Seville, 1548) and to rival the topographical histories that had already been produced for Germany, Austria, and Italy. Known as the *Relaciones histórico-geográfico-topográficas*, the project began in 1575 and succeeded in collecting information about more than 600 towns in Extremadura, La Mancha, and New Castile. Similar *relaciones* were planned for other parts of the kingdom but remained unfinished.[11]

In 1582 Philip helped Juan de Herrera, the royal architect, establish a scientific academy in Madrid offering instruction in cosmography and geography, among other subjects. The king's interest in these disciplines was even manifested in the throne room at the Escorial which, in 1591, incorporated a series of wall maps, evidently drawn from Abraham Ortelius' *Theatrum Orbis Terrarum*, first published in 1570. An Italian traveller also reported that Philip had wooden models of Spain's principal cities on display in Madrid's Alcázar.[12]

SIXTEENTH-CENTURY CITY VIEWS   Philip's passion for geography was by no means unusual for his time and was shared with other sixteenth-century rulers, including Cosimo I de' Medici, Pope Pius IV, and Elizabeth I. Royal interest in the subject seems to have begun with the dissemination of Ptolemy's *Cosmography* after its translation from the Greek into Latin in 1406, but was really sparked at the end of the fifteenth century by Spanish and Portuguese discoveries in Africa, Asia, and the New World. Curiosity about distant lands was matched by a corresponding demand for

11 For the history of the *relaciones*, see Manuel F. Miguelez, "Las relaciones histórico-geográficas de España," in *Catálogo de los codices españoles de la biblioteca del Escorial Relaciones históricas* (Madrid, 1917), 249–332. See also José M. López Piñiero, *Ciencia y técnica en la sociedad española de los siglos xvi y xvii* (Madrid, 1979), 216–219. Although the *relaciones* were never completed, they were deposited in the Escorial library and made available to scholars. They may in fact have been utilized by Diego Pérez de Mesa, who edited a revised edition of Pedro de Medina's topographical history in 1595. Medina, *Primera y segunda parte las grandezas y cosas notables de España* (Alcalá de Henares, 1595).

12 For this academy, see Agustín Ruiz de Arcaute, *Juan de Herrera* (Madrid, 1936), 98. Jean l'Hermite (ed. Charles Ruelens), *Le Passetemps* (Antwerp, 1890), II, 68. The models were said to be there as early as 1571. See Carl Justi, *Velázquez y su siglo* (Madrid, 1953), 184–185.

new and more accurate descriptions of places closer to home. The great political struggles of the day—Louis XI's invasion of Italy, Charles V's battles against the Lutherans, and the Habsburg-Valois wars—contributed to this demand: generals in the field required accurate maps as well as accurate views of the cities that they were ordered to besiege.[13]

Whatever the precise impetus, by the start of the sixteenth century map-making was transformed into a major industry in Italy, Germany, the Low Countries, and Portugal. Simultaneous advances in trigonometry and surveying also turned map-making, formerly the domain of artists, into a skill that required training in mathematics and the use of various kinds of instruments. Sixteenth-century map-makers increasingly used techniques pioneered by the makers of sea-charts and portalans and relied upon direct observation and mathematical projections. A sign of the times in map-making was the disappearance of sea-monsters, mermaids, and similar fanciful details, and the appearance of precise mathematical scales measuring distance. Map-making, in short, had developed into a science, and the most valued maps were those offering the greatest degree of topographical accuracy.

A similar shift occurred in the art of depicting cities. Here I follow Schulz, who has identified two distinct artistic traditions that apply equally well to city views and to maps. The first and oldest of these mapping traditions is that of the encomiastic or emblematic view. In this tradition topographical fidelity was subordinated to a larger message that views sought to communicate. Examples of this genre occur throughout the Middle Ages and include a 1344 view of Siena by Ambrogio Lorenzetti that appeared in the center of a now-lost *mappamundi* in that city's Palazzo Púbblico. The apparent purpose of the Lorenzetti view was to signify the unity of *urbs* and *orbis* and thus express Siena's universality.[14]

13 One example of the relationship of military concerns to city views is the sketchbook prepared by Francisco de Holanda for King John III of Portugal. In 1536 John sent Holanda to Italy "to see and make drawings of the fortresses and of the most famous and notable things in that country." Holanda returned in 1541 with a remarkable series of views that accorded special emphasis to the fortifications that Italy's cities had erected. For this commission, see John Bury, "Francisco de Holanda: A Little Known Source for the History of Fortification in the Sixteenth Century," *Arquivos do Centro Cultural Portugues*, XIV (1979), 163–220.

14 Jurgen Schulz, "Jacopo de' Barberi's View of Venice: Map Making, City Views, and Moralized Geography before the Year 1500," *Art Bulletin*, LX (1978), 425–474.

Another example of such an emblematic view is Taddeo di Bartolo's bird's-eye portrait of Rome (1413) which was also on display in Siena's Palazzo Púbblico. In this case the view of the Eternal City, which formed part of a larger mural cycle centering on the virtues essential to just government, was meant to exhort Siena's governors to follow the example of ancient Rome. The epitome of this particular tradition is Jacobo de'Barberi's majestic, if somewhat distorted, bird's eye view of Venice, first published as an engraving in 1500 and intended, in the words of Anton Kolb, its publisher, "principally for the glory [fama] of this illustrious city." Although its precise purpose remains undefined, the engraving was apparently meant to celebrate Venice as a great international maritime emporium.[15]

The second city view tradition defined by Schulz first emerged at the start of the sixteenth century. This scientific or topographical tradition placed a premium on accuracy and was inspired by the rediscovery of Ptolemy, Strabo, Pomponius Mela, and other ancient geographers; by advances in the art of making portalan charts based on direct observation; and by humanistic concerns for understanding the natural world in rational terms. One of its pioneers was Leonardo da Vinci, who helped to develop the ichnographic view in which the representation of a city is based a series of abstract, mathematical rules. On the whole, however, this topographical tradition is customarily associated with artists and cartographers from north of the Alps, especially those in Germany and Flanders.[16]

Too much may have been made of the northern origins of this tradition. On the one hand, there is little historical evidence to support the recent assertion that the Low Countries had a "mapping impulse" that Italy lacked. On the other hand, the topographical tradition of city views does seem to bear a close relationship to the political developments in northern Europe at this time. The Emperors Maximilian I and Charles V both tried to expand the power of imperial institutions at the expense of local autonomy and privilege. Cities in Flanders and in Germany resisted these initiatives, and in the course of this struggle many developed a new awareness of themselves as a *communitas perfecta*,

15 *Ibid.*, 462, 472.
16 John A. Pinto, "Origins and Development of the Ichnographic City Plan," *Journal of the Society of Architectural Historians*, XXXV (1976), 35–50.

each with a history, governing institutions, and traditions considered unique. The result was an outburst of local patriotism and a renewed sense of civic pride that found verbal expression in such works as Konrad Celtis's *Norimberga*, a panegyric originally presented to Nuremberg's governing council in 1495, and Felix Fabri's *Tractatus de civitate ulmensi* (1488), one of a new genre of local topographical histories.[17]

These same ideas found visual expression in engraved views of individual cities that were based on direct, personal observation. Their authors took special care to depict the local topography, individual buildings, and other details as faithfully as possible. Examples of this type of topographical view include Albrecht Dürer's views of Innsbruck and Trent (1495), Cornelis Massys' view of Brussels (1540), Cornelius Antoniszoon's bird's-eye view of Amsterdam (1544), and Conrad Morant's fish-eye view of Strasburg (1548), as well as Van den Wyngaerde's views of Amsterdam (1544), Dordrecht (1544), and Genova (1553).

Although this particular tradition soon spread to the south, the demand for this type of city portrait developed faster in Flanders, the Rhineland, and other parts of Germany than in Italy. Consequently, artists in these northern regions began to specialize in the production of these views at a time when their Italian counterparts were still engaged in the production of what Schulz has described as "moralized" views. In contrast, Van den Wyngaerde himself summarized the objective and purely visual aims of the new topographical genre in an inscription included in his 1553 engraving of Genoa: "Of all the pleasures offered by the delightful and ingenious [art of] painting, none do I esteem more highly than the depiction of places."[18]

The topographical tradition also found expression in a series of city atlases, geographical gazetteers, and travel books. Similar to the ancient *periegesis* in which authors used words to transport

17 Svetlana Alpers, *The Art of Describing: Dutch Art in the Seventeenth Century* (Chicago, 1983), 119–168. Gerald Strauss, *Sixteenth-Century Germany, its Topography and Topographers* (Madison, 1959), is invaluable for understanding the development of this genre.
18 Vasari's commentary on the *vedute* painted by Pinturicchio for Pope Alexander VI in the Vatican Belvedere in 1487 suggests that city views "in the Flemish style" had made their appearance in Rome before the end of the fifteenth century. See Giorgio Vasari (ed. Gaetano Milanesi), *Opere* (Florence, 1973), III, 498, For other examples of fifteenth-century views of Italian cities, notably those by Francesco Roselli, see Schulz, "Barberi's View of Venice," 429–430. The quotation by Van den Wyngaerde is cited in *ibid.*, 472.

readers from place to place, these books used city views to achieve a similar effect. Such books had existed in the Middle Ages, but the first to included accurate city portraits was probably Bernhard von Breydenbach's *Sanctarum Peregrinationum . . . Opusculum* (Mainz, 1486), with illustrations by Erhard Reuwich. Hartmann Schedel's *Liber Cronicarum*, published in Nuremberg in 1493, was a true city atlas with views of 116 cities, of which twenty-three are recognizable as representations of individual cities; the remainder are interchangeable and were intended simply to illustrate the concept of the city rather than a specific place. However, this travel volume was subsequently superseded both in terms of its accuracy and its geographical scope by Sebastian Munster's *Cosmographia*, first published in Basel in 1544, and then by such works as Braun and Hogenburg's great multi-volume compendium, which initially appeared in 1572, and the collection of maps, views, and battle scenes that Lafréry published in Rome around 1572. Armchair travel had come of age.[19]

The commission that Philip II offered to Van den Wyngaerde formed part of a burgeoning, European-wide demand for accurate maps and city views. Prior to this commission, the only existing views of Spanish cities were some rather crude and inaccurate woodcuts similar to those published in Medina's *Libro de las grandezas de España*. The inadequacies of these works helps to explain why Philip was so eager to bring Van den Wyngaerde to Spain. The king primarily envisioned this commission as a scientific enterprise designed to complement his other geographical projects. Such a commission represented Philip's efforts to obtain a comprehensive chorography of Spain—a detailed, close-up view of each of the individual cities and towns that comprised his kingdom. "The end of chorography," wrote Ptolemy, "is to deal separately with a part of the whole, as if one were to paint only the eye or the ear by itself. . . . Accordingly, therefore, it is not unworthy of Chorography, or out of its province, to describe the smallest details of places, while Geography deals only with regions and their general features." Chorography also differs from geography because, in "selecting certain places from the whole, it treats more fully the particulars of each by themselves—even

19 Antoine Lafréry, *Tavole moderne di geographia de la maggior parte del mondo . . .* (Rome, 1572?).

dealing with the smallest conceivable localities, such as harbors, farms, villages, river courses, and such like." According to Ptolemy, moreover, "Chorography needs an artist, and no one presents it rightly unless he is an artist."[20]

The chorographic quality of Van den Wyngaerde's views hardly requires demonstration. He kept extraneous embellishments to a minimum, eschewed the emblems, allegorical figures, inscriptions, and other devices that artists working in the encomiastic tradition used to invest cityscapes with some deeper meaning, and generally limited inscriptions to labels for principal monuments, important historical sites, and notable topographical features. Furthermore, instead of the profile views and jumbled topography characteristic of most medieval cityscapes, he used perspective in order to convey a sense of depth and to illustrate the city's relationship to the surrounding countryside. He also employed an elevated, oblique perspective that simultaneously allowed a view of the façades of principal monuments as well as a glimpse of the street plan. The use of this oblique perspective is particularly evident in his view of Barcelona as seen from an imaginary vantage point at sea, and in his panorama of Zaragoza viewed from the east (Fig. 2).[21]

Van den Wyngaerde's concern with topographical accuracy is further revealed in his working method. He normally began with a series of site plans and sketches of individual buildings that he would later incorporate into a finished view. His view of Granada, for example, was the painstaking product of no fewer than four or five preliminary sketches. Van den Wyngaerde, however, often exaggerated the size of buildings nearest the vantage point, a practice that is unavoidable when the cavalier perspective is employed. He tended also to increase the size and the height of churches, possibly to draw attention to the city as a *civitas christiana*, a tradition that was commonplace in the north of Europe. Yet there is little in his views to suggest that he purposely distorted the arrangement and scale of buildings. Even the choice of

---

20   Edward L. Stevenson (trans.), *Geography of Claudius Ptolemy* (New York, 1932), 26–27.
21   In his first Spanish views each important building was labelled individually, but, for the sake of clarity, beginning with the views prepared on his journey to Andalucia in 1567, Van den Wyngaerde provided an alphabetized key to serve as a guide to major monuments and other sites.

Fig. 2 Anton van den Wyngaerde, *View of Barcelona* (from the east), 1563.

SOURCE: Oesterreichische Nationalbibliothek, Cod. Min. 41, fol. 3.

cities appears to have been somewhat random, although the selection may have been dictated by the king. In addition to views
of Spain's major cities, all of which were royal, Van den Wyngaerde also depicted seigneurial towns (Alba de Tormes, Chin-
chilla, and Sanlúcar de Barrameda), and occasionally drew a small
village such as Ojen, near Marbella. If an overarching, predeter-
mined scheme existed, it was an attempt to include cities representative of each of Spain's major political divisions—Aragon, the
two Castiles, Valencia, etc.—in an effort to compile the comprehensive chorography that Philip apparently had envisioned.[22]

Nonetheless, Van den Wyngaerde's Spain was fragmented.
His vision was that of a Fleming whose political loyalties were
steadfastly local. Consequently, his Spain was a collection of independent cities rather than a united realm. Yet his vision was
also that of an objective observer: a chorographer whose task was
primarily to record what he saw. His scientific detachment was
especially evident in his drawings of classical ruins, such as those
at Italica (Seville) and Saguntum (Valencia) where he was simply
content to prepare a visual catalogue, making note of important
inscriptions and other historical material. A similar objectivity
infused his portrait of the *almadraba* or great tuna fishery at Zahara,
on the southwest coast of Spain, in which the inscriptions detail
the type and number of workers employed and offer a guide to
where various activities connected with the *almadraba* were carried
out: "here are the sheds where the tuna are dried"; "here are
where the merchants gather"; etc. (Fig. 3). Hoefnagle's contemporary view of the nearby *almadraba* at Conil reflected his interest
in genre scenes rather than topographical accuracy. In contrast,
Van den Wyngaerde's drawing was that of an enthnographer and
suggests that this was precisely the kind of detailed information
that Philip was seeking when he ordered this artist "to paint a
description of some of these most important towns."[23]

As a result of these concerns, Van den Wyngaerde compiled
a visual record of Spanish cities that was unique. At the time
nothing remotely comparable existed for other European states;

---

22 Without a contemporary inventory of Van den Wyngaerde's work, there is no way
of knowing whether he executed views of cities other than those represented in the
collections of Vienna, London, and Oxford. For a list of these cities and a map tracing
his itineraries across Spain, see Kagan, *Spanish Cities.*
23 Hoefnagle's view of Conil is printed in Braun and Hogenberg, *Civitates,* II, pl. 6.

Fig. 3 Anton van den Wyngaerde, *View of the Almadraba at Zahara de Los Atunes* (from the east), 1567?

SOURCE: Oesterreichische Nationalbibliothek, Cod. Min. 41, fól. 74.

Philip therefore could rightly boast of being the first European ruler to possess such a complete and accurate "description" of his realms. Furthermore, just as Philip's other geographical projects were intended to be made available for scholars, both then and in the future, Van den Wyngaerde's chorographic view of Spanish cities constitutes a rich cache of information about Spain that still awaits our exploration.

Architectural historians will be able to use these cityscapes to date and otherwise to reconstitute monuments that have long since disappeared. Similarly, those scholars interested in urban history can use these views to trace the development of Spain's cities during an epoch when many were beginning to shed their medieval plan in favor of Renaissance principles of urban planning and design. Economic historians will be interested in the information that Van den Wyngaerde provided about ships and shipping, Spain's building and textile industries, and the interrelationship of urban and rural space. Even social historians will find something useful here. The detailed sketch of a *juego de cañas,* a type of aristocratic joust popular in the sixteenth century, that Van den Wyngaerde included in one of his views of Jeréz de la Frontera, is among the earliest representations of this important pastime.

PHILIP AND POSTERITY   But was chorography the only thing that Philip had in mind when he invited Van den Wyngaerde to Spain? In 1560 Felipe de Guevara, one of Philip's courtiers, advised the monarch that royal support of Esquivel's cartographic project would represent a gift to scholarship and a deed that could only add glory to Philip's name and perpetuate his fame. Philip's humanistic education would already have taught him this valuable lesson, together with the need for princes to gather around them men of learning, science, and art. Indeed, this principle is one that Philip warmly embraced: he supported numerous artistic and scientific projects, built on a lavish scale, and took a personal interest in architectural design. Philip also ranked as one of the greatest collectors of his day, with tastes running the gamut from rare birds and exotic plants to ancient coins and medals, and the works of Titian, Jacopo Bassano, Roger Van der Weyden, and Hieronymus Bosch. With the help of Benito Arias Montano, a noted humanist, he simultaneously established in the Escorial one of the sixteenth century's largest and most comprehensive libraries of rare books and manuscripts, a collection of more than 14,000 volumes that incorporated works in Arabic, Chaldean, and Hebrew, as well as Latin and Greek. Within this context, the Van den Wyngaerde commission can also be understood as part of the monarch's desire to be remembered as a patron and protector of the liberal arts.[24]

Philip's concern for posterity was also expressed by his desire to impress contemporaries with the extent of his power and the magnificence of his deeds. He had seen the great Pannemaker tapestries celebrating the victory of his father against the Turks at Tunis that hung in 1555 in the nave of the cathedral in Bruges, and he himself may have been responsible for the engravings that recorded Spanish victories against the French in 1557 and 1558. Philip subsequently ordered Van den Wyngaerde to accompany the fleet sent to capture the Moorish stronghold of Peñón de Velez de Gomera in North Africa in 1564. "Current events" maps were a popular genre in the mid-sixteenth century, and Van den Wyngaerde's task was to record the various stages of the battle. The resulting drawings pointedly portray this little skirmish as a great triumph of Christianity over Islam and include royal banners proclaiming the victory as a personal triumph for Philip II. The king also had other artists, among them Rodrigo de Holanda, Van den Wyngaerde's son-in-law, decorate the Escorial with scenes of other Spanish victories.[25]

Did not the cityscapes displayed in the Pardo and in the Alcázar have a similar purpose? Although executed in accordance with the topographical tradition that we associate with Van den Wyngaerde, these vistas also belong to the older encomiastic tradition in which city portraits were invested with deeper meaning. Mural cycles of cities used for this purpose had existed in Italy since the end of the fifteenth century. The prototype was undoubtedly that painted by Pinturicchio for Pope Innocent VIII in the loggia of the Vatican Belvedere around 1487. The precise purpose of this particular cycle remains controversial, but the

24 Felipe de Guevara, "Comentarios de la Pintura," in Francisco J. Sánchez Cantón, *Fuentes literarias para la historia de arte en España* (Madrid, 1923), I, 174.

25 For more on Charles V's tapestries, see William Eisler, "Arte y Estado bajo Carlos V," *Fragmentos,* III (1984), 21–39; Lafréry, *Tavole moderne,* fols. 93–97; Julián Zarco Cuevas, *Pintores españoles en San Lorenzo el Real de El Escorial* (Madrid, 1931), 231.

loggia seems to have inspired the *camere della città* (the city rooms) that were subsequently incorporated into many of the Roman palaces built in the Cinquecento, including the Villa Farnesina, the Villa Guilia, and the Villa Medici, as well as the Farnese palace at Caprarola. Some of these *camere*, in keeping with humanists' concerns for the *vita contemplativa*, may have been intended simply for idle reflection, but most were meant to serve as an expression of the authority and territorial possessions of the family associated with the villa in question. Such was obviously the intention in the loggia at Caprarola where the decorative program, dedicated to the heroic deeds of the Farnese, incorporated views of ten Farenese territories, including Caprarola itself, and featured profile views of Parma and Piacenza, two jewels in the Farnese crown. Likewise, in the Villa Medici, the views decorating the apartments occupied by Cardinal Alessandro de' Medici in the 1590s were those of the major cities of Tuscany, the heart of the Medicean domain.[26]

Similar motivations explain the purpose of *camere della città* incorporated into other Italian palaces, notably those of the Palazzo Vecchio in Florence, where the decorative program of the quarters of Leo X built by Cosimo I de' Medici included a series of city views that were intended as a record of Medicean triumphs. Designed by Vasari beginning in 1555, the views in question were executed by Hans von der Straat, a native of Bruges who, as Giovanni Stradano, made Florence his adopted home. The frescoes in the Sala de Cosimo I included views of Tuscan cities that Cosimo had fortified, whereas those incorporated into the program of the Sala de Clemente VII honored Cosimo's military victories. Vasari and Stradano also joined forces to decorate Sala

26 For an explicit political reading of the Pinturicchio cycle, see Sven Sandström, "The Programme for the Decoration of the Belvedere of Innocent VIII," *Konsthistorisk Tidskrift*, XXIX (1960), 35–60. Sandström's idea is challenged in David P. Coffin, *The Villa in the Life of Renaissance Rome* (Princeton, 1979), 75. See also Schulz, "Pinturicchio and the Revival of Antiquity," *Journal of the Warburg and Courtauld Institutes*, XXV (1962), 36. In keeping with the tradition of using these city rooms for contemplative purposes, Paolo Cortese, author of *De Cardinaltu* (1510), specifically recommended that "a painted picture of the world or the depiction of its parts" was appropriate for the interior decorations of a palace's summer rooms. See Kathleen Weil-Garris and John F. D'Amico, "The Renaissance Cardinal's Ideal Palace: A Chapter from Cortese's *De Cardinalatu*," in Henry A. Millon (ed.), *Studies in Italian Art and Architecture, Fifteenth through Eighteenth Centuries* (Rome, 1980), 95. Coffin, *Villa in Renaissance Rome*, 294; Glen M. Andres, *The Villa Medici in Rome* (New York, 1976), I, 321.

de Gualdralda with a series of views of Florence, again with the intention of honoring the Medici. The first *cortile* of this same palazzo acquired yet another series of city views in 1565. Executed by artists from the north of Italy, the series, which depicted the imperial cities of Germany, was specifically commissioned to celebrate the marriage of Francesco de' Medici to Giovanna d' Austria.[27]

Although topographical accuracy came to be recognized as an integral part of the Italian *camera della città,* the city views in question were customarily subordinated to an overall decorative scheme designed to honor or somehow to demonstrate the power and majesty of a particular family. These *vedute,* in keeping with the encomiastic tradition, served principally as icons or emblems of fame. Topographical fidelity, although important, was a secondary concern.

The similarity between these "city rooms" and the city views hanging in the Alcázar adds yet another dimension to our understanding of why Philip brought Van den Wyngaerde to Spain. The king intended this artist's cityscapes to serve as emblems of Habsburg power, symbols of the vast empire under his personal control. But what remains to be established is how he came to the use of city views for this purpose.

Philip II was the first Spanish ruler ever to employ city views in this fashion; there is no record that city views had previously been used as decoration in any Spanish palace, royal or otherwise, prior to the Van den Wyngaerde commission. Philip could have learned about the *camera della città* from his agents and ambassadors in Italy, although there is no evidence of any such report. What

27 For a reconstruction of the *camera della città* that Francesco II Gonzaga, Duke of Mantua, included in his villa at Gonzaga in the 1490s, see Clifford W. Brown, "Francesco Bonsignori: Painter to the Gonzaga Court - New Documents," *Accademia Virgiliana di Mantova. Atti e Memorie,* XLVII (1979), 81–85. According to Schulz, "Barberi's View of Venice," 465–466, this room, with its alternating views of "inland" and "maritime" cities, may not have had a deeper political purpose. However, the *saletta della città* that the Gonzaga incorporated into their palace in Mantua in the 1590s does appear to have a program that reflects the family's glories. See Giovanni Paccagnini, *Il palazzo ducale di Mantova* (Turin, 1969), 152–156, Fig. 151. For a detailed description of the various cycles of city views in the Palazzo Vecchio, see Eitone Allegri and Alessandro Cecchi, *Palazzo Vecchio e i Medici. Guida storica* (Florence, 1980), 143–149, 166–174, 208–212, 277–281. Vasari's description of how he had to climb various hills in order to sketch the panoramic view of the city that was subsequently painted on the walls of the *sala de guardralda* may be found in his "Ragionaménto Primo," in his *Opere,* VIII, 174–175.

is certain is that Philip, en route to the Low Countries in 1548, visited the castle of Gian Giacomo de' Medici in Melegnano, a small town near Milan. Medici, who had served in the Emperor's army in Germany, redecorated this castle shortly before Philip's visit. In honor of the prince's father, he renamed the entrance hall the *sala dell' Imperatore* and commissioned local artists to copy on its walls views of seven imperial cities—Basel, Spire, Worms, Cologne, Erfurt, Fulda, and Frankfurt-on-the-Oder—previously reproduced in Munster's *Cosmographia universalis*. Since Philip would not have encountered anything remotely similar on his subsequent travels to Germany, the Low Countries, and England, it seems reasonable to conclude that the entrance hall in Melegnano served as the model for the views that he later had painted in Madrid's Alcázar.[28]

Philip seems to have had mixed motives when he invited Van den Wyngaerde to Spain. Scientific considerations mingled with dynastic and political concerns, and this combination, in conjunction with the topographical skills of the artist, resulted in a rare yet remarkably complete contemporary portrait of a sixteenth-century state. Thanks to these drawings, the physical appearance of the cities of sixteenth-century Spain can be established as never before. In terms of the genre of city views, Philip's commission to Van den Wyngaerde is of considerable historical importance because it represents a synthesis of the two great traditions of views—the encomiastic and the topographical. In the mid-sixteenth century such a synthesis was relatively new, but then Philip II was no ordinary patron. As a ruler of cities as

---

28 The only other contemporary use of city views as palace decoration in Spain were those painted during the 1570s in the courtyard of the palace of the Marquis de Santa Cruz's palace at El Viso. For the palace at Melegnano, see Giovanni Battista Sannazzaro, "For a Study of Some Woodcuts in the *Cosmographia Universalis*: Comparison with Lombardy Frescoes of the Sixteenth Century," *Print Collector*, XLIX (1979), 10–29. For Philip's visit to this palace, see Juan Cristóbal Calvete de Estrella, *El felicísimo viaje del muy alto y muy poderoso príncipe don Felipe* (Madrid, 1930), I, 91–92; Vicente Alvarez (ed. M. T. Dovillé), *Relation du beau voyage que fit aux Pays-Bas, en 1548, le prince Philippe d'Espagne, notre seigneur* (Brussels, 1964), 48. According to Alvarez, Philip, upon leaving Mantua, visited "une maison de plaisance" that belonged to the Duke of Mantua. This may have been the Gonzaga palace at Marimolo where he could have seen yet another *camera della città*. Munster, *Cosmographia universalis* (Basel, 1544).

widely dispersed as Brussels and Naples, Madrid and Milan, he was in a unique position to combine the Italianate *camera della città* with the topographical city views characteristic of Europe north of the Alps. Philip's ability to fuse these two genres in a single commission was not accidental. Rather, it reflected the breadth and sophistication of his artistic tastes.

Jonathan Brown

Enemies of Flattery: Velázquez' Portraits of

Philip IV Since antiquity, portraits of rulers have reflected the aspirations, ideals, and pretensions of those in power. Because these images epitomize a ruler's self-concept, they are valuable sources for understanding the personalities and programs of the sitters. The messages of ruler portraits can be decoded by standard methods of content analysis, but equally important is the subtlety of conception and the quality of execution, elements which were always appreciated by the shrewder princes and potentates.

In the seventeenth century, the period with which I am concerned here, many of the best artists were employed at the major courts, where they consolidated the traditions of princely glorification which had begun to take shape during the previous 200 years. In general terms, as the power of the absolute monarch grew, the images of the ruler became more assertive in their claims and richer in their references to the virtues embodied in the prince. As fashioned by artists such as Peter Paul Rubens, Anthony Van Dyck, and Charles LeBrun, the Baroque ruler portrait speaks tellingly of the golden age of the European monarch. How strange, then, that the portraits of Philip IV of Spain, one of the greatest rulers, painted by Diego de Velázquez, one of the greatest artists, should go against the grain of the prevailing trend. An examination of this phenomenon affords the opportunity to study concepts of kingship in the early modern period as they are reflected in official state portraiture.

It is a rare study of Velázquez which fails to comment on the restraint and sobriety of these portraits. Explanations of the phenomenon, however, are difficult to find. The one in widest circulation postulates that the painter was concerned with expressing the essence of kingly power, which made redundant the use of allegory. Undoubtedly, this observation is correct, but it does not

Jonathan Brown is Carroll and Milton Petrie Professor of Fine Arts at the Institute of Fine Arts, New York University. He is the author of *Diego de Velázquez, Painter and Courtier* (New Haven, 1986).

explain why this approach was favored by Velázquez and Philip IV and by virtually no other European ruler of the time. In this article, I offer several hypotheses to account for this unique style of royal portraiture in the Baroque age. But, first, it is important to define the differences by examining the complete range of Velázquez' portraits of the king.[1]

Velázquez settled permanently at the court of Philip IV in 1623, after an unsuccessful attempt to attract the attention of the king in the previous year. According to Francisco Pacheco, his father-in-law, Velázquez first painted Philip's portrait on August 30, 1623. The identification of this work has been much debated. I believe that it resembled the bust-length *Portrait of Philip IV* in the Meadows Museum, Dallas, if it was not this very work. However, it is also possible that this picture is a lifestudy, intended to serve as the model for a full-length portrait. This conjecture leads to another—namely, that this full-length portrait is identifiable with a picture repainted by Velázquez later in the 1620s and now partly visible beneath the subsequent alterations. This is the famous portrait in the Prado Museum (Fig. 1). With the passing of time and subsequent changes in the transparency of the pigment, it is easy to see, even with the naked eye, that Velázquez made important revisions in the pose. Fortunately, the original version was copied before the revisions were made and is represented in paintings in the Metropolitan Museum of Art, New York, and the Museum of Fine Arts, Boston. These images, in my view, are faithful records of Velázquez' initial portrait of Philip IV.

The stark simplicity of this portrait is self-evident. Almost nothing about the sitter indicates his regal status or his wealth and power. He displays only a single attribute, the insignia of the Order of the Golden Fleece, of which he was grand master. However, this discreet emblem is charged with meaning, for it indicates Philip's inherited status as defender of the Catholic religion, a principal and hereditary obligation of the Spanish Habsburgs. More elaborate examples of princely portraiture were undoubtedly known to Philip and his court, yet there is no sign of

---

1 José López-Rey, *Velázquez. The Artist as Maker* (Lausanne, 1979), 63–67. The following survey of Velázquez' portraits of Philip IV is based on Brown, *Velázquez*, 45–47, 85–88, 112–116, 132, 173, 229–230.

Fig. 1   Velázquez, *Philip IV.*

SOURCE: Museo del Prado, Madrid.

their impact on this work or the revised version done a few years later.

Velázquez' next portrait of the king was a large-scale equestrian portrait completed in 1626. This work no longer survives, but eyewitness descriptions suggest that it was not an elaborate composition. The horse, the rider, and a landscape background are the only elements mentioned in the three sources which described the work before it vanished in the fire in the Alcázar of Madrid in 1734. When completed, this portrait was placed in a newly created stateroom in the Alcázar, where it remained for only two years. It was then replaced by what might be called an up-to-date version of the subject by Rubens. Rubens, who was at the Spanish court from September 1628 to March 1629, executed a typical Baroque allegory with symbols and personifications which also fell victim to the Alcázar fire, but is still known from a copy in the Uffizi Gallery. Nevertheless, Velázquez was to have the last word on the subject of royal equestrian portraits (Fig. 2). His picture of Philip IV for the Hall of Realms in the Buen Retiro Palace, completed in 1635, answers perfectly to Palomino's description of the lost portrait of 1626: "The portrait showed His Majesty dressed in armor and mounted on a fine horse and was executed with the care and attention required for so great a subject, on a large canvas, life-size, and even the landscape was taken from nature."[2]

From 1629 to early 1631, Velázquez was in Italy on a trip undertaken to acquaint himself with Italian art. He visited Milan, Venice, Rome, and Naples, where he would have seen, among other things, a great variety of portraiture, and especially allegorical portraiture, in which the Italians excelled. But once back in Madrid, there were almost no traces of this experience in his royal portraits (although his technique had been wholly transformed). The *Portrait of Philip IV* in Vienna, completed by September 1632, is largely a workshop picture, but it appears to be based on a full-length prototype by Velázquez, which is known through a copy in the Hermitage. Once again, the king wears the habitual black costume and the Order of the Fleece and holds a petition in one hand. Some attempt to monumentalize the figure

2 Antonio Palomino, *El museo pictórico y escala óptica* (Madrid, 1947; orig. pub. 1724), 898.

Fig. 2 Velázquez, *Philip IV on Horseback.*

SOURCE: Museo del Prado, Madrid.

is apparent in the addition of a loggia in the right background and a heavy swag of drapery at the left. These elements, which appear to have been borrowed from Rubens' full-length portrait of the king (a copy of which is in the Galleria Durazzo-Pallavicini in Genoa), are devoid of symbolic content, although they do increase the impressiveness of the composition.

Between 1635 and 1638, Velázquez painted two more important portraits of the king. The first is *Philip IV in Brown and Silver* (Fig. 3). From a technical and coloristic standpoint, the picture is exceptionally brilliant. But iconographically it is again ultra-conservative. It is as if Velázquez had lifted the figure of the king from an earlier portrait and given him new clothes.

Fig. 3 Velázquez, *Philip IV in Brown and Silver.*

SOURCE: National Gallery, London.

More surprising still is the second portrait, *Philip IV as Hunter,* painted for the Torre de la Parada between 1636 and 1638 (Fig. 4). A comparison with Van Dyck's *Charles I as Hunter* makes the point clearly: the elegance of the latter portrait makes Philip look more like one of the beaters than the royal huntsman.

In 1644, Velázquez accompanied the king on campaign in Aragón and painted one of his best-documented pictures—the *"Fraga Philip"* (Fig. 5). The picture was executed during the month of June under difficult campaign conditions, while the royal army was assaulting Lérida to liberate it from the French. The siege was a success and in August the king entered the reconquered city. Meanwhile, Velázquez's portrait had been dispatched to Madrid, where the resident Catalan community requested permission to display it at a thanksgiving service.

Portraits of a ruler victorious in war offered an irresistible opportunity for painters in the seventeenth century; Louis XIV devoted the entire decoration of the Galerie des Glaces to his victories in the Dutch War. Admittedly, he had more cause to celebrate, but rulers were by no means adverse to having successful skirmishes magnified into glorious victories. But, except for the red costume and the fact that the king faces to his right instead of to his left, there is not much difference between this and Velázquez' other standing portraits of Philip IV.

The two final portraits of Philip IV date from the 1650s; they display an amazing lack of apparatus. Both portraits are bust-length and show the now-aged king posed against a plain black background. The earlier of the two (Fig. 6) was in existence by 1655, when it was engraved, whereas the second (National Gallery, London, costume completed by another hand) was painted before 1657, when it, too, served as the model for a print. Once again, an obvious, even blatant, comparison can be drawn— Hyacinthe Rigaud's 1702 *Portrait of Louis XIV,* which is as arrogant as Velázquez' portraits are modest. However, at the risk of vitiating this custom-made comparison, it should be pointed out that neither of the portraits of Philip was ever intended to be put on display. Rather, they appear to be life studies made for the workshop, which upon occasion incorporated the portrait into a grander format (Madrid, Prado no. 1219). Still, even the most ambitious of the workshop creations do not alter the traditional image of the king.

Fig. 4 Velázquez, *Philip IV as Hunter.*

SOURCE: Museo del Prado, Madrid.

Fig. 5 Velázquez, *Philip IV at Fraga.*

SOURCE: Frick Collection, New York.

Fig. 6 Velázquez, *Philip IV in Old Age.*

SOURCE: Museo del Prado, Madrid.

These few pictures constitute the corpus of Velázquez' portraits of Philip IV, and a remarkable corpus it is. In not a single
work does he display an attribute which could not have been
worn by a high-ranking nobleman. If we placed Velázquez' images of Philip IV alongside those, not of a powerful monarch like
Louis XIV or Charles I, but next to those of a regional princeling
like the Grand Duke Cosimo de' Medici, and did not otherwise
identify the subjects, we would be entitled to assume that Cosimo
ruled half the globe and Philip a small corner.[3]

Describing this phenomenon is easier than explaining it, for
no single explanation will suffice. Let us begin with one idea
which has already been introduced into the literature by Elliott
and myself in our book on the Palace of the Buen Retiro. There

3 For the portraits of Cosimo I de' Medici, see Karla Langedijk, *The Portraits of the
Medici. I: Fifteenth through Eighteenth Centuries* (Florence, 1981), 79–120, 407–530.

we note that the "Habsburg kings of Spain did not have to advertise their power and majesty in quite the same way as did lesser potentates—as heads of a world-wide empire, they were universally recognized as the most powerful monarchs on earth. The name of the king of Spain was synonymous with political might and grandeur. This may explain why Velázquez, for example, almost always dispensed with symbolic attributes when painting the king. The person of Philip was a completely satisfactory symbol of all that was regal." In other words, actions spoke louder than symbols.[4]

Proof of this observation is found in an unnoticed consequence of Rubens' visit to Madrid in 1628/29: he was not commissioned to execute a decorative ensemble in praise of the king. In 1622, Rubens' trip to Paris produced the Marie de' Medici cycle and plans for another series dedicated to Henri IV. His visit to London seven years later resulted in the commission of the Banqueting Hall ceiling in honor of James I. But in Madrid, his genius for allegory went entirely unappreciated. Indeed, his portraits of Philip IV, except for the *Equestrian Portrait,* show that even this irrepressible artist was weighed down by the taste in Spanish royal portraiture (see the *Portrait of Philip IV,* Kunsthaus, Zurich). Thus, a potential turning-point in the history of Spanish royal imagery was missed; allegory was rejected as an effective means of royal propaganda and the tradition of simple representation of the monarch continued without interruption.[5]

In addition to an apparent preference for understatement, another factor came into play. There is reason to believe that Philip IV insisted on scrupulous accuracy in representations of his person, as seen in the copies of Velázquez' first portrait of the king in Boston and New York. Velázquez, like any aspiring court painter, took pains to improve the king's appearance, primarily by reducing the length of the head and the thrust of the jaw. In the revision of the portrait (Madrid, Prado), however, the suppressed elements appear, which are both more realistic and less attractive. It is possible that among the reasons for the revision was a desire for greater truth to life.

4 Brown and John H. Elliott, *A Palace for a King: The Buen Retiro and the Court of Philip IV* (New Haven, 1980), 150.
5 See Frances Huemer, *Corpus Rubenianum Ludwig Burchard, Part XIX. Portraits* (London, 1977), I, 62–80.

This preference surfaces again in a document of October 1 and 3, 1633, ordering the court painters Vicente Carducho and Velázquez to inspect portraits of the royal family which are "not good likenesses, most of them, while others show indecent costumes and others are made too small with tiny figures. And it is not suitable that portraits be made, sold, and displayed in public which are not well made and like the persons represented and with the required decency." The constables of court were ordered to collect all images of the royal family on public display and bring them for inspection to the two painters. Eighty-four paintings were inspected, a majority of which were found to be wanting. Accordingly, the faces had to be erased and repainted to a better standard of accuracy and art. As this document suggests, quality and verisimilitude in royal portraits were a matter of concern to the court.[6]

A second occasion occurred in 1642, when the long-awaited bronze *Equestrian Portrait of Philip IV,* executed in Florence by Pietro Tacca, arrived in Madrid. The lifesize statue had been commissioned in 1634, and, in the interval, naturally, the king's appearance had changed. Thus, Tacca's son, Ferdinando, who had brought the statue from Italy, was ordered to rework the king's face to bring it into line with his present appearance.[7]

At about the same time, another equestrian portrait underwent a similar change. A full-size copy of Rubens' portrait of 1628/29 was made for some unknown purpose. However, again, the face was changed to reflect the inevitable toll exacted by the passing years; the king looks much as he does in the *Fraga Portrait* of 1644.[8]

Further proof of the desire for fidelity to appearance is found in an unpublished letter written toward the end of the king's life. The letter states his desire, for reasons of advanced age, never to be portrayed again. By implication, he seems to have resisted the use of a simple, if ultimately futile, way to disguise the ravages of old age—the services of a flattering portraitist. However, physiognomic accuracy and allegory were never mutually exclusive. Even the vain Sun King made concessions to the fading luster of

6 *Varia Velazqueña* (Madrid, 1960), II, 236, doc. 53.
7 Brown and Elliott, *A Palace,* 111–114.
8 See López-Rey, *Velázquez,* 434, where the painting of the head is improbably attributed to Velázquez.

his person precisely by having his portrait filled with magnificent finery and a showy setting. But Philip's lifelong concern with verisimilitude does indicate a hostile attitude toward exaggerating or distorting the facts of his appearance. Such an attitude might have made him wary of the traditional flattery of court portraiture. Cherubs with attributes of his glory were not constant companions; personifications of virtue never entered his chamber. To a literal-minded person, there could be no justification for including these elements in his portraits.

The weight of tradition was a heavy burden to Philip. His ancestors had been among the greatest princes of Europe and had assembled vast territories which he was obliged to defend and bequeath intact to his heirs. Yet, from the moment of his accession to power, the prospects for the completion of this mission were clouded and, as we know, the clouds descended, never again to lift. The imperial legacy also entailed an iconographical legacy which stemmed from Charles V, emperor and founder of the Spanish Habsburg dynasty. This paragon of princes was Philip's great-grandfather; and his grandfather was the almost equally redoubtable king, Philip II. The image of their greatness was always before Philip's eyes, both metaphorically and visually.

The visual image had been forged during the reign of Charles V. From the studies of Yates, we know how the emperor became the repository of ancient prophecies and modern dreams. There are also numerous studies of how these potent ideas were given form by artists in northern and southern Europe. Yet it has not been sufficiently stressed that there were two branches of Caroline iconography which evolved during the emperor's lifetime.[9]

The first branch took shape in Italy on two occasions during the 1530s. The solemn entry into Bologna in 1529 and the subsequent coronation ceremony in 1530 were the first times that the antique vocabulary of glorification was marshalled in praise of a modern prince. Of greater importance was the prolonged triumphal progress through the Italian peninsula, following the victories at Tunis and La Goletta. In October 1535, the emperor paraded through Messina where, beneath arches designed by Polidoro da Caravaggio, he began his northward progress, entering Naples on November 25. Here he was greeted by a series of

---

9 Frances A. Yates, *Astraea. The Imperial Theme in the Sixteenth Century* (London, 1975).

colossi, personifying Victory, Fame, and Faith. Following was the glorious entry into Rome, where, as Vasari notes, all the best and worst artists were commanded to work on the centerpiece, the triumphal arch at the Palazzo di San Marco designed by Antonio da Sangallo. According to Vasari, the decorations of the Roman entry were the training ground for a new generation of court artists—Francesco Salviati, Battista Franco, and Baccio de Montelupo—who were to be active inventors of princely decorations in the years ahead. Finally, the emperor entered Florence on April 28, 1536, to be greeted by the most elaborate decorations yet. Vasari, Niccolò Tribolo, Baccio de Montelupo, and others created temporary structures adorned with allegories, *imprese,* and souvenirs of the heroes and rulers of antiquity. In this way, a potent new language of princely glory was codified for use by successive generations of rulers great and small. An engraved portrait of the emperor, executed by Enea Vico in 1550, epitomizes the tradition of allegorical glorification in Italy during the 1530s, a tradition that was promulgated in Charles' northern realms as well.[10]

This tradition does not impinge in any way upon Velázquez' portraits of Philip IV, and for good reason, for they depend on the second branch of imperial portraiture—the famous portraits of Titian. Titian first met the emperor in 1530, upon the occasion of the coronation, and executed a simple half-length portrait in armor (lost but known through copies). Also at this time, Francesco Parmigianino, another important artist, painted the emperor's portrait. This work is preserved in a copy now on the art market and is cast in the form of an allegory. Here Charles is clad in full armor and attended by the infant Hercules, who offers him a globe as symbol of his dominion over earth. The other figure is Fame, who holds a laurel in one hand and a palm in the other, symbolizing worldly and spiritual victory respectively. Judging from his neglect of Parmigianino and his continued patronage of Titian, the emperor was not pleased with this literary approach to personal portraiture. His decision may also have been motivated by aesthetic factors. But there is reason to believe that he consciously rejected this mode of portraiture in favor of the

10 See André Chastel, "Les entrées de Charles Quint en Italie," in Jean Jacquot (ed.), *Les Fêtes de la Renaissance. II: Fêtes et cérémonies de Charles Quint* (Paris, 1975; 2nd ed.), 197–206. It is here that Chastel cites the references to Giorgio Vasari, *Le vite de' più excellenti pittori, scultori i architetti* (Florence, 1568), mentioned above.

straightforward approach used by Titian, who henceforth became his favorite painter.[11]

Thus, when the emperor and Titian met again in Bologna in 1533, the resultant portrait was *Charles V with a Hound,* which appears to have been copied from a painting by Hans Seisseneger. A work of disarming informality, it is clearly the inspiration for Velázquez's *Portrait of Philip IV as Hunter.*

In the most famous portrait of the emperor, *Charles V at Muhlberg,* painted in Augsburg in 1548, Titian again resorted to understatement. Panofsky has interpreted the picture as depicting the emperor as a Christian warrior through subtle allusions to classical antiquity. But it is the eloquent understatement and re-strained sense of grandeur which make the greatest impression and which are revived in Velázquez' *Equestrian Portrait of Philip IV.* From these two portraits and another masterpiece of under-stated majesty (Munich, Alte Pinakothek), also painted in Augs-burg in 1548, it can be deduced that the emperor made a conscious decision to avoid rhetorical excess in his official portraits. This decision was to prove binding on the Spanish House of Habs-burg.[12]

However, there is still some distance between the restrained portraits of Charles V by Titian and the often austere portraits of Philip IV by Velázquez. None of the known portraits of the emperor represent him in the stern black costume seen in the images of Philip IV. This element was introduced into the icon-ography of the Spanish Habsburgs by Philip II. During the first half of his reign, Philip II was portrayed with simplicity, but also with elegance. Titian's portrait of the prince in armor painted between 1550 and 1551 (Madrid, Prado) is based on the lost portrait of the emperor and exemplifies this stage of the devel-opment. There is an even more ambitious *portrait d'apparat* (Cin-cinnati, Art Museum), which shows Philip II wearing a crown and holding a scepter. It was not until around 1580 that the first "black" portrait of the king appeared in a work attributed to Alonso Sánchez Coello (Madrid, Prado). Although his Flemish

---

11 Harold E. Wethey, *The Paintings of Titian. II: The Portraits* (London, 1971), 18–22, 35–38, 85–91, catalogue nos. 20–22. Sydney J. Freedberg, *Parmigianino. His Works in Painting* (Cambridge, Mass., 1950), 112–113. As of this writing, Parmigianino's painting of Charles V is on loan to the Art Museum of Princeton University.

12 Erwin Panofsky, *Problems in Titian. Mostly Iconographic* (New York, 1969), 84–87.

subjects continued to make limited use of allegory in representations of the king, Philip's Spanish painters thereafter followed this
model, culminating in the spectral portrait attributed to Pantoja
de la Cruz (El Escorial). The distance between this late portrait
of Philip II and Velázquez' first portraits of Philip IV is not great.[13]

Yet there is more to this similarity than meets the eye because, to the best of my knowledge, there is no portrait of Philip
III that bridges the gap between grandfather and grandson. Almost without exception, Philip III was portrayed standing,
dressed in half-armor, and holding a scepter. Indeed, the very
lack of variety is amazing. In matters of royal iconography, as in
statesmanship, the reign of Philip III is marked by a lack of
initiative and imagination.[14]

The stagnation of Philip III's reign was reversed when his
son, Philip IV, came to the throne in 1621. Under the guidance
first of Baltasar de Zúñiga, and then of his nephew, Gaspar de
Guzmán, the Count-Duke of Olivares, a clean break with the
immediate past became a cornerstone of a new regime dedicated
to restoring the fading glory of the Spanish monarchy. Thus, it
is no surprise that the reformers cast a longing eye backward to
that moment when Spanish power and reputation still held sway,
the reign of Philip II. The conscious emulation of Philip II at the
start of the new reign was noted in a letter from the imperial
ambassador in Madrid, dated May 2, 1621:

> The death of the Christian, saintly king [Philip III] has saddened
> us more than can be said, but if the new king . . . follows up on
> his good beginnings and has a long life, the Spanish Monarchy will
> recover. . . . The king wishes to model his government on that of
> his grandfather, Philip II, and to this end has removed all the
> benefits from his ministers and has installed everywhere ministers
> who still remain from that majesty.[15]

In artistic terms, the consequences of the revival of the era
of Philip II are dramatically seen in two portraits of Philip IV

---

13 For Titian's portraits of Philip II, see Wethey, *Paintings of Titian,* 126–133, catalogue
nos. 78–84.
14 For a representative selection of portraits of Philip III, see Ciriaco Pérez Bustamante,
La España de Felipe III (Madrid, 1979).
15 Elliott, *El Conde-Duque de Olivares y ha herencia de Felipe II* (Valladolid, 1977), 68.

done only a few years apart. Rodrigo de Villandrando's portrait of *Prince Philip with the Dwarf Soplillo* (Madrid, Prado), probably executed around 1620, shows the sitter dressed in the elaborate finery of Philip III's reign. In Velázquez' portrait of 1623, the king is dressed in solemn black and unaccompanied by attributes or other figures, just as his grandfather appeared in his late portraits. The startling change of format may be interpreted as a signal of the rigorous policy of reform articulated by Olivares at the start of the reign, a reform which, among its lesser features, sought to eliminate the costly, showy style of dress of the previous regime. To contemporaries, this portrait would have exemplified the deliberate contrast between the new king and his indolent father, who had allowed Spanish power to wane while he did nothing.

Symbols sometimes outlive the circumstances which inspired their creation, and this was to be the fate of the austere formula of Spanish Habsburg portraiture. By the end of his reign, Philip IV recognized that his monarchy had withered, not prospered. Thus, it is tempting to interpret the simple black costume work in Velázquez' late portraits as a sign of melancholy, not of optimism. But by then, all meaning had been drained from the motif and it had become simply the uniform of the King of Spain. Charles II, the enfeebled successor to Philip IV, frequently was portrayed in this guise (see the portraits by Carreño de Miranda in Madrid, Prado and Gemäldegalerie, Berlin-Dahlem), although he presided over a marked decline of Spanish power. The symbol even managed to survive the extinction of the Spanish Habsburgs at his death in 1700 and was given a new, if short, lease on life by the Bourbons, who were clearly oblivious to the original significance. In the first portrait of Philip V, executed in 1701 by Rigaud (Versailles), the new Bourbon monarch wears the now-anachronistic black costume and *golilla* (simple collar) which appears in Velázquez' early and late portraits of Philip IV, as if to claim legitimate succession to a dynasty not his own.

Thus, behind Velázquez' simplified portraits of Philip IV lies the eventful history of a man, a reign, and a dynasty. By evoking the memory of the great princes who preceded him, Philip thought he needed no further help from a complicated symbolic apparatus in staking his claim to glory. It is for this reason that the portraits strike a retrospective note. For Philip, the key to the future lay in the past. Despite the efforts of Olivares to modernize the Spanish monarchy, the king failed to recognize that new circumstances required new policies. By the mid-1650s, the favored portrait type accurately reflected the inability to adapt to the shifting world of early modern Europe and the impending decline of Spain within that world.

Simon Schama

The Domestication of Majesty: Royal Family
Portraiture, 1500–1850

More than the passage of time separates Edwin Landseer's *Windsor Castle in Modern Times* (1841–1845) from Jean Nocret's *Allegorical Portrait of the Family of Louis XIV* (1670) (Figs. 1 and 2). They stand at opposite ends of a process that transformed the image of a reigning dynasty from a clan of deities to a domestic parlor group. In the 1670s, when Louis XIV's brother, Monsieur, commissioned Nocret's picture for his house at St. Cloud, there was not yet any conception of a royal *family*. By the middle of the nineteenth century, as calotypes and daguerrotypes were already transmitting images of Victoria, Albert, and their children to their subjects, the identification between dynasty and family had become a serviceable cliche.

This is not the whole story. Recently, Cannadine, in a rich and suggestive contribution, has argued that the British monarchy owes its current appeal primarily to the "reinvention of tradition" at the end of the nineteenth century in the form of the elaborate coronation ceremonial. The resilience and popularity of the monarchy, it is further argued, has been the result of this reinvigorated program of ritual and spectacle. No one old enough to remember the imperial scale of the coronation of Elizabeth II in 1953 could question the basic truth of this contention. But it may not be the whole truth.[1]

Those monarchies that have survived into the late twentieth century have done so through a calculated combination of the ritual and the prosaic; of high ceremony and bourgeois demystification; garden parties along with the anointing oil. Landseer, who was the most intimate of Queen Victoria's court artists—her drawing master as well as her obedient servant—understood this

Simon Schama is Professor of History at Harvard University. He is the author of *The Embarrassment of Riches: An Interpretation of Dutch Culture in its Golden Age,* forthcoming.

1   David Cannadine, "The Context, Performance and Meaning of Ritual: The British Monarchy and the 'Invention of Tradition,' 1820–1977," in Eric J. Hobsbawm and Terence Ranger (eds.), *The Invention of Tradition* (Cambridge, 1983), 101–164.

Fig. 1   Edwin Landseer, *Windsor Castle in Modern Times,* 1841–1845.

Fig. 2   Jean Nocret, *Allegorical Portrait of the Family of Louis XIV,* 1670.

SOURCES: Fig. 1—The Collection of Her Majesty the Queen. Fig. 2—Musée Historique, Versailles.

balance of sensibilities perfectly. Accordingly, he incorporated romantic and fanciful elements in *Windsor Castle*: the Prince Consort's bag of game improbably strewn about the floor, and his *Freischutz* boots. But the sharply drawn distinctions between manly sports and womanly delicacy (signified by the posy held in the Queen's hand), and the hunting and house dogs are those of the Victorian marriage, not the Victorian crown. For in Landseer's view of the Green Drawing Room, it is the standing wife-queen who attends on the seated husband-prince. And this vision of the domestic virtues, and of family piety, is completed by the distant prospect of the queen's mother, the Duchess of Kent, being solicitously wheeled about the park in a bath chair.[2]

The rise of the concept of a royal family was accompanied by the rise of the royal family portrait. Indeed, no firm distinction existed between the image and the political reality. For, once the means of mass production and distribution of such images was available, allegiance (or at least the sentimental bond forged between monarch and subjects) depended on a steady flow of appealing images. Beside the continuing importance of military uniform and coronation robe portraits, the genre of nursery album pictures and conjugal portraits became the stock-in-trade of the monarch-mongering business. Along with the traditional celebration of the monarch's birthday, a whole calendar of domestic events—births, christenings, betrothals, weddings, and comings-of-age—was transferred to the public domain.[3]

This essay examines the dramatic alteration of representations of royalty as a family group. To take that process for granted as an axiomatic historical process is to assume that in this case imagery followed obediently behind social reality; form hid function. It also implies that the domestication of royal family portraiture may conveniently be explained as an obvious consequence of the inexorable rise of the companionate family. But, in fact, the nineteenth-century royal families were, in all their essentials, the very opposite of the image that they projected. They held

2 For a full account of this painting, see Richard Ormond, *Sir Edwin Landseer* (Philadelphia, 1982), 150–152. *Windsor Castle* took Landseer four years to complete between 1841 and 1845 but, in the end, the queen called it "a very beautiful picture and altogether very cheerful and pleasing."

3 On the change of court fashion from formal dress to riding coats and uniforms, see the fine article by Philip Mansel, "Monarchy, Uniform, and the Rise of the *Frac,* 1760–1830," *Past & Present,* 96 (1982), 103–132.

tenaciously to the rules of patriarchal dynasticism, arranging marriages with the good of the dynasty paramount and without any thought of affectionate consent on the part of the partners. A reasonably typical case was that of Princess May of Teck who, when her betrothed, the Duke of Clarence, died of influenza, was summarily transferred to his brother George, the future George V. Despite the stock images turned out by Winterhalter of the queen-as-mother blissfully surrounded by her troop of happy infants, Victoria's feelings about the pleasures of a large family were decidedly mixed.[4]

It is not only the disparity between social reality and representation that is at issue here, but also the absence of inevitability in the process by which dynastic images became domestic. For, if there were some reason to want to promote a public image that would embody values and virtues dear to the solid middle class on whom the throne rested, then there was quite as much reason to ensure a decent area of separation between the realms of the ordinary and the magnificent. In some ways, it is less surprising that the family group did not come to monopolize pictures of royalty, to the exclusion of coronation and parade-ground images, than that the image of a domestic tribe came to be so popular at all.

What explains this change? To treat the issue purely as illustrated history would be to seek explanations external to imagery. Apart from the onward and upward march of the nuclear family, a different, although related, account might see the increasingly bourgeois quality of royal imagery as a defensive response against the tide of domestic sensibility that reached a climax in the French Revolution. There is no doubt that the emblems of republican sovereignty, although expressed primarily in neoclassical allegory, did make room for domestic idylls alongside pikes, liberty hats, carpenters' levels, eyes of surveillance, and the fasces of unity. Rousseau's virtuous family, dressed *a la sans culotte*, replaced

---

4 Kenneth Rose, *George V* (London 1984), 25. See, for e.g., Frans Xaver Winterhalter, *Queen Victoria and her Family in 1846*. Queen Victoria's diaries suggest a great deal of tender feeling and love for her small children. But she loathed and dreaded the ordeal by which they were brought into the world, and took little pleasure in infants while they were incapable of anything more than "that terrible frog-like action." See Christopher Hibbert (ed.), *Queen Victoria in her Letters and Journals* (New York 1985), 92.

Louis, the impotent and betraying *pater patriae*, and the vicious and ruthless *putaine autrichienne* as the repository of patriotic feeling.[5]

The image of the French monarchy had changed considerably during the eighteenth century. But it had altered less out of any nervous reaction to opposition polemics on virtuous or vicious families than to the pervasive influence of a purely representational fashion: the conversation piece. Royal portraiture was not, then, a weak field onto which was impressed whatever message or ideology happened to be current; it was an important genre in its own right. Its variations were fed by values and forms peculiar to the traditions of that genre, as well as by contemporary historical exigencies. It is only by taking the genre seriously as an active agent in shaping the historical self-consciousness of monarchy that the success or failure of its outward appeal can properly be understood.[6]

Once a tradition of imagery is allowed to become the primary focus of enquiry, the route from dynasticism to domesticity immediately becomes more tortuous and indeterminate than the axioms of family history might indicate. Instead of one kind of portraiture obliterating an earlier form, the latter seems to evolve from the former. Even in the striking contrast between allegorical formality and domestic informality, there remain equally striking affinities. There is, for example, a relationship, albeit distant, between Nocret's *Family of Louis XIV* (Fig. 2) and Landseer's portrait of Victoria and Albert dressed as King Edward III and Queen Philippa (Fig. 3). Unlike Charles Le Brun's allegorical compositions where the Sun King's Apollonian attributes are presented with the utmost literalness, in Nocret's painting the be-

5 On the sources of these symbols, see Ernst Gombrich, "The Dream of Reason: Symbolism of the French Revolution," *British Journal for Eighteenth-Century Studies*, II (1979), 187–205.
6 Most surveys of court portraiture succumb to the temptations of illustrated royal history, rather than considering the cultural implications of changing form and manner. There are, however, some distinguished exceptions: Michael Levey, *Painting at Court* (New York, 1971); Oliver Millar, *The Queen's Pictures* (London, 1977); and everything written on this subject by Roy Strong, e.g., *Van Dyck: Charles on Horseback* (London, 1972). John H. Plumb, *Royal Heritage* (New York, 1977) is an outstanding example of a popular survey that integrates consideration of both institutions and imagery in an illuminating account.

holder is meant to see the contemporaries as costumed, rather than transubstantiated, into divinities. Both paintings are transparent in that the contemporaries are deliberately recognizable beneath their fancy dress. Given the semi-public nature of the two commissions—one for the younger brother of the king (but for conspicuous display in his house), the other to commemorate a costume ball—that transparency was an essential part of their commission. But there resemblances end.[7]

What is revealed in these two paintings are strikingly different relationships between family and sovereignty. The Nocret picture might be thought a benign lie about the nature of Monsieur, notorious for his pederasty. But through an artful choice of mythical persona it also served to link family relationships to the ritual pecking order at Versailles. It was Monsieur for example who was the first to wait on the king at the *entrée familière* during the interminable ceremonies of the daily *levée*. Although the king is dressed as Apollo, his brother has the attributes of the morning star that precedes (though in the deferential sense of the herald) the ascent of the sun's course in the heavens. The familial element in the painting further draws on Flemish and Dutch group portraits of the period that immortalized dead infants as angels. There are allusions, through allegorical attributes, to the recent and troubled history of the Bourbon dynasty. Anne of Austria, Louis XIV's mother, for example, is dressed as Cybele, matriarch of the gods, and the even more forlorn figure of Henrietta Maria, the widowed queen of England, carries the maritime attributes of trident and coral. Notwithstanding all of these intimate references, the family feeling of the painting is swamped by the formal, iconic representation of terrestrial divinity. Even aside from Louis' fixation with the cult of Apollo, it was in the guise of gods on earth that absolute monarchs of the seventeenth century appeared to courtiers and ambassadors. Versailles began as a mise en scene for a court masque and ended as a governmental barracks.[8]

7 For a detailed description of Nocret's painting, see Eudoxe Soulie, *Notice du Musée National de Versailles* (Versailles, 1881), II, 198.
8 For a perceptive and detailed discussion of the daily ceremonies and ritual at Versailles, see Norbert Elias, *The Court Society* (New York, 1982). On the Flemish and Dutch group portraits, see the examples by Jan Mytens and Nicolas Maes given by William Robinson, "Family Portraits of the Golden Age," *Apollo* (Dec. 1979), 494–495.

In Nocret's group, family relationships are a function of dynastic hierarchy. In the Landseer painting (set in 1842, but completed in 1846), the opposite seems to be the case. Although Prince Albert was consort and in no sense equal in sovereignty with the queen, their particular choice of fancy dress, as in the Windsor group, has the effect of reversing that relationship. Just as the transparency of the costumed portrait revealed an official court ethos, in the Landseer portrayal (and in the queen's own water color study of the same costume) it is a bourgeois marital idyll that is at its controlling center. That was fitting since the ball was, at least ostensibly, meant to benefit the depressed silk industry at Spitalfields through a kind of altruistic display of conspicuous consumption. Moreover, the monarchs that they chose to identify with had a very particular resonance for nineteenth-century sentimental history. It was thought to have been by a display of wifely devotion and with an appeal to conjugal tenderness that Philippa intervened with her victorious husband to spare the lives of the "Burghers of Calais." Their appearance before the king with ropes about their necks echoed the prostrate humility of the queen's intercession. And no one at the ball who saw Victoria and Albert in that guise, or indeed who subsequently saw Landseer's painting, could fail to be reminded of those earlier paragons of a happy royal marriage.[9]

The appeal of the Landseer painting from one devoted royal couple to their remote lineal ancestors was a useful fiction. In the fourteenth century there could have been no comparable pair portrait that proclaimed simultaneously the status of dynasty and the virtues of marriage. The closest approximation would have been the donor portrait or the tomb effigy that laid husband and wife together in a recumbent attitude of prayer. Pendant portraits appear at the Italian courts, but in a tradition that arose from civic, rather than dynastic commissions. The imperial aura that Renaissance princes appropriated for themselves was inhospitable to any representation of shared authority. Yet at least those princes who were most exercised about dynastic pedigree made their lineage the subject of public works of art.

9   Ormond, *Landseer*, 156. See the full report on the ball in *London Illustrated News* (May 14, 1842).

Fig. 3 Edwin Landseer, *Prince Albert and Queen Victoria as Edward III and Queen Philippa,* 1846.

Fig. 4 Remigius van Leemput, *The Families of Henry VII and Henry VIII* (copy after Hans Holbein), 1675.

SOURCE: Figs. 3 and 4—The Collection of Her Majesty the Queen.

The most emphatic dynastic group portrait was the mural that Hans Holbein produced for Henry VIII for the Privy Chamber in Whitehall. Although destroyed in the fire of 1698, a 1675 copy by Remigius van Leemput, a Flemish artist, together with the cartoon, provides some sense of the original (Fig. 4). The king, who was concerned to present himself as a Tudor synthesis of the houses of Lancaster and York, is shown with his father and mother, Henry VII and Elizabeth Woodville, who represented, respectively, the two embattled dynasties. Out of their union, it is necessarily implied, flowed peace and authority. The king is himself supported by the queen, Jane Seymour, who had provided him with a Protestant male heir, and stands in his distinctive heroic pose (derived from Donatello's Orsanmichele St. George): legs astride, resplendently costumed, a massive, frontal princely icon. As Strong suggests, he is, in this style, both *imperator* and *chevalier*.[10]

To characterize the dynasty gathered about the altar as a family group would be anachronistic, despite the intimate detail of the queen's lap dog nestling in her train. It is rather a dynastic tableau that proclaims the continuity of royal succession: that preoccupation which perhaps more than any other determined the king's policies. A later group portrait in somewhat the same manner, executed after Henry's death, was meant to supply the same kind of dynastic pedigree for his insecure successor, Edward VI. In this case, the incorporation of the young prince and his mother within the central canopied area of the enthroned king reinforced the directness of the male line. The princesses Mary and Elizabeth, both stigmatized by disgraced queen mothers, are relegated to the wings (though not excluded outright, from the line of succession).[11]

Formally disposed in the manner of a bas-relief or frieze, these dynastic ensembles were closer in spirit to heraldic history painting than to group portraiture. Even when their subject was the legitimacy of queens and female issue, the figure of the patriarch prince was indispensable to their symbolic purpose. For within the Renaissance and ideology of kingship there persisted a renovated version of a more archaic theme: Adamic descent. If

---

10 Strong, *Holbein and Henry VIII* (London 1967), 34–37, 42.
11 See A. Geoffrey Dickens (ed.), *The Courts of Europe* (London 1977), 37.

the Divine Right theory, as it appeared in baroque apotheoses like Peter Paul Rubens' Whitehall ceiling for James I, transported the monarch to Olympian status, it also relied on the scriptural language of Old Testament progenitive patriarchy. Robert Filmer's *Patriarcha* (London, 1680), the canonical text for this manner of royal argument, used the succession from Adam not just as a metaphor, but also as the literal historical basis on which unconditional obedience to divinely ordained monarchy should be grounded. In his speech to Parliament on March 21st, 1609, James I stated flatly that "in the Scriptures, Kings are called Gods and so their power after a certain relation compared to the Divine power. Kings are compared to Fathers of families: for a King is trewly *Parens patriae,* the politique father of his people." Conversely, it may not be altogether fortuitous that the seventeenth-century succession that was compelled to justify its legitimacy in terms of a marriage—that of William and Mary—also signified the victory of constrained over unconstrained prerogative, and of diluted matrilineal dynasticism over concentrated patrilineal absolutism.[12]

It would be rash to equate the beginnings of royal family portraiture proper with the weakening of absolutism. Diego de Velázquez' portraits of the children of Philip IV and, more particularly, Anthony Van Dyck's two portraits of the children of Charles I confound any such easy assumption. At the Stuart court, especially, there prevailed a neo-chivalric gallantry that made much—in masque, verse, and image—of the bonds of love between Charles and Henrietta Maria, and extended its tender sentiment to embrace the royal family. Those ties of affection, however, were still very much connected to the traditional concerns of lineage and succession. Even the otherwise startlingly intimate family group done for Charles I by Hendrik Pot proclaims those concerns. For it poses the royal parents together with attributes of *their* own parental and dynastic stock—emblems of peace for James I and of martial valor for Henry IV.

For all of Charles I's keen interest in Dutch art, as both patron and collector, the Pot group portrait was an innovation without much consequence. For the most part, it was either Flemish painters like Van Dyck and Rubens, or those Dutch artists who spe-

12   Charles H. McIlwain, *The Political Works of James I* (Cambridge, 1918), 307.

cialized in formal court and state portraiture—Gerrit Honthorst, Daniel Mytens, and Michiel Miereveld—who ranked high in commissions and favor. Predictably, it was on the great dynastic projects that celebrated the marriage connections of Orange and Stuart, such as the decoration of the Huis ten Bosch outside The Hague, that such artists were most suitably employed. The program for the *Oranjezaal* at the stadholder's small palace was in some sense a work of conjugal piety, being dedicated to Frederick Henry by his widow, Amalia van Solms. But the execution was grandiloquent and baroque, in the manner of the dynastic apotheoses of Pietro da Cortona at the Pitti Palace, and Rubens in Whitehall.

Ironically, it was that same connection between Orange and Stuart that, in the person and under the patronage of William III, brought Dutch taste much more systematically to the royal collections in the 1690s. The mainstream of that taste might be said to have been significantly more patrician than dynastic. Furthermore, there was in the patriotic ethos of the Dutch a strongly anti-dynastic strain, that had almost cost the House of Orange the stadholderate. Its own group portraiture was intensely concerned with the display of family power and status, but always in the context of civic, rather than dynastic authority.[13]

Although much of court portraiture was concerned to separate as remotely as possible the aura of majesty from the hearth and home of common subjects, the representation of republican space in Holland did exactly the opposite. Indeed, it was unique in seventeenth-century art in bringing together, in so self-conscious a fashion, patriotic monuments and the citizens who were to be instructed by their posterity. Paintings like De Witte's version of the tomb of William the Silent in the Nieuwe Kerk at Delft, and De Hooch's interior of the Burgomaster's Chamber in the new Amsterdam Town Hall assumed a common purpose between city fathers on the one hand and the families who were

13 It was in the aftermath of William II's attempts to purge the Dutch oligarchies of regents opposed to his military policy in 1650 that Johan de Witt attempted to preclude the House of Orange from monopolizing both the stadholderate and the captain-generalcy of the Republic. At a deeper level, early Dutch history chronicles deliberately polarize their account of the war against the Spanish in terms of a "home defense" of hearth and family against the atrocities inflicted by mercenaries who were themselves the tools of tyrants. For the implications of these atrocity chronicles see Schama, *The Embarrassment of Riches: An Interpretation of Dutch Culture in Its Golden Age,* forthcoming.

their protective concern on the other. The prince is shown here not as dynast but as tutor and moral exemplar, posthumously gratified by the act of charity that takes place in his presence; the "court" of the burgomasters as a schoolroom in civic instruction.[14]

Given this idealized conjunction of domestic and patriotic sensibilities, it is not surprising to find Dutch art offering the first instances of public men displaying their status in the context of family pleasures. A striking example is Gerard ter Borch's painting of Adriaen Pauw on his way to Munster for the peace negotiations that led, in 1648, to Spain acknowledging the independence of the Dutch Republic. The patrician pleipotentiary has chosen to have himself represented, not in princely entourage, but in a simple carriage along with his wife and daughter as though on a Sunday outing. No image could possibly speak more eloquently to the immense distance between the formal court hierarchies of dynastic display, and the disconcerting informality by which private virtues and public office were related in the Netherlands.[15]

Despite this apparently irreconcilable dichotomy between republican families and princely dynasts, a strange and paradoxical interfusion occurred toward the end of the seventeenth century. During the tenure of the King-Stadholder William, high Dutch taste was subjected to the scrutiny of apostles of classical refinement like Gerard de Lairesse. For the dwindling numbers of self-consciously old-fashioned vernacular genre painters in the 1690s this purification of taste was unhappily close to aping the French, with whom the Republic was almost continuously at war for forty years. As if to return the compliment, French classicism was itself confronted with the more expansive and fluent Flemish

14 Ilse Manke, *Emmanuel de Witte, 1617–1692* (Amsterdam, 1963), catalogue no. 27; Peter C. Sutton, *Pieter de Hooch* (Oxford, 1980), 97. De Hooch set two other paintings in the galleries of the new Town Hall (*ibid.*, nos. 67, 68) which, although less obviously taking public space and its pedagogies as their subject, were no less remarkable for freely drawing on public architecture as the setting for an ostensibly domestic interior, without losing plausibility.

15 On these themes, see Mario Praz, *Conversation Pieces: A Survey of the Informal Group Portrait in Europe and America* (University Park, Pa., 1971), 19–24. Praz begs an important issue by assuming this kind of art to be "the art of the bourgeoisie." He offers some important examples of Italian "conversational portraits," in particular Andrea Mantegna's *Ludovico Gonzaga among his Relatives,* but they remain relatively scarce compared with the much more profuse genre in the north. See also A. Staring, *De Hollanders Thuis. Gezelschapstukken uit drie eeuwen* (The Hague, 1956).

baroque influence that fueled the contention between followers of Nicholas Poussin and followers of Rubens.

A generation of artists toward the close of Louis XIV's reign, most notably the Antwerp-trained Nicolas de Largillierre, began to produce court and society pictures that were more informal in style than had hitherto been academically acceptable. This period coincided, not altogether fortuitously, with the French discovery of Dutch genre painting and the creation of the first great aristocratic collections of northern Netherlandish art. In that taste, French society had been anticipated by the English and there too the more celestial and iconic conventions of early Stuart portraiture were being diluted with more directly contemporary references and a more informal tone. James Thornhill's work for the Painted Hall at Greenwich Hospital, for example, was an uneasy compromise between the manner of high baroque mythology in the style of Pietro da Cortona's ceilings at the Pitti Palace, and the need to depict the altogether earthier motifs of the Glorious Revolution of 1688 and the Hanoverian succession. In contrast to James I's familiarity with the immortals and the divine authorization of his rule at Whitehall, William III and George I both appear at Greenwich as monarchs invited by Parliament rather than appointed by God.

In both France and England, conversation pieces in the Dutch manner began to be commissioned by aristocratic society, but not as a consequence of any imagined or real penetration of the nobility by an upwardly mobile bourgeoisie. Royal ministers such as Nicholas Fouquet and Jean Baptiste Colbert liked to bask in the reflected glow of the royal aura and either emulated the highest baroque style or else ministerially inserted themselves into an unconvincingly self-effacing corner of a royal apotheosis. It was, in fact, at the highest tier of court society, that of the heirs apparent, that opportunities arose to offer a view of the royal clan as family rather than dynasty. The restive relations of royal sons with their fathers may have produced an early acceptance of informal style as a conscious escape from the rigidly hierarchical conventions of the court. At any rate the first royal family group in France to discard allegory altogether was Pierre Mignard's group portrait for the Grand Dauphin in 1687. Likewise, it was Frederick, Prince of Wales, George II's son, who had Philippe Mercier paint his portrait in 1733 along with his sisters before the retreat of the Dutch House at Kew, in a style that economically combined two old conventions of family painting: the harmonious assembly and the outdoor party.[16]

The canonical reference point in the inauguration of an authentically royal family portrait is Largillierre's painting of Louis XIV's family, now in the Wallace Collection (Fig. 5). Together with the king and the Duchesse de Ventadour are assembled the dauphin and his son, the Duc de Bourgogne, both of whom were

Fig. 5 Nicolas de Largillierre, *The Family of Louis XIV.*

16 Mercier also did a pendant of the same group in concert at Hampton Court. See Millar, *Queen's Pictures,* pl. XVI. There was more than an element of wishful thinking in these images of sibling harmony, for Frederick apparently quarrelled with his sisters (as with his parents). Plumb, *Heritage,* 157.

to die within a few months of each other, making the ensemble a poignant counterpart to the heroic masquerade of the Nocret allegory. The Largillierre painting represents a bold departure from the iconographic conventions of the Sun King, although it is not correct to describe it as an "elimination of allegorical allusions," the image of Apollo's car being discreetly retained on the wall. Notwithstanding the dogs and the relatively informal *contrapposto* of both the dauphin and the Duc de Bourgogne, it would be going too far to see this painting as a royal conversation piece. Nor was it, as a drastic recasting of the image of the Bourbons as a family group, a particularly fruitful initiative. Louis XV, who for all the scandalous reputation of his menage at the *Parc aux Cerfs,* was certainly more sensitive than his great-grandfather to the role of *pater familias.* But the informal taste in aristocratic portraits that became more widespread during his reign did not extend to images of the royal family itself.[17]

That such a development should have occurred so decisively during the reign of George III, the Hanoverian most exercised by niceties of title and prerogative, seems on the face of it unlikely. But Dutch taste, that had made an impact on the late Stuart court through artists like Peter Lely and Godfrey Kneller with Netherlands roots and traditions, had become more pervasive as conversation pieces began to be bought and then commissioned in polite society in the 1730s. A number of William Hogarth's most important commissions in this period—for example, for the Cholomondely and Cavendish families, both the cream of the Whig elite—were executed in the informal Dutch style of the late seventeenth century that mingled anecdote and emblem in a relaxed and ingratiating manner. The shift from a dynastic, pseudo-military, or courtly presentation of status to a more urban, patrician style of display was in keeping with an elite that cultivated its pleasures as much in town as in its Palladian parks and villas. Typically, the royal family itself preserved archaic conventions longest; George II, the last English king to lead his armies in battle, was content to be depicted in traditional poses, much like

17 For some time this painting was attributed to François de Troy, but is now considered again to be by Largilliere. I am grateful to Antoine Schnapper for this information. See Schnapper, "The Position of the Portrait in France at the End of the Reign of Louis XIV," in Nan Rosenfeld et al., *Largilliere and the Eighteenth-Century French Portrait* (Montreal, 1981), 81.

his Stuart predecessors, either in coronation regalia or, more improbably, as the equestrian *rex et imperator*. There is only the hint, in an unfinished sketch by Hogarth, now in Dublin, of a royal family group that, if completed, would have been the first such royal conversation piece. It may have been successfully obstructed by William Kent for precisely that reason.

It was left to George III, the son of Frederick, Prince of Wales, himself an enthusiastic collector and patron, to inaugurate the new manner most decisively. Paradoxically it was the minister who was most detested by the Whig polemicists—the Marquess of Bute—who was the link to a new style. As the king's early tutor and a devotee of Viscount Bolingbroke's *Patriot King*, Bute had no wish to fashion an image of the monarch that was particularly concessionary. In fact, he probably reinforced suspicions of a Caledonian design against the Revolution of 1688 by having the Scottish painter Allan Ramsay paint the king's coronation portrait in the style of the grandiose full length picture he had done of Bute himself. Although the Ramsay portrait was in the most uninhibited rococo manner of Hyacinthe Rigaud and Carle van Loo, it was a formidable success, as the many demands for copies testify. But if this represented the majestic side of George III's new royal assertiveness, Bute was also instrumental in commissioning the young Johan Zoffany, who saw in his commissions an opportunity to create an altogether different kind of ensemble. It was apparently Bute's enthusiasm for Zoffany's painting of David Garrick in *The Farmer's Return* that prompted his commendation to the king. With his work for the theater and his mastery of small-scale conversation pieces, Zoffany had revived two of Hogarth's most successful genres. For the king himself he produced a strikingly relaxed portrait, despite the insignia of the Garter and the traditionally ready sword, especially compared with Van Loo's historicizing images of the martial Louis XV. In 1770, the process was taken a step further with a full-scale family group posed in a park setting that was repeated both as an engraving and as statuettes in Derby porcelain biscuit.

There is, however, something odd about the 1770 portrait that betrays either Zoffany or, more likely, his patrons as reluctant to present the royal family merely as another domestic ensemble. Although this is a family portrait, its allusions are deliberately anachronistic. The Van Dyck costume of the royal children has been extended to their father, who, ominously for Whig pessimists, wears the fallen lace collar of Charles, king and martyr, below his impeccably Hanoverian wig. Yet for all of its ostentatious historical trappings which the king favored to identify himself with his ancestors, this is not a dangerously dynastic picture. The costumes already appear self-consciously dressed-up, much as the first awkward efforts of William Kent to produce a new school of British history painting were notable for their clumsy archaisms.

This pictorial nostalgia was made even more innocuous when Zoffany's two most important contributions to royal family portraiture are considered: the 1764 painting of the Prince of Wales and the Duke of York, and the 1765 painting of the two princes, in costume, interrupting the queen at her toilet in Buckingham House (Figs. 6 and 7). Quite apart from the "fancy picture" charm of the portraits, their decor is significant in the relaxation of more bombastic conventions of royal representation. Millar has noticed that, although Zoffany carefully reproduced details of the so-called Warm Room at Buckingham House in the earlier painting, he invented some of the wall portraits, emphasizing the informality of the scene by retaining case covers on the sofa and chairs. The two Van Dyck portraits of Charles I's and of the Duke of Buckingham's children represent much less an ideological reaction than the beginnings of a sentimental revivalism. They also testify to the important fact of their repossession in 1765 into the royal collection itself. Historical nostalgia and the collector's enthusiasm for domestic decor and family feeling were all cunningly linked together in the painting by Zoffany. If the king and queen did actually hang their new Van Dycks in the Warm Room, Zoffany conceived their portraits to preside over royal children dead and royal children living, so that lineage and parentage melted into one set of harmonious associations.[18]

The 1765 painting of the queen with the two princes is bolder still in making the imagery of royal home life acceptable. There is some evidence from a royal household inventory that the roles the Prince of Wales and the Duke of York were playing were, respectively, Telemachus and a Turkish Sultan. But it would be

18 Millar, *The Later Georgian Pictures in the Collection of Her Majesty the Queen* (London, 1969), catalogue no. 1200; Mary Webster, *Johan Zoffany 1733–1810* (London, 1976).

Fig. 6   Johan Zoffany, *The Prince of Wales and the Duke of York,* 1764.

Fig. 7   Johan Zoffany, *Queen Charlotte at her Dressing Table,* 1765.

SOURCE: Figs. 6 and 7—The Collection of Her Majesty the Queen.

entirely out of keeping with the tone of the painting to embark on elaborate speculation about the significance of the allotted roles. Unlike Nocret's carefully designed allegorical parts, the princes are here merely costumed by their mother for family diversion. Paintings like this are the antecedent for Victoria and Albert in historical costume at the Buckingham Palace ball.

Zoffany's work initially found favor with his royal patrons. The King bestowed the unusual distinction on him of a personal nomination to the Royal Academy, thus obviating the requirement of election by the fellows. Ironically, it was not a royal portrait at all, but the bravura masterpiece of the Uffizi *Tribuna*—another official commission—that cost him his special place at court. That his conversational style may have caught on in Europe is suggested by a similarly intimate portrait of the Habsburg Archduke Pietro Leopoldo and his family done during his stay in Florence.

Informality did not wholly replace formality as the dominant public image of the reigning monarch in Britain. Probably the most popular and enduring of all the images of George III remained the grandiloquent coronation portrait by Ramsay. But the king's other favored artists—Benjamin West and Thomas Gainsborough—both provided family groups, either singly or in series, in the new, relatively informal manner. Many of these paintings, it is true, were for private, rather than public audiences. An artist who was insensitive to the difference, or who pushed informality to the edge of disrespect, could expect abrupt discouragement. When Thomas Lawrence, a virtuoso of brilliant palette (and a great favorite of the Prince Regent), persuaded Queen Charlotte to sit with her hair unpowdered and *décoiffée* and with a loose shawl over her shoulders, the result, though one of the most beautiful of all royal portraits, displeased the king so much that the portrait was rejected outright.

There was no precise moment at which private domestic images of the monarchy became acceptable public ones. But toward the end of the eighteenth century there is substantial visual evidence, especially from the graphic arts, that informal, and even satirical images of the king and queen became charged with positive as well as negative connotations. Their identification with John Bull's foreigner-hating bluff simplicity, especially during the French wars, however grotesquely rendered in some of James

Gillray's caricatures, became something of a patriotic asset. That the king might be lampooned without any real threat of serious *lèse majesté* was a unique situation in a Europe of increasingly defensive *ancien régimes*. In 1787 the poet John Woolcot could write of George III's visit to a brewery by applauding his common touch: "Thus to the world of *great* whilst others crawl,/ Our Sovereign peeps into the world of small." The visual equivalent of that irreverent but unthreatening backhanded compliment was Thomas Rowlandson's famous drawing given the title *King George and Queen Charlotte Driving Through Deptford,* where the monarch is reduced to no more than the minutest and least significant figure at the extreme right of a composition dominated by the likes of the Duchess of Devonshire and John "Orator" Henley.[19]

In France, by contrast, the notion that royal domesticity could be depicted comically without subverting its authority was unthinkable. It is not surprising, therefore, that it was not until the beginnings of Louis XVI's disgrace in 1791 that the transformation of divine right royalty into contractual constitutionalism took place, and then in a context of aggressive hostility. But this is not to say that court conventions, or the art that serviced them, remained rigidly archaic throughout the last years of the old regime. The writers, Edmond and Jules Goncourt, were not far from the mark in emphasizing the rococo pleasure in smallness of scale, intimate interiors, and pastoral informality. Even at Versailles, Madame de Pompadour's mark was left on the Trianon and in the salon of L'Oeil de Boeuf rather than in the grandiose spaces that Le Brun organized according to an allegorical program.

It was also during Louis XV's reign that Jean–Baptiste Greuze made his spectacular reputation in the Salons, beginning with *Un Père de Famille lit la Bible a ses Enfants* in 1755. Scene after scene thereafter drew on the bottomless well of moist-eyes *sensibilité* with which Greuze irrigated his family dramas. In contrast to the emotionally indifferent and sensually driven manners that were

19 Draper Hill, *Mr. Gillray* (London 1961), 44–46. On the rehabilitation of George III's image and its importance as a rallying point for patriotic sentiment, see Linda Colley, "Loyalty, Royalty and the British Nation, 1766–1820," *Past & Present,* 102 (1984), 94–129. John Woolcot, "Instructions to a Celebrated Laureat," in Roger Lonsdale (ed.), *The New Oxford Book of Eighteenth-Century Verse* (New York, 1984), 739.

supposed to prevail in aristocratic society, Greuze offered the spectacle of parental tenderness and connubial innocence. The village idyll, *L'Accordee de Village,* that showed a Protestant notarized wedding in the simplest of circumstances, corresponded closely to the familial obsessions of Diderot's *"drames bourgeois,"* among them *Le Fils Naturel* (1757) and *Le Père de Famille* (1758). Diderot was the most extravagant enthusiast of the moral seriousness and dramatic truth of Greuze's painted narratives, which remain the touchstone for taste polarized between a whimsically hedonist and self-consciously decorative rococo manner on the one hand and a morally charged domestic didacticism on the other. Diderot's famous diatribe against François Boucher in 1765 for his offences against truth and decency has contributed particularly to the impression that there was an element of social, as well as moral, opposition at work. Although court and aristocratic art was synonymous with the amoral rococo style, Greuze's repertoire of demure brides; solicitous, tutorial parents; devoted (or, if errant, remorseful) children and fecund mothers obediently breast-feeding their babes in arms, were all images that were bourgeois in market appeal as well as in tone.[20]

This almost manichean view of the taste wars of the mid-eighteenth century is excessively simplified. Greuze was far from despised by the aristocratic elite. It was at the very top of French society, rather than at the bottom, that the maternal nursing prescriptions of François Tronchin and Jean Jacques Rousseau had their most immediate effect. Greuze's *Mère Bien Aimée,* representing a rhapsody of superabundant bliss in the nursery, was, in fact, a dramatized portrait of (and commissioned for) a family of royal financiers, the Labordes, who were far from bourgeois (Fig. 8). Diderot praised it as being "excellent on two counts: as a work of art, and an example of the good life. It preaches population and depicts with great feeling the inestimable happiness and value of domestic felicity." Many of the high nobility embraced the *sensibilité* narrated in Greuze's pictures as enthusi-

---

20 See Denis Diderot (ed. Jean Seznec and Jean Adhemar), *Salons* (Oxford, 1957–1967), 4v.; Seznec, "Les Salons de Diderot," *Harvard Library Bulletin,* V (1951), 267–289. For a brilliantly challenging interpretation of Diderot's account of these paintings, see Michael Fried, *Absorption and Theatricality: Painting and Beholder in the Age of Diderot* (Berkeley, 1980). For a different perspective, see Norman Bryson, *Word and Image: French Painting of the Ancien Regime* (Cambridge, 1981), 122–203.

Fig. 8 Jean-Baptiste Greuze, *The Well-Beloved Mother,* 1769.

SOURCE: Collection Laborde, Madrid.

astically as they took to vaccination, breast-feeding, looser clothing, and parental instruction for their young. It seems likely that
there was a "new world for children" in eighteenth-century France
as well as in England. Indeed, the royal families of both Louis
XV and Louis XVI thought of themselves as exemplary in their
parental concerns.[21]

Explanations of the French Revolution that featured a reac-
tionary and socially impermeable aristocracy alienating a thwarted
bourgeoisie have all but collapsed against the weight of empirical
evidence. The more plausible view of a nobility that was socially

21 Diderot, *Salons,* I, 155. See also Carol Duncan, "Happy Mothers and Other New
Ideas in Eighteenth-Century French Art," in Norma Broude and Mary D. Garrard (eds.),
Feminism and Art History (New York, 1982), 201–220. Plumb, "The New World of
Children in Eighteenth-Century England," *Past & Present,* 67 (1975), 64.

and culturally fluid might suggest that the pre-history of revolutionary culture might actually be discovered within the *ancien
régime* rather than outside it. It is not that the French monarchy
did not follow the British in replacing dynasty with family in
their portrayed self-image. But certainly some of the same elements—the sudden surge in popularity of Dutch genre interiors;
the invasion of conversational domestic taste; the onslaught of
literary and visual *sensibilité*—all played some part in the significantly more informal tone of royal portraits in the 1780s. What
Zoffany and Lawrence were to the late Hanoverians, Vigee-Lebrun was to the court of Louis XVI.[22]

Many of Vigee-Lebrun's society portraits—the Marquise de
Pezay and the Comtesse de la Châtre, for instance—are genuine
examples of fashionable informality and studied simplicity, posed
and *décoiffée,* or with broad brimmed hats, flowers, books, and
all the other obligatory props of unaffected, natural *sensibilité.* Her
most important patroness, Marie-Antoinette, whom she painted
a number of times, was, however, another matter. The first portrait of 1778, intended for her Habsburg family in Vienna, was a
highly formal full-length study, complete with a formidable
hooped skirt and a high-plumed, dressed and powdered *coiffure.*
But thereafter, roses, lace, and pastoral attitudes prevailed. Portraits that were meant for grand public commissions retained a
more august manner, but it is naive to suppose that the more
intimate half-length studies, commissioned for friends, but more
often for ambassadors (in London and Constantinople, for example), were in any sense meant as private works. Where else
was there so important a place for public propaganda and conspicuous display, if not at an embassy? In that context, these
portraits may reasonably be supposed to reflect the queen's sense
of how she wished her authority and personality to be represented.

One such portrait by Vigee-Lebrun was hastily commissioned in 1787 as a replacement for an unsuccessful and much
more formal version by Adolf Ulric Wertmüller, the Swedish
court artist, and was displayed in the Salon, where it was greeted
with as much vocal hostility as admiration (Fig. 9). Baillio has
argued persuasively, that the representation of the Queen with

---

22 See Joseph Baillio, *Elisabeth Louise Vigee-Lebrun, 1755–1842* (Forth Worth, 1982).

Fig. 9 Elisabeth Louise Vigee-Lebrun, *Marie Antoinette and her Children,*
1787.

SOURCE: Musée Historique, Versailles.

her children was meant to offset her scandalous reputation as a
woman of extravagant tastes, haughty demeanor, and insatiable
appetites. A portrait that represented her not as a spendthrift
wanton, but as the incarnation of maternal tenderness, was deliberately designed to launder this soiled reputation. The end result,
however, was an awkward compromise between the majestic and
the maternal. For, unlike Zoffany's relaxed observation of family
caprice at Buckingham House, Marie Antoinette was seated, un-
repentently one presumes, before an immense jewel chest in the
Salon de la Paix, enfiladed off from, of all places, the Hall of
Mirrors. Although it may be debatable whether her expression

was as authoritative as has been suggested, there is no question that Vigee-Lebrun tried to do the impossible by offering what was simultaneously meant as a regal and a domestic image.[23]

The French monarchy experienced considerable difficulty in devising a persona for itself that could manage to be both authoritative and accessible. In the light of this difficulty it is not so surprising that the greatest history paintings of the Revolution eschewed the ineffectual harmonies of domestic narrative. Calling on antique models of republican patriotism, Jacques-Louis David's *Oath of the Horatii* (retrospectively taken into the revolutionary canon) and his *Brutus* superseded family solidarity with images of national loyalty. David's stoical heroes witness the destruction of sentimental bonds in the name of political rectitude and patriotic sacrifice in the most militant and unyielding manner. The feminine and maternal ties connecting domestic groups in both Zoffany and Vigee-Lebrun are sundered by the imperatives of heroic masculinity in David's depictions. In these opposed schemes, it is mothers who personify the unities of family and fathers who break them apart in the name of politics.[24]

In the most compelling compositions of the 1780s and 1790s, fathers replace mothers as the fulcrum on which moral decision turns, even when the martyrs of republican patriotism—Belisarius, Seneca, and Socrates—are surrogate fathers: old captains, tutors, and teachers. Their tragedies were meant to speak to the disgrace by which the *patrie* seemed orphaned of its proper *pater,* an image that Louis XVI had attempted to reverse with acts of ritualized paternalism during the *guerre des farines.* The Roman stoical patriotism, that the Jacobins sought to substitute for homage to the throne, proposed, in effect, that families should define themselves in terms of their selfless devotion to the *patrie,* and not see in the Republic a sentimental family writ large.[25]

23   *Idem,* "Marie Antoinette et ses Enfants par Madame Vigee-Lebrun. Le Dossier d'Une Oeuvre Actualite Politique," in *L'Oeil* (Mar. 1981), 34–41; (May 1981), 52–61.

24   The literature on David is vast. It is, therefore, all the more surprising that even the more recent accounts—for example, Schnapper, *Jacques Louis David* (Fribourg, 1975) and Anita Brookner, *Jacques Louis David* (London, 1982)—have not paid much attention to what might be called the sexual politics of David's great history paintings.

25   Louis XVI had attempted to assuage the anger of the rioters on the Ile de France by a traditional act of symbolic largesse: the distribution of bread and small sums of money from the terrace at Versailles. See Musée Carnavalet, *La Révolution Française. Le Premier Empire. Dessins du Musée Carnavalet* (Paris, 1982), 39–41.

It was surely not accidental that the tension between family feeling and patriotic sacrifice in David's own career collapsed together the worlds of private life and public art. His friends of the 1780s and the subjects of his dazzling dual portrait of an idealized companionate marriage had been destroyed by revolutionary incrimination. Antoine Lavoisier, the scientist, patron, and exemplary husband, had been guillotined for being a tax farmer. David's own marriage had been dissolved thanks to the republican institution of divorce. It was only after his own career as Jacobin pageant-master and Robespierrean devotee had ended in prison that the virtues of family life and public duties could be reconciled. Notwithstanding their estrangement, it was David's wife who interceded with Thermidorean politicians to secure his release. During his recuperation with his in-laws, the Seriziats, David turned to imagery of domestic happiness, producing portraits of *plein-air* innocence that also reflected his Theophilanthropic beliefs in the harmonic affinities between nature and love. It was in the same year, 1795, that David began work on *The Intervention of the Sabine Women,* that repaired the plastic unities which he had broken in the *Brutus* and the *Horatii.* It was the *Sabine Women,* completed four years later, that reinstated the sovereignty of family feeling over political and martial contention.

Given this background, it was not so extraordinary that it fell to David, the survivor of these revolutionary contradictions, to attempt, as imperial court painter, a work that brought together family feeling and the authority of state. In his epic account of the imperial coronation in Notre Dame, David finally succeeded in creating an image of a French royal family (Figs. 10 and 11). In all the innumerable commentaries on this canonical work, curiously little attention has been paid to the importance of the fact that it represents the crowning of the empress rather than Napoleon himself. This lack of comment is even odder since one of the few (and characteristically terse) remarks that Napoleon is known to have made about it, when he saw the completed painting, concerned the portrayal of Josephine. It is her centrality, together with the prominence of the Bonapartes in the picture (despite the manifold allusions back to earlier imperial regalian rites, Carolinian and Byzantine), that classify the painting as a family portrait, albeit on a monumental scale.[26]

26 The other, more often cited remark made by Napoleon was to congratulate David

Fig. 10 Jacques-Louis David, Detail from *Oath of the Horatii*, 1785.

Fig. 11 Jacques-Louis David, *Detail from the Coronation of Josephine*, 1806–1808.

SOURCE: Figs. 10 and 11—The Louvre, Paris.

It was significant that David's sketches showing Napoleon crowning himself in the manner of Constantine were rejected in favor of the crowning grace of the imperial husband. Given the not always harmonious climate that prevailed in the Bonaparte clan, it was important to promote the myth of a unified family, gathered around its presiding genius. This impression of tribal solidarity (even more Corsican then French) was further reinforced by adding the presence of Letitia Bonaparte, *Madame mère,* to the painting, even though she was in Rome, not Notre Dame, at the time of the ceremony in December, 1804. In this guise, Napoleon personified the emperor of the *Code Civile* who had restored, in the most emphatic manner, the patriarchal rights of the husband and father that he thought the Revolutionary law codes had damaged. But, in his view, these rights were always conditional on the recognition of certain mutual obligations within the little governance of the family.

It was in keeping with these assumptions that Napoleon supposed that the successful implantation of a new imperial dynasty would only be secured by attending to the prescription and regulation of the bourgeois family: paternal and conjugal guardianship; the deprivation of the property rights of illegitimate children; and the whole somber canon of institutionalized family authority. His remark to David about the depiction of the kneeling Josephine might have been an epigraph for his views on the necessary conjunction of social and political virtues. He expressed his gratitude to the artist for having "transmitted to posterity the proof of the affection that I have wanted to bestow on her who shares with me the burdens of government.[27]

Ironically, it may have been David's zeal to oblige Napoleon by concentrating on his act of husbandly largesse that contributed to his failure to be awarded the Decennial Prize (won by Baron Antoine Gros for his *Pestiferes de Jaffa*) in 1810. In that year, Napoleon was in the process of divorcing Josephine and replacing her with Marie Louise, the Habsburg princess who was to complete the imperial-bourgeois menage by supplying an heir. In those delicate circumstances, it would have been embarrassing to

---

for having "divined my intentions" by making the emperor a *"chevalier français."* The comments are given in Etienne J. Délecluze, *Louis David, Son Ecole et son Temps* (Paris, 1855), 313.

27 *Ibid.*

have given the palm to a painting the heroine of which was yesterday's consort. Napoleon's attempt to reinforce the imperial family with some authentically dynastic blood was merely the prelude to his demise. Although his nephew, Napoleon III, commissioned Winterhalter to do the same kind of nursery album pictures for Eugenie that he had produced for Queen Victoria, the discrepancy between the imagery of bourgeois virtue and the reality of the plutocratic demi-monde was too much for the mythology of art to disguise.

How important were these alterations in historical self-representation? It would be idle to pretend that the fate of the European monarchies hung on the degree to which their incumbents replaced dynastic totems with family interiors, presenting themselves as devoted fathers and doting wives, rather than mounted warriors or imperial judges. Nor do I mean to suggest that the domestication of the royal aura made the ceremonial forms of its magnificence redundant. The late nineteenth century was as much the heyday of the imperial military parade and the pompous coronation, as it was that of the publicly displayed royal family. In 1953, Pietro Annigoni's imperially crowned Queen Elizabeth succeeded to Jacopo Amigoni's Queen Caroline, draped in baroque robes and surrounded by cherubim.

In so far as the survival of monarchy into the twentieth century has depended on its success at embodying a patriotic mystique, it came to be important that the institution should be seen to be the family of families, at once dynastic and domestic, remote and accessible, magical and mundane. (Indeed, the apologetic metaphor for the post-imperial British Commonwealth was that it was a "family of nations.") As imperial power atrophied, so the family fetish loomed ever larger as part of the royal mystique. The matriarchal spirit seemed so benignly personified by George VI's widow that the title of "Queen Mother" became coined as though it had had always been part of the dynasty's hierarchical nomenclature. Its calendar, followed with popular devotion, now consists as much of the calendar of domestic life as the more formal ceremonies of state. Just as the evolution from dynastic to domestic ethos was served, and defined, by imagery, so the further marriage between public and private life has come to depend on the transmission of images.

Antoine Schnapper

The King of France as Collector in the

Seventeenth Century The Renaissance worked actively
and effectively to make the arts and patronage of the arts essential
to the magnificence of princes. Having recovered numerous ancient texts, from Aristotle to Pliny, which established the necessity
of this linkage, humanists suggested that the grandeur of a king,
although established by war, was maintained by peace. The fruits
of peace, they claimed, were commercial prosperity and progress
in the arts, which in turn immortalized the prince's glory. A vast
body of encomiastic literature, spanning many countries and centuries, celebrated the actions of princes on behalf of the arts in
the hope of encouraging them even further. Unfortunately, this
support was not always and everywhere forthcoming: Pevsner's
classic study of academies of art gives considerable evidence of
artists who sought a patronage that many princes failed to grant.
In France, the Royal Academy of Painting and Sculpture escaped
penury only when, after fifteen years of difficulty and entreaty,
Jean Baptiste Colbert, minister to Louis XIV, offered to protect
it.[1]

Recent historiography has paid considerable attention to cultural politics at all levels of society. Every act of a prince, in the
arts as in other fields, is given what is essentially a rather simple
political interpretation: its purpose is to demonstrate the grandeur
and power of the prince in the eyes of his subjects, of foreigners,
and of posterity. Nobody would deny that there is some truth to
this line of interpretation, but I am concerned about its systematic
and uncritical application to the specific phenomenon of collecting. Such an approach parallels directly the narrow sociological
treatment that has come to explain the collections of the aristoc-

Antoine Schnapper is Professor of Art History at the University of Paris-Sorbonne. He
is the author of numerous articles, books, and exhibition catalogues, mainly on seventeenth-century French painting.

1 Nikolaus Pevsner, *Academies of Art Past and Present* (Cambridge, 1940).

racy or the bourgeoisie mainly as efforts to affirm or ameliorate social status. In France, the numerous disciples of Bourdieu, who share his obsessions but not always his talent for detailed social analysis, discern in the libraries of the great *parlementaire* families "one of the privileged instruments of the strategy by which the bourgeoisie, and more particularly their ennobled elite, try to involve culture in their self-affirmation against the aristocracy" as a means "of transmitting the values, virtues and capabilities which confer legitimate membership in the bourgeois dynasties." As for kings, if they gathered objects together in a cabinet of curiosities or in an art collection, they did so in order to affirm their prestige, to impose it on their subjects, or to intimidate foreigners by a display of wealth.[2]

Alpers' recent book, which, for example, attempts to integrate seventeenth-century Dutch painting into the whole of the "visual culture" of the times, says that: "The products of both nature and man once assembled to celebrate the glory and power of a monarch like Rudolph [II] are now the possession, and decorate the lives and households of the Dutch merchants." Her sentence is particularly interesting because it does not presume to be original, but rather summarizes what now is assumed to be standard and incontrovertible knowledge. Yet this assumption is questionable in two respects. First, there was no time lag between the assembling of cabinets of curiosities by sovereigns and by the bourgeoisie; quite the contrary, what Pomian calls "the culture of curiosity" appeared simultaneously among princes and the educated classes in the second half of the sixteenth century, the heyday of cabinets of curiosities. Second, there is no proof (if anything, the opposite) that Rudolph II built his collection to celebrate his glory and his power. Indeed, recent attempts to give Rudolph's cabinet of curiosities a truly imperial significance are fragile.[3]

---

2 Jean Viardot, "Livres rares et pratiques bibliographiques," in Roger Chartier et al. (eds.), *Histoire de l'édition française. II: Le livre triomphant, 1660–1830* (Paris, 1984), 448. The second part of the sentence is a quotation from Pierre Bourdieu.
3 Svetlana Alpers, *The Art of Describing: Dutch Art in the Seventeenth Century* (Chicago, 1983), 111; Krzysztof Pomian, "La culture de la Curiosité," *Le Temps de la Réflexion*, III (1982), 337–359; Thomas DaCosta Kaufmann, "Remarks on the Collections of Rudolf II: the *Kunstkammer* as a Form of *Representatio*," *Art Journal*, XXXVIII (1978), 22–28; idem, *L'Ecole de Prague. Le peinture à la cour de Rodolphe II* (Paris, 1985), 25.

The recently published inventory of 1607 to 1611, organized by categories of objects, does not prove that Rudolph's cabinet was laid out in the same fashion. Many seventeenth-century inventories and descriptions impose an order on a collection, the actual presentation of which was completely different because of the practical necessities of placing objects primarily according to size—in contrast to the more or less logical order of the written accounts. If one wishes to measure the difference, one need only compare the few engravings of these cabinets with the catalogues or descriptions that they illustrate (e.g., the *Museum Wormianum*, 1655).[4]

It is unwarranted for an argument reinterpreting the entire cabinet of curiosities to be based solely on those few articles commissioned by Rudolph which appear to celebrate imperial power, such as the fountain of Wenzel Jamnitzer or the paintings of Giuseppe Arcimboldo. The distinction between the role of the patron and that of the collector is essential, and is discussed below. Also, there is much contemporary evidence that access to the cabinet was very difficult, notwithstanding that the Emperor did admit some distinguished foreign visitors. This argument assumes, but does not show, that Rudolph's cabinet differed (in more than its size) from the many others which sought to assemble as complete a microcosm as possible; did all these lawyers, doctors, and apothecaries also seek to dominate the world? At the end of his life the Emperor fled the world, seeking refuge in his collections, somewhat like Charles I of England, who preferred the world of the arts to the administration of his kingdom.[5]

4 Rotraud Bauer and Herbert Haupt, "Die Kunstkammer Kaiser Rudolfs II in Prag. Ein Inventar aus den Jahren 1607–1611," *Jahrbuch der Kunsthistorischen Sammlungen in Wien,* LXXII (1976).
5 See, among others, Erwin Stresemann, *Die Entwicklung der Ornithologie von Aristoteles bis zur Gegenwart* (Berlin, 1951), 29. Robert J. W. Evans, *Rudolf II and his World: A Study in Intellectual History, 1576–1612* (Oxford, 1973), unfortunately quite sketchy on the collections, insists on the sovereign's taste for secrecy (196–242) and notes "the marked unwillingness to share his collections with outsiders." Kaufmann, "Collections of Rudolf II," ascribes too much importance to the banal remark of one of the rare visitors, Cardinal d'Este, who mentions a "*tesoro degno di chi il possede*" (a treasure worthy of the owner). See, too, Peter W. Thomas, "Charles I of England. The Tragedy of Absolutism," in A. Geoffrey Dickens (ed.), *The Courts of Europe. Politics, Patronage and Royalty, 1400–1800* (London, 1977), 191–211. Thomas suggests without hesitation that "the Kunstkabinett itself was a form of propaganda" (201).

These, then, are the kinds of problems that are raised by the current scholarly literature on royal collecting. There is no easy means of resolving them, and indeed it would be difficult at this point to propose a general theory about the collections of princes and kings. It would be better, instead, to start with a study of individual cases, without at the same time forgetting the opposite phenomenon—the many princes who were not collectors—so as to put into better perspective those who gathered natural curiosities, antiques, or works of art.

It also seems appropriate to study the meaning of princely collections in the framework of dynasties and territorial units. For example, when Francesco I d'Este, Duke of Modena from 1629 to 1658, and then his son, Alfonso IV, who died prematurely in 1664, displayed a remarkable fervor for collecting all sorts of curiosities, their main intention was probably to connect themselves with the traditions of their Ferraran ancestors. Rather than adopting generalizations unquestioningly, we would do better to examine the realities of specific cases. The seventeenth-century kings of France (Henry IV, Louis XIII, and Louis XIV), who are of particular concern here, were not short of advisors interested in the collection of antiquities and works of art, but they themselves behaved individually. A study of their actions permits us to sort out the true from the false in the topos of collection-propaganda by recognizing the importance of different conditions and temperaments.

In France, there was a royal tradition of collecting art and curiosities—magnificently exemplified by Francis I—which was marked by boundless admiration for, and rivalry with, Italy. Yet Francis' purchases of paintings, statues, and ancient art should not be confused with his creation of a major artistic center at Fontainebleau, where Italians played the prime role and where royal glory could be celebrated in language that was so complex as to be understood only by a small elite. As early as the next century, it had become incomprehensible, and remained so until it began to challenge our modern iconologists. Besides great works of art, the collection of Francis I also contained minor antiques, coins, and engraved stones, to which were added the later collection of Catherine de' Medici. Francis was likewise interested in exotic objects, plants, animals, and Indian artifacts, which travellers

brought back in large quantities—curiosities that continued spo-
radically to attract French monarchs.[6]

After Francis I, however, significant royal patronage of the
arts in the sixteenth century declined. Henry IV, the first of the
seventeenth-century kings, was primarily interested in architecture; decorative painting played a considerable but nonetheless
secondary role. We have no hint of the king acting as art collector.
However, we do know of a serious attempt to persuade him to
collect antiques and medals. The instigator of the project was
Pierre-Antoine de Rascas de Bagarris, a lawyer from Aix-en-
Provence. He was a leading figure in the small world of erudition
and collecting in Provence, one of those who initiated Nicolas
Peiresc into the study of antiquity, and someone who himself
owned a noteworthy collection of medals and engraved stones.
While in Paris from 1599 to 1613 he tried to persuade the king to
create a collection. We have a document that he drew up in 1602
which includes a list of ancient marbles, statues of various sizes
(either complete or needing restoration), busts of the twelve Cae-
sars, and a series of medals which were offered to the king for
purchase. Bagarris seems to have received the title of keeper of
the king's medals and ancient works, but he made only one
important acquisition: 746 medals by François Dupérier, a friend
of François de Malherbe. Further proof of the king's scant interest
in the project is the fact that Bagarris had to proceed indirectly,
arranging for the Estates of Provence to buy the medals to present
to Henry IV in 1608.[7]

6   Gustave Loisel, *Histoire des Ménageries de l'Antiquité à nos jours* (Paris, 1912), 3 v.; Jean
Adhémar, *Frère André Thevet* (Paris, 1947); Jean Baudry's introduction to his new edition
of the 1558 text *Singularitez de la France antarctique* (Paris, 1981); *idem, Documents inédits sur
André Thevet cosmographe du Roi* (Paris, 1982). Pierre Dan, *Le Trésor des merveilles de la
Maison royale de Fontainebleau* (Paris, 1642), 84–85, describes the later decay of Francis's
collections.
7   On Henry IV, see Ludovic Lalanne, "Inventaire des Tableaux et autres curiosités au
Louvre en 1603," *Archives de l'Art Français, Documents,* III (1853–1855), 49; Joseph Guibert,
"Inventaire des curiosités trouvées en différens endroits de la Bibliothèque du Roy (mai
1684)," *Archives de l'Art Français,* I (1907), 330–356; Jean-Pierre Babelon, *Henri IV* (Paris,
1982), pt. 3. On Bagarris, see Philippe Tamizey de Larroque, *Les correspondants de Peiresc,
XIII: Pierre-Antoine de Rascas, sieur de Bagarris* (Aix, 1887); "Abrégé d'inventaire des pièces
que le sieur de Bagarris a en mains pour dresser un Cabinet à Sa Majesté de toutes sortes
d'antiquitez, suivant le commandement donné audit sieur de Bagarris par S.M., tant de
bouche que par lettre de 22 mars 1602," Bibliothèque Nationale, Ms Français 9540, fo.
226. On the sale of the Dupérier collection, Edmond Bonnaffé, *Dictionnaire des amateurs
français au XVIIe siècle* (Paris, 1884). One should not discount the possibility that the

Eventually, Henry seems to have been convinced of the potential importance of gathering in Paris some ancient works—those that had once belonged to Francis I as well as new acquisitions. Indeed, the decoration of the "Grande Galerie," Henry's main achievement in the Louvre, was accompanied by the creation of a "Salle des Antiques," the splendors of which were acclaimed by travellers and by Sauval in the early 1650s. This room, paved with marble in 1608, and containing in its niches some famous statues, such as the so-called Diana of Ephesus, was, as Sauval tells us, "similar to a reliquary or to the highly decorated German cabinets." In 1677, Félibien still praised Henry IV for furnishing the "Salle des Antiques," which had also been intended "to house other figures which were to come from Italy," even though the principal antiques had been transported around 1667/68 to the Tuileries. Unfortunately, the room was barely finished when Henry IV, who had hardly been eager in pursuit of these acquisitions, was assassinated.[8]

In 1608 Bagarris had presented another idea to the king, in a speech which he published in 1611. According to Bagarris, the profiles of sovereigns and great men, placed on coins, were the surest way to eternalize their memory—an argument that is consistently used by medal collectors who seek recognition for the importance of their collections. The recommendation was that Henry not only collect coins, but also put his portrait on copper coins—a notion that met with the determined opposition of Poullain, of the Royal Mint, who feared that the coins, to be made of copper, would debase the currency. As a result, the project came to nothing.[9]

Henry IV's interest in painting seems to have been limited to portraits and to large-scale decorative schemes; he showed little inclination to collect generally. The attitude of Louis XIII was just as limited, which is surprising since we know that he had a personal fondness for painting. Félibien even reports with satis-

monarchy came into possession of the gift of medals only in 1622, on the occasion of Louis XIII's visit to Provence.

8 See Babelon, "Les Travaux de Henri IV au Louvre et aux Tuileries," *Paris et Ile-de-France, Mémoires,* XXIX (1978), 119–124; Henry Sauval, *Histoire et recherche des Antiquités de Paris* (Paris, 1724), II, 42; André Félibien, *Tableaux du Cabinet du Roi. Statues et Bustes Antiques des Maisons Royales* (Paris, 1677; new ed. 1679), foreword.

9 Bagarris, *La Nécessité de l'usage des médailles dans les monnoyes* (Paris, 1611); Henri Poullain, *Traitez des monnoyes* (Paris, 1621; rev. ed. 1709).

faction that Louis had had lessons in pastels with Simon Vouet. Again according to Félibien, even before Vouet's return from Italy in 1627, the King had given him a stipend because he had been "so inclined by the Queen his mother, who had been apprised of Vouet's beautiful manner." Nevertheless, during the Regency and the first years of Louis XIII's reign, the best painters left France, where they could not find suitable conditions for work or study, and went to Italy; that was the case with Valentin de Boulogne, Vouet, Nicolas Regnier, Nicolas Tournier, and Claude Vignon (not to mention the Lorrainers, such as Claude Gellée and Charles Mellin). In the early 1620s, Nicolas Poussin, Claude Mellan, and Jacques Blanchard also departed for these reasons. The king seems to have played no role in the awakening of interest in painting in Paris between 1620 and 1625. In this area, too, Louis remained a discreet monarch, disinclined to glorify his person or his power; it has been noted that he even gave up the venerable tradition of the ceremonial Royal Entries, which did not reappear until the time of the Fronde. The galleries of this period devoted to the glory of the monarchy and its government derive from Cardinal Richelieu and from Pierre Séguier, not the king.[10]

In the absence of an inventory, the history of the royal collection of painting remains so little known from the death of Francis I to the beginning of the personal reign of Louis XIV because it is not a very rich history, with probably less than 100 paintings acquired in more than a century. However, in the 1620s Marie de' Medici and her entourage showed a renewed interest in painting, for the queen had brought with her from Italy her family's traditional taste for the arts. Yet, even though she commissioned a sizable number of paintings, portraits, and decorative works, there is no evidence that she had a real collection. Still, she had enough of a reputation as an art lover to convince her nephew, Duke Ferdinando Gonzaga, that he could do nothing better to please her than to give her the series of ten decorative canvases by Giovanni Baglione which he commissioned in 1620 and which arrived in Paris in 1624. It is around the decoration of her new Luxembourg Palace, around her son Gaston d'Orléans, and around Richelieu, the superintendent of her household, that

10 Félibien, *Entretiens sur les vies et les ouvrages des plus excellens peintres anciens et modernes* (Paris, 1688), II, 183, 185.

the signs of interest, not only in painting, but in collecting, begin to multiply. Peter Paul Rubens was made aware that Richelieu himself would be happy to own some examples of his talent; various letters by Maugis, chaplain and artistic advisor to the queen, reveal the interest of this milieu in painting; and 1621 marks the first mention of the greatest commission of the queen's career, the cycle of allegories of her life by Rubens. Marie also sought to acquire works of art in Italy for Gaston and herself in 1626. On his own account, Gaston had several cases full of antiques and paintings sent from Italy in 1630.[11]

Starting around 1630, Richelieu, too, developed a large personal collection, mostly of ancient works and paintings. At the time of his death, his Parisian palace alone housed approximately 150 paintings (not counting the series of portraits and decorative works commissioned from Vouet, Philippe de Champaigne, Poussin, and the young Charles Le Brun), of which a large number were early and contemporary Italian paintings. Richelieu also owned collections of medals, bronzes, porcelain objects, tables in Florentine stones, and other such objects. The antiquities were particularly numerous, in his houses in Paris and at Richelieu. We also hear in the 1630s of several large collections, in Paris and elsewhere, that belonged to men connected with Richelieu, including the archbishop of Bordeaux, the bishop of Albi, the Duke of Liancourt, and the Duke of Créqui, upon whose death in 1638 Richelieu bought several important paintings.[12]

Richelieu, seconded by Sublet de Noyers, tried to convince the king of the value of a real policy for the arts. He may have been involved in the recall of Vouet in 1627; he was certainly involved in Poussin's return to France and in an accompanying

---

11 Madeleine Laurain-Portemer, "Opposition et propagande. Paris au temps du sacre de Louis XIV," in idem, Etudes mazarines (Paris, 1981), 155–174; Deborah Marrow, The Art Patronage of Maria de'Medici (Ann Arbor, 1982). Among the letters, see the one sent by Maugis on 14 Aug. 1621, in Nouvelles Archives de L'Art Français (1885), 113–115; also Max Rooses and Charles Ruelens (eds.), Correspondance de Rubens et documents épistolaires concernant sa vie et ses oeuvres (Antwerp, 1898), II, 316–319. For the acquisitions in Italy, see Antonino Bertolotti, "Objets d'art transportés de Rome en France du Seizième au Dixneuvième siècle (1541–1864)," Nouvelles Archives de l'Art Français, II (1880–1881), 57–82.
12 We have learned more about Richelieu's collection from "L'inventaire après décès du Cardinal de Richelieu," Archives de L'Art Français, XXVII (1985), 9–83. The part dealing with the sculptures was published previously, in Arthur de Boislisle, "Les collections de sculptures du cardinal de Richelieu," Mémoires de la Société nationale des Antiquaires de France, XLII (1882), 71–128.

plan for the arts that was probably supposed to include the creation of a Royal Academy of Painting and Sculpture, which came into being only in 1648. The chief impulse, as usual, came from a proposal for a vast painted decoration—this one was envisioned for the "Grande Galerie" of the Louvre—but the aim was larger. The mission of Fréart de Chantelou to Italy in 1640, sent after laborious negotiations that had been going on since 1638, was supposed not only to "seek out the best painters, sculptors, architects, and other famous artisans," but also to buy works of art, chosen either for their quality or for their low price, and in addition to have molds made of the chief ancient bas-reliefs. This mission may have been more successful than is often thought, for Philippon, later engineer to the king, wrote of having been employed in Rome to buy the statues and bas-reliefs. Yet the works did not arouse much interest in Paris, except from Gaston; some apparently went to his collection at Blois, to return to the monarchy in 1670, when heavy crates, the exact contents of which—though definitely sculpture—remain a mystery, were sent from Blois to Paris, part of Gaston's legacy to his nephew, Louis XIV.[13]

Jules Mazarin, even more than Richelieu, was a great collector and lover of art, one of the foremost in Europe. Before settling in Paris in 1639, he had acted as agent for Richelieu and had proposed himself as superintendent of the cardinal's collections, which he expected to enrich with such items as busts, statues, paintings, desks, and tables. In 1634, he had brought Richelieu several paintings and other articles—presents from Cardinal Antonio Barberini, who would again send gifts in 1638 on the occasion of the birth of the dauphin. The importance which Richelieu attached to the paintings, and his efforts—all in vain—to incline the king in the same direction, can be seen from his donation of some famous canvases to Louis XIII, first in a gift of 1636 and then in his will. Moreover, Richelieu and Mazarin were

13 Jacques Thuillier, "Académie et classicisme en France: les débuts de l'Académie royale de peinture et de sculpture (1648–1663)," in Stefano Bottari (ed.), *Il mito del Classicismo nel Seicento* (Messina, 1964), 181–209; Charles Jouanny "Correspondance de Nicolas Poussin," *Archives de l'Art Francais,* V (1911); Laurain-Portemer, "Mazarin militant de l'art baroque au temps de Richelieu (1634–1642)," *Bulletin de la Société de l'Histoire de l'Art Français* (1975), 65–89, whose conclusions I do not share; Georges Dethan, *Mazarin, un homme de paix à l'âge baroque, 1602–1661* (Paris, 1981), 49–50; Sauval, *Antiquités de Paris,* II, 55. Adam Philippon, *Curieuses recherches de plusieurs beaux morceaux d'ornemens antiques et modernes* (Paris, 1645).

equally great collectors of manuscripts and books (Mazarin's library was already famous before he left Rome), but here again royalty hardly followed its ministers' example prior to the intervention of Colbert.[14]

The beginning of the personal reign of Louis XIV marks an upheaval in the policy for the arts. Since texts almost by definition honor the king by ascribing to him all initiatives, it is difficult to determine exactly what part the king's personal wishes played. There are many indications, however, that Louis XIV had little personal interest in his collections until some time in the 1680s or, more precisely, until the installation of the court at Versailles. And even after that date, in keeping with the practice of his predecessors, he paid more attention to architecture and interior decorating than to sculpture or painting, as is seen from his active role in the construction of the Marble Trianon and the record of his orders, kept by the superintendent, Jules Hardouin-Mansart, for the years 1699 to 1703.[15]

As chance would have it (the event is both historic and symbolic), Gaston d'Orléans died just before Louis XIV took the reins of government, and left the king his collections—although the will did not specifically mention either paintings or the large botanical garden and aviary at Blois (now known mainly through some remarkable illustrations on vellum). From that time on, thanks to the energy of Colbert, who became superintendent of buildings and was himself a great lover of books, the collections of the king were to undergo a prodigious change. Although it cannot be discussed in detail here, the first steps in that change are clear: the purchase of paintings, sculptures, crystal, agate, and, especially, tapestries from the Mazarin collection; the purchase in 1662 of the first part of the Everard Jabach collection (essentially Italian paintings); the legacy of Hippolyte de Béthune; the purchase of works from Nicolas Fouquet; the purchase in 1665 of

14 Laurain-Portemer, "Mazarin militant"; Abbé Jourdain, "Mémoire historique sur la bibliothèque du Roy," *Catalogue des livres imprimés de la Bibliothèque du Roy: Théologie, 1ᵉ partie* (Paris, 1739); Léopold Delisle, *Le Cabinet des Manuscrits de la Bibliothèque Impériale* (Paris, 1868), I.

15 Bertrand Jestaz, "Le Trianon de Marbre ou Louis XIV architecte," *Gazette des Beaux-Arts* (Nov. 1969), 259–286. For Hardouin-Mansart's records, see Archives Nationales, O¹, 1869.

the first collection of the Duke of Richelieu (a treasure because of its thirteen famous paintings by Poussin); and the gift of important paintings by Cardinal Pamphili. This momentum was paralleled by a surge of interest in the purchase of manuscripts and books, as well as medals, engraved stones, and prints, which were the usual complement of a good library.[16]

The development of the royal collection during the first third of Louis XIV's personal reign is rather more problematic than is usually supposed. Collecting was distinctly secondary to major architectural projects, as is apparent if one analyzes the contents of the series of engravings commissioned from Israel Silvestre in March 1663. According to the king's instructions, Silvestre was to engrave "all his palaces, royal houses, the most beautiful views and aspects of his gardens, public assemblies, Carrousels, and outskirts of cities." In 1667, the project was enlarged and other engravers were charged to represent the "plans and elevations of royal houses, their painted and sculpted decoration, the paintings and antique sculpture from the Cabinet of His Majesty, or those which were to be found elsewhere, and also pictures of plants and animals of every species and other rare and unique things." In both cases, it was mainly the royal houses which were to be publicized.[17]

These official publications, later known by the misleading name of "Cabinet du roi," were begun in 1670, and included a series of engravings reproducing royal entertainments (starting with the Carrousel of 1662), the splendors of Versailles, and the king's victories, as well as collections of scientific essays demonstrating the work of the royal academies and some maps. What place did collections have in this encyclopedia of royal patronage of the arts, literature, and the sciences? Not a small one, certainly, since they are well accounted for in the program. But not a great one either, especially if the full extent of these publications is kept in mind. Only a single anthology of art works was published, the *Tableaux du Cabinet du Roi: Statues et Bustes Antiques des Maisons*

16 Schnapper, "Jabach, Mazarin, Fouquet, Louis XIV," *Bulletin de la Société de l'Histoire de l'Art Français* (1982), 85–86.

17 *Idem,* "From Politics to Collecting: Louis XIV and Painting," catalogue of the exhibit *The Sun King: Louis XIV and the New World* (New Orleans, 1984), 119–126; Georges Duplessis, "*Le Cabinet du Roi:* collection d'estampes commandées par Louis XIV," *Le Bibliophile Français*, II (1869), 87–105; André Jammes, "Louis XIV, sa Bibliothèque et le Cabinet du Roi," *The Library*, XX (1965), 1–12.

Royales, comprising a total of forty plates, accompanied by texts by Félibien. The foreword resembled the foreword to the first anthology (*Les Tapisseries des Elements et des Saisons*), published in Paris in 1670, in which Félibien proclaimed the virtues, not of painting, but of engraving, which was an unrivalled means of publicity: "it is again by means of these prints that all nations can admire the sumptuous edifices which the king has built everywhere, and the rich ornamentation which embellishes them." It is indeed the "excellent public works which the king commissioned" which primarily hold one's attention, and even Félibien could produce only one small sentence to explain why the contents of the collection were also being reproduced: "because the paintings and statues sought by the great Prince are priceless and singularly beautiful."[18]

A major turning point in the attitude of the royal collector came after his move to Versailles. From then on, Louis XIV began to live in direct contact with the collections gathered under his orders; within a few years, a genuine, semi-private museum was organized in his small apartment and right next door. The operation was accomplished in two stages: between 1682 and 1685, a sumptuous *Cabinet des Curiosités* was set up adjacent to the "Salon de l'Abondance," which was decorated during the same era. In the Cabinet's elaborate, refined decor were assembled twenty-four paintings (for the most part small ones), vases of semi-precious stone, and the engraved stones and medals that were brought from the royal library of Paris. The medals were placed in twelve special cases, ordered from Gilles Oppenord and delivered in 1684, along with the gold batons with which the king enjoyed sorting through his medals after coming from Mass. The dream of Bagarris was finally realized, for the king was thereafter interested in antique medals and had the great episodes of his reign commemorated by new ones. These medals of the history of the reign were reproduced in a collection of engravings published in 1702: images of images, they increased the chances of survival of the bronze originals.[19]

Other small rooms, which are virtually unknown except through the 1687 description by Tessin, were added to the *Cabinet*

18 Félibien, *Tableaux du Cabinet du Roi,* foreword.
19 See Alfred Marie, *Versailles—Son histoire. II: Mansart à Versailles* (Paris, 1972), 2 v.

des Curiosités; they were filled with filigrees, crystals, and agates. Two rooms fitted out in 1685 in the same area, at the end of the king's small apartment, received the paintings. Almost the entire collection that previously had been in Paris was brought to Versailles, where by 1690 less than 100 paintings remained. The creation of this new museum spurred new acquisitions, which were extraordinarily numerous between 1684 and 1685, before the difficulties of the War of the League of Augsburg slowed them down. A multitude of vases in semi-precious stone and rock crystal were bought through a middleman at prices running from about 1,000 to 2,000 livres apiece. The big cameo of the *Apotheosis of Germanicus,* valued at 7,000 livres, came as a gift from the Monastery of Saint-Epvre at Toul. The king owned 181 articles of semi-precious stone in 1681 and 350 by 1701. Numerous paintings were acquired over the same period: a whole set came from the Marquis of Hauterive, and there were purchases of a series of Albanis and Poussins (thirteen of whose works were acquired between 1683 and 1693). In the year 1685 alone, 92,500 livres were spent on buying paintings. In September 1693, the architect André Le Nôtre gave the king his twenty-one most beautiful paintings and his bronzes and busts.

By constant shifting of the new acquisitions, a larger and better organized "Museum of Louis XIV" was formed. At the end of 1684, Madame de Montespan's fall from favor allowed the king to reclaim the "Petite Galerie" and the two end salons which she had occupied and to annex them to his small apartment. Pierre Mignard then decorated the ceilings, and luxurious wall decorations were prepared, using tortoise shell and mirrors framed in lapis lazuli. In 1692, this ornamentation was dismantled and replaced by a very simple arrangement, punctuated by pilasters on which paintings were hung. At the same time, a small building was erected in the adjacent, interior courtyard, perpendicular to the "Petite Galerie." This building joined the "Petite Galerie" with the apartment of the king, and added two new rooms to the "museum": the "Salon Ovale" and the "Cabinet des Coquilles," for which Mignard designed ceiling paintings which, however, were never installed.[20]

20 Pierre Francastel and Ragnar Josephson, "Relation de la visite de Nicodème Tessin à Marly, Versailles, Clagny, Rueil et Saint Cloud en 1687," *Revue de l'histoire de Versailles et*

Henceforth, the king could enjoy the treasures of his collection on a daily basis in his new museum and in the various rooms of his private apartment. Thus Louis became a true collector with rather traditional tastes. However, it should be noted that these treasures were kept in a part of Versailles which, if not strictly speaking closed to the public (their beauty was mentioned in descriptions of Versailles published from 1701), was nonetheless in the most private section of the palace. A striking sign of the new royal attitude was the preparation of inventories of the collection, which were made with increasing frequency after 1683, and which allow us to trace its growth. Also striking is the timing of this development: Louis XIV turned into a collector at the very moment when Colbert died (1683)—when the effort to disseminate the image of royal glory ceased to be a well-organized endeavor, and when the difficult period of the reign began. With the completion of the "Galerie des Glaces" and the two adjacent Salons of War and Peace, the great projects of decorative painting (the Invalides and the Chapel of Versailles) were conducted in remarkable disorder, with hesitations, struggles for power, and about-faces that attest to the absence of a firm hand on artistic policy after the disappearance of the Marquis of Louvois. Moreover, one should not exaggerate Louis XIV's passion for his own collections: from the time that the private museum was finished, around the year 1695, until his death twenty years later, acquisitions ceased almost completely.[21]

The collecting of paintings, then, was a brief interlude in the king's long reign, and by no means his most important royal artistic activity. Paintings were considered a suitable adornment of a great king, but contributed to his glory only in a vague, indefinite way, especially when compared with buildings. Colbert is explicit on this point: "Your Majesty knows that in the absence of brilliant feats of war, nothing does more to signal the grandeur and intelligence of princes than buildings, and all posterity measures them by the yardstick of these superb houses which they

de Seine et Oise, XXVIII (1926), 283; Schnapper, "Two Unknown Ceiling Paintings by Mignard for Louis XIV," Art Bulletin, LVI (1974), 82–100; Jules Guiffrey, Inventaire général du mobilier de la Couronne sous Louis XIV (1663–1715) (Paris, 1885–1886), I, 171–220.

21 Guiffrey, Inventaire; Fernand Engerand, Inventaire des tableaux du Roy rédigé en 1709 et 1710 par Nicolas Bailly (Paris, 1899); Schnapper, Jean Jouvenet (1644–1717) et la peinture d'histoire à Paris (Paris, 1974), 103–128.

construct during their lifetime." Note also his comment of 1665, reported by Chantelou: "He had said to His Majesty that even should he find no pleasure in beautiful things, it was incumbent upon a great prince to show that he appreciated them, and to commission all these types of works." Here Colbert makes the important distinction between collecting existing works of art and commissioning new works, a vital if oft-forgotten difference. Commissioned works clearly serve more effectively to glorify a prince and proclaim his status as patron of the arts.[22]

Yet even the relationship of royal patronage and royal propaganda was not without complications. For instance, it is commonplace to say that the enlightened protection of Louis XIV finally enabled France to supplant Italy as the leading country for the arts. But, it is also well known that Colbert favored national production in order to limit costly imports, including works of art. Finally, there is the testimony of Félibien's *Entretiens,* which proclaimed the establishment of a genuine French school of painting. The publication of the seventh *Entretien* in 1685 (the first appeared in 1666), which is entirely devoted to Poussin, is the real cornerstone of the argument.

But this evidence is in some ways misleading, especially if it is held that a royal policy for painting was in place at the start of Louis XIV's personal reign. For example, it has recently been pointed out that a museum of sorts was created between 1666 and 1671 in the Galerie des Ambassadeurs, or the Galerie de Diane, in the Louvre, near the large apartment of the king. The decoration of the vault consisted partly of a copy of the Carracci Gallery in the Farnese palace in Rome, executed for the most part by the first pensioners of the French academy in Rome (founded in 1666). To this scheme were added other compositions—probably pastiches of the Carracci—by the young painters Charles de La Fosse, Gabriel Blanchard, and Claude Vignon the younger. The walls were hung with a group of Italian paintings from the royal collection. This ephemeral arrangement unfortunately is known to us only through a passage in Félibien which cites the names of Raphael, Giulio Romano, Perino del Vaga, Leonardo

22 Pierre Clément, *Lettres, instructions et mémoires de Colbert* (Paris, 1861–1865), V,269; Chantelou (ed. Lalanne), *Journal de Voyage du cavalier Bernin en France* (1885; repub. Paris, 1981), 181. This distinction explains Colbert's desire to economize on purchases of ancient sculptures or paintings.

da Vinci, Giorgione, Titian, Paolo Veronese, Correggio, the Carracci, and Caravaggio and his pupils. Félibien describes a sumptuous arrangement: "big, magnificent cabinets, tables of precious stones, plaques, end tables, incense burners, and countless other silver vases." In addition, the principal antiques of the king were likewise placed in the Tuileries.[23]

The decoration of the Galerie des Ambassadeurs is remarkable for the absence of French painters and an explicit political program. What better place to display the power and virtue of the king, or to advertise the merits of the French school of painting, than in a room designed for the reception of foreign ambassadors? Just at this time, in fact, Louis had acquired no less than thirteen paintings by Poussin from the Duke of Richelieu (1665). These included the *Four Seasons* and the unfinished *Apollo and Daphne.* Yet not one of these was placed in the new gallery. Nor was any place accorded to Le Brun's *History of Alexander,* an elaborate and flattering tribute to the king. In 1660 and 1661, Le Brun had started with *The Queen of Persia before Alexander,* the allusions and intentions of which were explained by Félibien in a special brochure. Nevertheless, it is almost stupefying for twentieth-century historians, so adept at discerning the coherence and the continuity of monarchical propaganda, to see that no place could be found in any of the royal palaces for these immense poems to the glory of Louis XIV. It was only through the work of engravers that they were seen.[24]

The idea—in my view, largely erroneous—that a picture collection is an important means of propaganda comes from the con-

---

23 Louis Hautecoeur, *Le Louvre et les Tuileries de Louis XIV* (Paris, 1927), 108–111, includes plans of the buildings; Nicolas Sainte-Fare-Garnot, "La galerie des Ambassadeurs au palais des Tuileries (1666–1671)," *Bulletin de la Société de l'Histoire de l'Art Français* (1978), 119–126; Félibien, *Entretiens,* II, 3–5. The Galerie des Ambassadeurs was preceded by a short-lived installation of part of the collection in the new quarters that Louis Le Vau built in the Louvre around the Petite Galerie in 1661–1664. See Charles Patin's *Epitre au Roi* of April 1, 1661 (Paris, 1661), which was republished as a supplement to the second edition of his *Introduction à l'Histoire par la connoissance des Medailles* (Paris, 1667).

24 Jacques Thuillier, "Pour un *Corpus Pussiniannum,*" in André Chastel (org.), *Actes du Colloque Nicolas Poussin, 1958* (Paris, 1960), II, 197; Thuillier, "Pour André Félibien," *XVIIe siècle,* XXXV (1983), 88–89. In his unpaginated preface to the *Entretiens,* Félibien said about Poussin "that he had taken the science of painting out of the arms of Greece and Italy to bring it to France." See, too, Félibien, *Les Reines de Perse aux pieds d'Alexandre. Peinture du Cabinet du Roi* (Paris, 1663).

fusion of two distinct, albeit related, notions: collecting and patronage. Commissioning a new work, and thus having control
over its iconography, is not the same thing as acquiring an existing
work. When a monarch, or one of his advisors, wishes to decorate
a gallery, a large salon, or a formal apartment with paintings, it
is entirely natural for him to envisage an iconographic program
that will glorify the king and his kingdom. A major step in this
direction was taken by Louis XIV when he revived a practice
adopted by the Farnese in the sixteenth century in the decoration
of the villa at Caprarola. In the Grande Galerie at Versailles,
instead of a disguised glorification of the monarch, showing him
personified by Hercules or Apollo, there is a direct representation
of the great achievements of the reign.

But even in the case of commissions, one must not forget
that paintings can also serve simply as furnishing or decoration.
In the history of the building of the palace of the Buen Retiro,
Brown and Elliott have effectively contrasted the complex program of the Hall of Realms (where the depiction of royal victories
is associated with the labors of Hercules) with the massive purchases and commissions made in order to furnish an enormous,
empty palace as quickly as possible. The huge growth of the
Spanish royal collection during the reign of Philip IV (about 2,000
paintings) includes commissions which do not appear to have any
deep iconographic significance, despite the still-unpublished
claims of Barghahn, who seems to push the currently fashionable
zeal for interpretation to the point of caricature. In a similar vein,
when Louis XIV, half a century later, commissioned a large series
of paintings to adorn the Marble Trianon, he was not at all
concerned with iconography, nor even with the choice of painters.[25]

As far as art collections are concerned, they are really, at best,
no more than secondary means of royal propaganda. In seventeenth-century France, a certain number of advisors, who were
either minor or illustrious collectors themselves, believed that
collecting was one of the attributes of a great king; but we have

25 Jonathan Brown and John Elliott, *A Palace for a King. The Buen Retiro and the Court
of Philip IV* (New Haven, 1980); Barbara von Barghahn, "The Pictorial Decoration of the
Buen Retiro Palace and Patronage during the Reign of Philip IV," unpub. Ph.D. diss.
(New York Univ., 1979). Schnapper, *Tableaux pour le Trianon de Marbre, 1688–1714* (Paris,
1967).

to wait for Colbert and Louis XIV before such views were adopted by the Crown. In a country where the highest form of cultural expression was literature or, alternatively, architecture, to be a connoisseur was not in itself considered a royal attribute. At least until the 1680s, works of art continued to be regarded simply as accessories to buildings. Moreover, however large the payments for art commissions were, these sums were meager compared to the amount spent on buildings. If one were seeking glory in the seventeenth century, building a Versailles was a greater expression of magnificence than owning all the Titians in the world.

Raymond Grew

Picturing the People:
Images of the Lower Orders in Nineteenth-
Century French Art

If the images that artists create directly connect to the culture of their time, then the pictures painted, etched, and drawn in France between 1815 and the 1860s should be rich in representations of the people—of the people as peasants and workers, of the people seen as the lower orders in crowded slums or rural hovels, and as the *classes dangereuses* who filled social commentary.

The expectation that the lower classes should be frequently depicted in nineteenth-century French art would rest on more than the naive assumption that art must illustrate its era, for the sights of that age—thousands of immigrants and endless construction while the population of Paris trebled, new machines and industries, political demonstrations, barricades, and revolution—might well have stimulated the artistic eye. The culture as a whole was greatly concerned about these matters. They were the subject of novels (many of which are still read) and of systematic field studies (now remembered primarily for contributing to the birth of modern social science). They were the object of important political and religious movements and of innumerable programs for reform. They were discussed at the meetings of the Académie des Sciences Morales et Politiques, in sermons, in parliament, and in pamphlets and daily newspapers. Not only were pauperism, prisons, crime, illegitimacy, and illiteracy recognized as critical problems for modern France, but contemporary French history was also believed to have played a peculiarly exemplary role in the course of modern civilization.[1]

Raymond Grew is Professor of History at the University of Michigan and is editor of *Comparative Studies in Society and History*.
The author wishes to thank, without implicating them in any way, Marvin B. Becker, Philippe Bordes, Hilarie Faberman, Thomas W. Gaehtgens, and Carl E. Schorske for their helpful comments on this article.

1 Stephen Bann, *The Clothing of Clio* (Cambridge, 1984), 53.

Art and artists were particularly prominent in French society. Well-established artists had many connections to the writers, *académiciens*, statesmen, and journalists who devoted so many words to the lower orders. In these circles history paintings (which necessarily implied some social content) were the most admired; but works of every sort were exhibited at the annual salons, which drew over a million visitors during the July Monarchy, and were reviewed by many of the leading intellectuals of the day. As caricaturists, artists like Henri Monnier, Charles Philipon, Gavarni, Honoré Daumier, and the young Gustave Doré literally earned their living by commenting on the social scene. Not surprisingly, some artists had ties to Saint-Simonians, Fourierists, or Proudhonians; a number believed that popular art and formal art were or should be fundamentally related, that humble themes were suitable to great art, and that serious art ought to be accessible to the people—beliefs restated from the Revolution to the Third Republic. The advocates of such an art could cite impressive precedents for the choice of scenes from daily life, including Michelangelo Caravaggio (then one of the most admired Italian painters), Diego de Velázquez, Bartolomé Murillo, and Francisco de Goya among Spanish painters, and well-known examples from the Dutch tradition in addition to the work of French painters like the brothers Antoine, Louis, and Mathieu Le Nain, Jean Baptiste Chardin, and Jean Baptiste Greuze.[2]

There is reason to expect from this period a variety of images of the lower orders in France—images created by artists who were active participants in the culture of their time and were keenly aware of notable artistic traditions that encouraged inclusion of the lower orders. Such images were made all the more likely by the new popularity of lithography (which encouraged flowingly drawn, rapidly reproduced, and widely disseminated images) and by the presence of so many people (perhaps more than in any previous society) who considered themselves professional artists.

2 William Hauptman, "Juries, Protests, and Counter-Exhibitions before 1850," *The Art Bulletin,* LXVII (1985), 95–109. Elizabeth Gilmore Holt (ed.), *The Triumph of Art for the Public: The Emerging Role of Exhibitions and Critics* (New York, 1979), xxv; A. Tabarant, *La vie artistique au temps de Baudelaire* (Paris, 1942), 503–514. Gabriel P. Weisberg, *The Realist Tradition: French Painting and Drawing, 1830–1900* (Cleveland, 1980). See also, Charles Edward Gauss, *The Aesthetic Theories of French Artists from Realism to Surrealism* (Baltimore, 1973), 9–15; Robert Rosenblum, *The International Style of 1800: A Study in Linear Abstraction* (New York, 1976), 223–224.

Théophile Thoré's call in 1836 for an art *"social et progressif"* would seem to have had every chance of being answered.[3]

Consider images of the lower orders, for the moment overlooking important distinctions of medium, style, or broad purpose. In its dull concreteness such an approach acknowledges the relentless literalness of pictures, which once begun create a frame that must be filled, figures that must be clothed, and gestures that must be completed. The representational artist may be eager to show the curve of a single outstretched hand; whatever his aesthetic, dramatic, or symbolic intention, he must then make a number of choices about the other hand and the body to which both are attached. He may include an object that evokes feelings broadly shared in the larger society even when those feelings are not necessarily central to the work of art. Although there may always be some conflict between historical reality and artistic images that serve other purposes and are embedded in their own traditions, the literal search for pictures of the poor can largely ignore that problem.[4]

When one turns to the great outpouring of images in this period—to paintings neoclassical, romantic, and realistic; to genre scenes and landscapes; to lithographs, drawings, prints of subjects literary, historical, picturesque, and commonplace—it is astonishing how infrequently there are figures in worker's blouse or peasant garb and how much rarer still are scenes that depict a group of them acting together. Although French culture gave visual art a central place and also reverberated with writings about the poor, the poor were not commonly depicted in art.[5]

3 For the range of these images and their multiple connections to society see Beatrice Farwell, *French Popular Lithographic Imagery, 1815–1870* (Chicago, 1981). Harrison C. White and Cynthia A. White, *Canvases and Careers* (New York, 1965), 33–46, estimate that there were 3,300 painters in France by 1863. Thoré is cited in Holt, *Exhibitions*, 389.
4 Ronald Paulson, *Representations of Revolution (1789–1820)* (New Haven, 1983), 24. The historian's use of art to find out about society is in a sense the obverse of the social history of art. See T. J. Clark, *Image of the People: Gustave Courbet and the 1848 Revolution* (Princeton, 1982), 9–20.
5 Notice how few representations of the lower orders are to be found even in such socially sensitive and recent exhibitions as *French Painting 1774–1830* (Detroit, 1975); Farwell et al., *The Cult of Images: Baudelaire and the 19th-Century Media Explosion* (Santa Barbara, 1977); Peter Fusco and H. W. Janson (comps.), *The Romantics to Rodin: French Nineteenth-Century Sculpture from North American Collections* (Los Angeles, 1980); Weisberg, *Realist Tradition. Idem, Social Concern and the Workshop: French Prints from 1830–1910* (Salt Lake City, 1974), 14.

We can explore this paradox by considering the various kinds of images that were created of workers, peasants, poor people, and crowds. The existence of such images lends weight to the problem, for they are an important reminder that, however discouraging official taste, censorship, or the market may have been, artists could choose such scenes. A visual vocabulary was available that might be adapted to any increased interest in portraying the life of those at the bottom of society. After all, every painter of battle scenes, or at least his assistants, had spent considerable time painting the lower classes. Historical paintings, so fashionable in salon and academy, necessarily expressed an interpretation of history and in effect required artists to take a stand on the historical role in major events played by popular crowds (often a controversial matter). Centuries of landscapes and genre scenes offered other models.[6]

In addition, three types of prints (primarily lithographs) that became popular in the period from 1820 to 1850 included visual statements about the lower orders. One of these types consisted of scenes of provincial France, the grandest series of which was the *Voyages pittoresques et romantiques dans l'ancienne France* (1819–1879), a title that nicely captures an urban, bourgeois, and romantic sensibility. In the tradition of landscapes these scenes often included some country people. Forever bending to the cycle of seasons, birth, and death, yet always there, peasants provided a lesson in resignation. They were part of nature, as timeless as trees; and they went about their business apparently as indifferent to social relations as the Italian peasants in Giovanni Battista Piranesi's prints, who stolidly ignore the elegant foreigners invading their fields to exclaim over some marble fragment. As in many Dutch and English landscapes, these French peasants were usually small, distant figures. Literally marginal, they helped to set a scene. When peasant figures were more prominent in these French images, it was often their costume that mattered as a means to establish the locale; their visual function remained the same: a decorative evocation of pastoral calm and rural simplicity, part of the "interesting sights," the "noble memories" and the "poetic customs" of one's ancestors.[7]

6 Albert Boime, "The Quasi-Open Competitions of the Quasi-Legitimate July Monarchy," *Arts Magazine*, LIX (1985), 100–102.
7 See Bonnie L. Grad and Timothy A. Riggs, *Visions of City and Country: Prints and*

Colorful peasants or ones performing ageless tasks in the dim distance do not require that either artist or viewer take any stand on the social question. Nor are these peasants, so much at home in the pages of the albums of *Voyages pittoresques,* the peasants who agitate or engage in politics. Surprisingly, townlife is not very different. Just as cottages sit harmoniously by streams, whole villages nestle into the landscape. If in cityscapes figures suggest the noise, bustle, and variety of life in town; if they provide a colorful and softening vitality in contrast to the hard surfaces of stone buildings and narrow streets, that is enough. There is not in such scenes much Hogarthian interest in the specific tasks that individuals perform.[8]

Quaintness, local color, traditions (and processions) that express social order, fields and streets that illustrate the wholesome happiness possible where spontaneity never threatens to become disorder—these were attractive themes; such scenes nevertheless remained a minor part of nineteenth-century French art. Only rarely were they deliberately used as propaganda. For the most

---

Photographs of Nineteenth-Century France (Worcester, 1982). On Dutch influences within the French tradition, see Petra Ten Doesschate Chu, *French Realism and the Dutch Masters* (Utrecht, 1974), 18–79. Meyer Schapiro, "Courbet and Popular Imagery," *Journal of the Warburg and Courtald Institute,* IV (1941), 186, notes the sense of peasant resignation. A characteristic example is the lithograph by Alexis Victor Joly, *Ruins of the Château Gaillard* (1824). Richard Brettell, "The Impressionist Landscape and the Image of France," in *A Day in the Country* (Los Angeles, 1984), 38, mentions that earlier in the century rural figures were "tiny and distant from the viewer." Contrast the eighteenth-century interest in more realistic depictions of peasant life: D. G. Charlton, *New Images of the Natural in France* (Cambridge, 1984), 188–189. John Barrel, *The Dark Side of the Landscape* (Cambridge, 1980), argues that in English landscapes even these half-hidden figures served an ideological purpose, 36, 83–85, 97ff., 156. Philippe-Auguste Jeanron, *Les paysans limousins* (1834), is an example of attention to local costume. Grad and Riggs, *City and Country,* 17.

8   The series of *Voyages pittoresques* is well discussed in Weisberg, *Realist Tradition,* 15–25. Consider Paul Huet's etching, *The Keeper's House* (1833) and Eugene Isabey's lithograph, *Apse of the Church of Saint-Nectaire* (1831). Weisberg suggests that, prior to 1830, landscapes were likely to be dominated by a building and that after that date man-made edifices increasingly blended into the landscape itself, and he adds that realist painters were not much inclined to depict rural huts (21, 94). Richard Parkes Bonington's lithograph, *The Rue du Gros Horloge in Rouen* (1824), evokes an English tradition in the careful mixture of classes held together by their urban frame and their general busy-ness. Guillaume de Bertier de Sauvigny finds Marlet more useful to the historian than Augustus Pugin or Bacler d'Albe where "les personnages ne sont là que pour donner l'echelle ou animer les tableaux": introduction to Jean-Henri Marlet, *Tableaux de Paris* (Paris, 1979); Marlet did include prisoners (as did some others, including Monnier), a rat poison salesman, coal carriers, etc.

part peasants, when they appeared, remained distant and dour; and townsfolk were indistinct. Yet within that tradition there were seeds of another view that would begin to emerge in the 1840s. The interest in the picturesque implied recognition that society was changing, and these prints edged toward while still largely avoiding more direct social comment.[9]

Another tradition of popular images looked much more directly at the workingman, presenting the various *métiers* of France in a kind of visual catalogue. Fashionable in the eighteenth century, these pictures (usually woodblocks or etchings) continued to be produced in large numbers; and those stiff portraits of anonymous butchers, woodworkers, washerwomen, watercarriers, and women sweeping apparently seemed up-to-date to those who continued to buy them. Paradoxically, however, they had changed little with the French Revolution or industrialization.[10]

Not only did the often anonymous artists who made these prints choose to depict traditional occupations; they also presented the subject didactically, usually with one figure per occupation and one occupation per picture—a worker seen full face in a stiff pose that made his attributes (awl, anvil, or broom) and costume rather than his personality or action the focus of the picture. These depictions tended to be as coldly categorical as illustrations of army uniforms, except that the equipment of a given trade was often represented with an affection for detail reminiscent of the great *Encyclopédie*. From that distance, it was easier to argue for the importance of sanitation than to say something about society. In all the series on *métiers et professions* and despite all the talk of representing the popular classes, it would be difficult to find in these prints "political shoemakers" or working-class agitators of any sort.[11]

9 The opportunity for propaganda is illustrated by two commissioned works of 1817: Fleury-François Richard, *Madame Elisabeth de France Distributing Milk*; Louis Hersent, *Louis XVI Distributing Alms to the Poor*. Here the peasants are humble and their children clean. The theme was a traditional and familiar one; note François-Frédéric Lemot, *Henry IV Distributing Bread to the People of Paris*, a bronze relief commissioned by Louis XVIII for the Pont Neuf; Isadore Pils, *Soldiers Distributing Bread to the Poor* (1852); and the refinement of the theme in works commissioned by Napoleon III. Boime, "The Second Empire's Official Realism," in Weisberg (ed.), *The European Realist Tradition* (Bloomington, 1982), 92–95.
10 On the similarities of the earlier work by L. S. Mercier or Edmé Bouchardon, see Weisberg, *Realist Tradition*, 1–9.
11 Note how in J. G. V. de Moleon's lithograph of 1828, *Details of Some of the Slaugh-*

These pictures of artisans and working men and women were closely related to the popular series of *physiologies* that, with inexhaustible fascination, portrayed the various types of human animal to be found in Paris. Often advertised as a kind of Balzacian inventory, they were rooted in the pseudo-scientific claims of phrenology as well as sociology. Like the popular pamphlets and books known as the *Cris de Paris*, they sought to capture the colorful variety of Parisian life, treated activity in the capital as a form of theater, and focused more on the physical types associated with particular occupations than on their sociological origins. As the pamphlets' ironic prose made clear, this was largely a bourgeois view of Paris despite the popular tone. It was one more interested in the concierge, the *flâneur*, or the office clerk than the laborer, and one that looked at all of them from above.[12]

In text and drawing these illustrated pamphlets contributed to the explosion of caricature that was one of the glories of Paris in the 1830s and 1840s. Cartoons became sharply satirical, their

---

terhouse Operations at Montfaucon, the figures are subordinated to carcasses and a shed. See Judith Wechsler, *A Human Comedy: Physiognomy and Caricature in 19th Century Paris* (Chicago, 1982), 115–123; Eric J. Hobsbawm and Joan Wallach Scott, "Political Shoemakers," *Past & Present*, 89 (1980), 86–114. Sculpture—a still more formal and public art—waited another generation before depicting the worker. John M. Hunisak, "Images of Workers: From Genre Treatment and Heroic Nudity to the Movement of Labor," Fusco and Janson, *Romantics to Rodin*, 52.

12 The prototype for those studies was Johann Caspar Lavater, *Essai sur la physiognomonie destiné a faire connaître l'homme et à le faire aimer*, published first in Germany and then, between 1781 and 1800, in France. For a discussion of the genre and its relation to the tradition of mime, see Wechsler, *Human Comedy*, 42–52. In England the depiction of a crowd could become an essay in phrenological types: Mary C. Cowling, "The Artist as Anthropologist in Mid-Victorian England: Firth's *Derby Day*, *The Railway Station*, and the New Science of Mankind," *Art History*, VI (1983), 461, 466–467. The titles of these works reflect their view of Paris itself as a kind of diversion: *Promenades pittoresques et lithographies dans Paris et ses environs; Les Français peints par eux-mêmes; La musée pour rire; Le muséum parisien; Les pétits français*. Carle Vernet's *Cris de Paris* (1825) picked up elements from Chardin, Greuze, and Jean Antoine Watteau in the depiction of everyday life. Weisberg, *Realist Tradition*, 24–25. In Monnier's *Six Districts of Paris* (1828) popular life manages to seem festive and at least petty bourgeois. Louis Huart's *Physiologie du Tailleur* (Paris, 1841) is typical in saying almost nothing about tailors but much about their customers. Although the five volumes of *Français peints par eux-mêmes* include more than a score of distinctly lower-class types, the comment on "l'homme du peuple" is to ask what kind of an occupation is that. On Pierre Charles Baudelaire's "gaze of the flâneur," Walter Benjamin, "Paris—Capital of the Nineteenth Century," *New Left Review*, XLVIII (1968), 84. Grad and Riggs, *City and Country*, 27, mention the echo of eighteenth-century *fêtes galantes*. Something similar is true of the scenes of Paris done by Victor Adam and in other contemporary views as noted in Berbier de Sauvigny, *La Restauration, 1815–1830* (Paris, 1970).

wit exposing the painful gap between appearance and reality by piercing the hilariously thin veil on which appearance depended. Their satire was about social roles and the pretensions of the upwardly mobile. As such, it was primarily about the middle class—lawyers and politicians especially. Environment, Honoré de Balzac had argued, created the social type, but "today the individual gets his physiognomy from himself." The fascination of caricature lay in that creation of one's own presence, and it was difficult to imagine that the poor—except when deceitful—created their physiognomies. Only occasionally (and more in the 1840s than earlier) did the theme of the social mask show a direct link to the lower orders and then primarily in terms of the sad clown, a favorite nineteenth-century motif. Significantly, it was the theater and circus more than social programs that provided this bridge from satire of the middle classes to comment on the poor.[13]

For the most part the lower orders were not the subject of caricature. We feel their presence, in Daumier especially, because we are placed as observers with our noses, too, pressed against the window. In seeing the emptiness of authority, the hypocrisy of magistrates, and the dishonesty of politicians we recognize that the poor could also see all that. So we imagine them looking over Daumier's shoulder; we credit him with justified subversion and them with understandable bitterness. But he usually achieved that effect without actually showing us those lower orders whose presence we feel.

They appeared more often in the cartoons of Gavarni, where they became a target for laughter. Gavarni's workers are amusing in their pretensions: a father telling how he captured Lombardy; peasants who talk as if they understood high finance; the worker who warns the bourgeois that Poland will never forgive him— men with crude faces and wrinkled clothes playing at geopolitics or denouncing each other's opinions. It is rare that one of them speaks as a worker, like the man who mounts the rostrum to declare, "L'Etat c'est moi." Even Gavarni's famous character, Viroloque, the ragpicker who recalls popular images of the wandering Jew, is the perpetual outsider, a street philosopher whose

---

13 Wechsler, *Human Comedy*, 29. Martin Meisel, *Realizations: Narrative, Pictorial, and Theatrical Arts in Nineteenth-Century England* (Princeton, 1983), 201–225, 434.

apolitical skepticism of politics (there is something a bit Poujadist about Gavarni) and dialect as thick as Mr. Dooley's are reminders that here the unseen audience is middle class. Monnier drew his pompous, bourgeois M. Prudhomme from photographs of himself. Thus even in genres explicitly tied to peasants, workers, occupations, the human comedy, Parisian streets, and social satire the French art of the first half of the nineteenth century suggests some unspoken constraint in its concrete portrayal of society's lower orders.[14]

Some important art created in this period did take the lower orders as its subject. These works, often by artists now universally acclaimed, were part of a change in the visual treatment of workers and peasants, a shift with earlier roots but one that became apparent in the 1840s and found its greatest expression in the 1850s with the work of Gustave Courbet and Jean-François Millet. Seen in artistic context, this achievement becomes all the more impressive and the question of how the poor were portrayed becomes all the more significant.[15]

For those who chose so to employ it, there was a cultural wardrobe of images—religious, historical, literary, and anecdotal—that could evoke shared values while referring to the lower classes. These images could be called on in order to present the poor with sympathy, especially in scenes of the aged and the very young, or of mother and child. There was a classical tradition of powerful nudes, whose very nudity avoided issues of social class while universalizing human dignity. And there was a tradition of religious painting in which farmers and fishermen were God's agents, families were an expression of His design, and suffering was the path to Redemption. Only the combination of that visual vocabulary with contemporary concerns can explain Heinrich Heine's response to Léopold Robert's painting, *The Arrival of the Harvesters in the Pontine Marsh* (Fig. 1), as a revelation, an apoth-

14 Gavarni (Guillaume Sulpice Chevallier), *La mascarade humaine* (Paris, 1881) is a good anthology of his cartoons, primarily from the 1850s. One of Viroloque's favorite expressions is "Misère-et-corde," simultaneously a reminder of Christian charity and the lower orders' amusing ignorance. On Monnier, Wechsler, *Human Comedy*, 115.
15 Pierre Georgel, "Les transformations de la peinture vers 1848, 1855, 1863," *Revue de l'Art*, XXVII (1975), 62–77; Robert L. Herbert, *Barbizon Revisited* (Boston, 1962), 37–40, both emphasize the impact of the revolution of 1848. The continuity across that divide is a reminder that cultural history also has its own periodization.

Fig. 1 Léopold Robert, The Arrival of the Harvesters in the Pontine Marsh, 1831.

SOURCE: Reprinted with permission of the Louvre, Paris.

eosis in which "men are holy, yea, deified." Sentimental pictures
of young children (especially girls) and the aged (especially men),
which were so popular in the nineteenth century, drew on the
viewer's sympathy for the helpless (and therefore blameless)
whose purity included being innocent of social relations beyond
the family.[16]

The possibilities for social comment became more powerful
in pictures about victims. On *The Raft of the Medusa* (Fig. 2)
Théodore Géricault placed a mass of tangled bodies nude enough
to make a multiple Laocoon: men and women sharing a common
fate, together yet separate, victims of the sea and the state's choice
of an incompetent captain—devices that would be echoed in Eugène Delacroix's *Shipwreck of the Don Juan* (1840). Daumier's relief
of *The Emigrants* (1848/49) similarly shows a struggling group cut
off from ordinary society. Refugees from famine brought together
by desperate choice to share a fate if nothing else, they are the
victims of more than nature. So too is the man in a nightshirt
who sprawls against his bed (in his own flat) on *Rue Trasnonain*
(1834); he could almost be the victim of drink except for the
blood, the child's body underneath him, the woman's body a
little distance away—a (working-class) family victimized (by
Louis Philippe's militia) in the silence of their home—a shocking
juxtaposition of violence and powerlessness.

Peasants were not just a part of nature but its victims too as
in Gustave Brion's *Gathering Potatoes during the Flood of the Rhine*
(Fig. 3). Genre paintings could combine the bonds of family and
the pathos of poverty in picturing a family forced by the tragedy
of their horse's death to halt in the snow as the mother bundles
her baby, an old man huddles in the wagon, and the father stares
disconsolately at the inadequate fire while his children gather
wood. These were victims of society as well as nature; so were
the peasants of Millet. Often shown close up like artisans in the
traditional woodcuts of the *métiers,* their massive figures bend
with the endless rhythm of brutalizing work. Their eternal toil,
part of the "idiocy of rural life," has come to seem a harsh fate.
Yet these figures also echo the dignity of Michelangelo and are
done in colors and costumes that recall biblical scenes. Millet's

16 Heine is cited in Holt, *Triumph of Art,* 309–310. The distance was not very great from
romantic anecdote to touching scenes of daily life in the street. Weisberg, *Realist Tradition,*
41–49.

Fig. 2 Théodore Géricault, *The Raft of the Medusa,* 1819.

Fig. 3 Gustave Brion, *Gathering Potatoes during the Flood of the Rhine in 1852*, 1852.

SOURCE: Reprinted with permission of the Beaux-Arts Museum, Nantes.

Peasant Couple Going to Work (1863, 1866) look like the expulsion from Eden. Their own religion, however (and at a time when most religious scenes were comfortably historical or sentimental), remained as dull and habitual as their work. Still, Millet's peasants displayed a domestic life that reasserted their humanity and laid claim to the century's affection for the family, for he had creatively pulled together many of the themes of contemporary art and some of the themes of contemporary social concern.[17]

Realists went beyond the *physiologies* to do real portraits of anonymous peasants and workers. Fascination with *saltimbanques* became more psychological than theatrical and allowed a kind of special claim for those who survive on society's fringe. Visual conventions of occupational types or the *Cris de Paris* were now used for studies of everyday life done with deeper purpose. By the 1840s and 1850s work itself tended to be presented more warmly than before in pictures of artisans absorbed in their labor and of unskilled workers whose movements held more interest and suggested more energy than mere routine. The life of labor was acknowledged to have its separate world and its own rewards in the cozy interior of home or tavern.[18]

These workers remained artisans, their shops small, and their recreations those of the village more than of the city. The few attempts to depict industrial labor recall the stiffness of the older series on *métiers*. Precise attention to costumes and tools obscures personality; and the huge, angular machinery that dictates where the workers stand somehow lessens the credibility of their movements. Rarely do the paintings of François Bonhommé, painstak-

---

17 The picture described, Jean-Pierre Antigna's *The Forced Halt* (1855), so much like a battle scene, contrasts with Horace Vernet's earlier *Scene of the French Campaign of 1814* (1826) in which a peasant woman supports her dying husband while soldiers set fire to her house and drive off her cattle. The difference is more than one of style. Vernet's are the victims of the chances of war, of a sudden intrusion; Antigna's the victims of permanent poverty and therefore, in a sense, of society. Consider Millet's *L'Angelus* (1858) and the comments in Herbert, *Jean-François Millet* (Paris, 1975), 103–105. Balzac's reminder that primitive man could be seen among French peasants may have been particularly influential among painters. Grad and Riggs, *City and Country*, 16.

18 Wechsler, *Human Comedy*, 91–97, contrasts the catalogue of expressions in *Les pétit grimaces* with its predecessors. Francis Haskell, "The Sad Clown: Some Notes on a 19th-century Myth," in Ulrich Finke (ed.), *French 19th-Century Painting and Literature* (Manchester, 1972), 2–16. François Bonvin, *Interior of a Tavern* (1859), and the more famous *Monday* (1859) of Jules Breton were criticized both as too realistic and too bland. See *The Second Empire, 1852–1870: Art in France under Napoleon III* (Philadelphia, 1978), 256–261.

ingly executed for admiring industrialists, capture the heat and noise of the factory or a sense of human engagement in a compelling process. Nor did the visual possibilities inherent in the proud rituals of guilds attract major artists.[19]

The missing element is not so much specific occupations as society itself. Symbols of harvest, mankind's dependence on food, biblical references, and romanticism had all been invoked to convey a more considered and a more complex vision of peasant life; but wage labor was not so clearly situated in visual convention or literature. The important step from a catalogue of tasks to the portrayal of toilers at work had stopped short of depicting social relations. Even realism, which provided powerful devices for demythologizing contemporary life, proved an awkward vehicle for conveying social purpose or communal values. Rural life, thickly wrapped in myths to wipe away, offered realism the setting for its greatest achievements. Thus the separate interests of Courbet's *Peasants of Flagey* (1850) suggest a society not functioning very well, an ironic contrast to Robert's festive and pious Italian peasants. The villagers conducting Courbet's *Burial at Ornans* (1850) imply a society unmasked, or about to be, and it was the ambiguous meaning of that portrayal which infuriated critics. After considerable talk about a social art, there were now at least a few examples of what such an art might be like; its unpopularity is understandable. But the question remains of why the logical next step toward an art revealing modern social life among the urban lower classes (a step that would seem both to follow from and to have been made easier by the achievements of artists like Daumier, Millet, and Courbet) was not taken.[20]

That this step was not taken may tell us something about French society in the nineteenth century and about the special challenges

19 See the amateur examples in Jean Cuisenier, *French Folk Art* (Tokyo, 1976), pl. 340, 344, 353. The Barbizon painters' rejection of industrialization was quite a different matter: Herbert, *Barbizon Revisited*, 64–65. The artistic community was eager to participate in the industrial exhibition of 1855: Tabarant, *Vie artistique*, 230, 240–265. But contrast the scenes of English industry, including the work of Philip de Loutherberg from Strasbourg, commented on by Francis D. Klingender, *Art and the Industrial Revolution* (London, 1968), 59–113.

20 In Robert's *The Harvest*, flaying the wheat is like a dance; the great wagon seems to be on parade and peasant life an arcadian festival. Compare his *Pilgrims Returning from the Feast Day of the Madonna dell'Arco* (1827) with Courbet's peasants returning from the fair. Clark, *Courbet*, 80.

that artists faced, for we know that there continued to be (especially in Paris) novelists, socialists, religious crusaders, working-class radicals, and liberal reformers who were willing to broadcast their observations of lower-class life. Elements of these descriptions can be recognized in vignettes of city life and in familiar scenes of urban architecture and occupational types. Written commentary usually insisted, however, on the altered relations among individuals and between groups as a critical change that made the modern city the harbinger of a new era. Prior to Claude Manet French artists seem not to have found a consistent means of expressing what was sinister and exciting in the city that was *"le douleureux et glorieux décor de la civilization."*[21]

Perhaps the attractiveness of Paris made that challenge more difficult for artists grateful to be there, but there must be a deeper explanation for the curious fact that Géricault, Gavarni, and Doré were prompted more by visiting London than by living in Paris to portray the hopelessness of life in the slums. Conditions in London may have been worse or at least more graphic; probably the traditions of English art from William Hogarth through Thomas Rowlandson were an equally important stimulus. New environments are likely to be visually exciting, and maybe it is always easier to see the face of injustice etched upon a foreign society. But possibly it was more difficult to depict the poor of Paris because, in France, simple reporting (or seeming acceptance) of such a social system would not do; any picture of it would necessarily imply a cause or suggest a solution. Without any social theory adequate to the task, visual symbols were unlikely to move beyond the coldness of stone and the silence of darkness.[22]

---

21 Balzac and Eugène Sue are among the best-known novelists; the range of contemporary observation can be sampled in Louis Chevalier, *Classes laborieuses et classes dangereuses* (Paris, 1958) and Jean-Baptiste Duroselle, *Les débuts du catholicisme social en France (1822–1870)* (Paris, 1951). Baudelaire is cited in Michelle Hanoosh, "Painters of Modern Life: Baudelaire and the Impressionists," in William Sharpe and Leonard Wallock (eds.), *Vision of the Modern City* (New York, 1983), 175; his important influence could encourage overlooking the lower classes. Marshall Berman, *All That is Solid Melts into Air: The Experience of Modernity* (New York, 1983), 137–139.

22 A. Hyatt Major, *Prints and People: A Social History of Art* (Princeton, 1971), 671–672; Anne Renonciat, *La vie et oeuvre de Gustave Doré* (Paris, 1983), 194–203; Ralph E. Shikes, *The Indignant Eye* (Boston, 1969), 142–144. Even Alphonse Legros' bitter recollections of peasant life were done from memory after he had settled in London. Grad and Riggs, *City and Country,* 170. Adam's lithographs were unusual in that they included the poor on Parisian boulevards and even dramatic moments in the revolution of 1830, presented

One visual approach to city life was, in the tradition of picturesque landscapes, to emphasize urban space. English artists in France were especially comfortable with this device, which could be extended to Paris with the arrangement of space and some characteristic figures suggesting the rhythm of the capital. In village scenes quaint architecture established the locale, and faceless groups of people were almost incidental to the mysterious darkness of the streets or the water lapping in the harbor. On the whole these works were socially more attentive than the formulaic Parisian scenes of Giuseppe Canella which had been popular earlier in the century. Clearly, there was more to be said. Crime and criminals were found fascinating in literary and journalistic circles; and, visually, criminal scenes might have been used to suggest a sense of threat, of imminent conflict, or of social unpredictability. Portraying robbers, however, forces an artist to concentrate on a single dramatic moment and, worse, is likely to be perceived as observing social conflict from one side or the other. Daumier could soften that with humor, as when a suspect figure emerges from the dark to ask a startled burgher for the time. But human figures, and especially figures from the lower classes, risked making the sense of peril too concrete, too much like a social (and bourgeois) accusation. To evoke the evils of the city without seeming to blame the poor, it may have been wise to leave them out of the picture.[23]

It is interesting, given the general absence of such realistic depictions, that in the 1850s and 1860s a kind of expressionism was used instead to convey a more general mood and a broader social accusation. The startling results include Charles Meryon's disgusted gargoyle watching Paris below while vampires circle above, Félicien Rops' satan sowing sin above the city (Fig. 4), or

with deliberate matter-of-factness. See, in addition to the famous series on Paris, the examples in Farwell, *Cult of Images*, 21–22, 23, 39, 69–73.

23 Augustus W. Pugin and L. T. C Ventouillat, *Paris and its Environs . . . Two Hundred Picturesque Views* (London, 1831). Grad and Riggs, *City and Country*, 65–78. Canella's primary interest was not his human subjects. Having left Paris in 1826 "persuaded that the good period for painting [was] past," he returned to Milan, where in 1832 he held an exhibition of "pictures all sold and among these there are four in which the figures are planted almost as if the principle object: what the result will be heaven knows." Cited in Robert Bassi-Rathgeb, *Il pittore Giuseppe Canella (1788–1847)* (Bergamo, 1945), 17. Géricault in *L'Affaire Fualdès* (1818) met the same problem by placing his figures in the mountains outside an established social context.

Fig. 4 Félicien Rops, *Satan Sowing Evil Grain.*

Doré's semi-fantasies of slum street and specters as the setting for a suicide.[24]

Outside their living quarters, the lower orders could most easily be observed at work; but scenes of peasants or of laborers working generally kept their interactions to a minimum and left the quality of that interaction uncertain. Most of Millet's peasant figures stand alone, their relationship to others unstated even when a second or third figure is placed in equal isolation within the same frame. Their faces are often averted, and the men rarely look directly at the viewer—a pose likely to evoke some measure of social distance. Part of the power in Courbet's *Stonebreakers* (1851) lies in the uncertain symmetry of those figures. We can be more confident, as Courbet said, that the young man was destined someday to look like the old one, than we can of how the two of them felt about each other. Courbet may well have hidden their faces because he realized that he did not understand their feelings, but almost any glance that they could have cast risked opening up questions about their relations to each other and to the society that put them there. It has often been noted that most of Courbet's workers—tinker, knife-grinder, or faggot-gatherer—performed preindustrial tasks; but these members of the rural proletariat may have attracted the artist in part precisely because their position in the economic order was only loosely defined. Similarly, Millet's gleaners can be seen as working together or in lonely desperation; they bend over the same field much as the survivors of the Medusa cling to the same raft. This wrenching ambiguity was a significant achievement.[25]

Outdoors in the fields, these uncertain relationships shock the viewer and draw the eye (and mind) back again and again, but in the workshop the effect is likely to be awkward and stiff. Indoors the device of showing laborers from behind or with gaze averted (as in so much of Courbet's and Millet's work) can come to seem contrived, for the walls of the workshop close workers off from any private life and imply that those depicted must interact. Their placement, in practice arranged by task and title and only secondarily by the artist, invites some explantion. Perhaps the artist cannot tell us whether his workers are motivated

24 Grad and Riggs, *City and Country*, 93–132.
25 Clark, *Courbet*, 74.

by pride or driven by fear, but, by not suggesting their relation-ship to each other, he also avoided stating whether they were cooperating craftsmen or a proletariat of wage slaves. Pictures of the workshop therefore remained in the didactic tradition of the older illustrations of *métiers*. Admittedly work is difficult to de-pict, but these images contrast with the more relaxed scenes of women ironing in which the compulsion of poverty, traditional chores, maternal warmth, and the domestic workplace comfort-ably mix. Growing awareness of the tension between employer and wage laborer meant that scenes of labor were likely to be read as propaganda for one side or the other, a possibility that may have inhibited serious artists.[26]

Such subjects invited new directions. There was one, long established as suitable for artistic effort, that also invited visual presentation of the lower classes: great crowds that included the poor. Doré was willing to depict the throngs hailing Giuseppe Garibaldi in Naples; Rowlandson could represent the rather mo-tley greeting given King George III; John Zoffany chose to paint the crowd that had sacked the royal wine cellar in the French Revolution. But overpopulated Naples was united behind a hero already universally known; the boisterous humor of the English crowd implied no political threat; and the French Revolution was over. Crowds in contemporary France were a different matter. At a time when the crowd was among the strongest of cultural signs (but with diverse meanings of legitimacy, nationalism, shared religion, democracy, socialism, and revolution) and one endlessly presented in historical writing, in fiction, and on stage, sizable groups of the contemporary poor were not a major theme of French art.[27]

There are pictures, most often prints, of crowds at public ceremonies such as a ribbon-cutting or waiting for a train or

---

26 In *ibid.*, 80, Clark says that work is "too obvious and too obdurate for form: painters avoid it." Domestic labor was a popular motif that appeared in sculpture well before any figure of a male worker (although James Pradier's figure, which suggests something of a Greek goddess, was not exhibited. Hunisak, "Images of Workers," 54.

27 Paulson, who comments on Rowlandson and Zoffany in *Representations*, 151–153, notes that in England a crowd was the central image of the French Revolution, 39–45. The distrust of crowds was an important theme of French nineteenth-century thought. See Chevalier, *Classes dangereuses*; Susanna Barrows, *Distorting Mirrors: Visions of the Crowd in Late Nineteenth-Century France* (New Haven, 1981). On the crowd as an opportunity for English artists, see Cowling, "Artist as Anthropologist," 466–467.

boat—all occasions that predict behavior and, when a speech concludes or a train arrives, will justify the doffing of hats in a gesture once more commonly reserved for royal processions. There are even many images of the barricades of 1830 and 1848. Like the battle scenes that they recall, they are about a past event and the action that they record is largely independent of the larger outcome. For that reason and because a picture of men shooting and dying requires no political stand, it may have implied less of a social statement to show revolutionaries at the barricades than lower-class crowds at peace. Even the image of Archbishop Denis Affre dying on the barricade in 1848 is wonderfully neutral; everyone is simply horrified at the awful moment.[28]

Crowds of the common people had usually made their way into high art as participants in festivals, battles, royal or religious processions, and history paintings. In festival and battle, assigned costumes, more or less fixed roles, the momentary quality of the event, and its distance from centers of political power deprived even violent action by the masses of disturbing implications for contemporary society. One could savor the excesses and even the satire of peasant revellers or shudder at the accidents of death on the battlefield without pondering the social order. But in that historically self-conscious age, for people all but obsessed by history and its implications for the future, for people whose eyes were accustomed to probing historical paintings for every hint of interpretation, pictures in which crowds were not so visually constrained were likely to seem provocative. An individual ragpicker could be a colorful object of interest or humor, contempt or sympathy; but a crowd of them would seem to be going somewhere or about to do something.

When there was confidence in their historic role, then the people as a crowd or as a single symbolic figure could move to

28 Note the festive air in Adam's *Trip to Saint-Cloud by Steamboat* (1830). Goya's *Disasters of War* (1801–1826) was probably the single most influential model for the scenes of revolt. Adolphe Hervier, *L'Hôpital du Midi* (1848) and Ernest Meissonier's magnificent *The Barricade* (1849) let the dead and wounded make a point. Adolphe Leleux, *Le Mot d'Ordre* (1849) and *La Sortie* (1850) are more anecdotal but point to the next decade in their emphasis on the subject's feelings. Clark, *The Absolute Bourgeois: Artists and Politics in France 1848–1851* (Greenwich, 1973), 17–24, sees in these portrayals a new intimacy with the worker; they certainly contrast with Adolph Menzel, *Public Funeral of the March Revolutions of 1848* (1848). However, Georgel, "Transformations de la peinture," 73, says that if there was a radical style of 1848 it must be sought in "Oeuvres marginales, voire secrètes." René Perrout, *Les Images d'Epinal* (Paris, n.d. [1923]), 86–87.

the very center of the work of art. In Delacroix's *Liberty Leading the People* (1830/31) the figures are arranged in a trimphant pyramid of power (a common geometry in representations of popular victory) on a pedestal of corpses; they move forward with natural ease across the blood of the moment toward the future. History marches on. In that context ambiguity becomes possible and powerful. Liberty is simultaneously a goddess come to earth, a female force of nuturing and of revolutionary anger, and a figure of the people. To conservative critics Delacroix clearly took his models from the rabble, and his figures shared "the repugnant appearance that vice and crime imprint." Liberty reminded Heine, too, of the women "who swarm of evenings on the Boulevards," but that made the connection from goddess to society and therefore history, for there was

> also that little chimney-sweep Cupid, who stands with a pistol in either hand by this alley-Venus . . . and . . . the hero who storms onward with his gun, the galley in his features, [who] has certainly the smell of the criminal court in his abominable garments. And there we have it! a great thought has enobled and sainted these common people, this *crapule*, and again awakened the slumbering dignity of their souls.[29]

Daumier's bourgeois figures in parliament or the bourse, his refugee emigrants (at a time of famine and plague), or his wash-

---

29 Paulson, *Representations*, 21–22, cites Maurice Agulhon and Lynn Hunt on female figures as representations of revolution that associate domesticity and Venus with sexual energy. André Tardieu is the conservative quoted in *French Painting, 1774–1830*, 382. Heine is cited in Holt, *Triumph of Art*, 300. Boime, "Competition of the July Monarchy," 101–102. Delacroix's association of Liberty with other historical moments is further suggested by the similarity of her sisters in *Death of Sardanapalus* (1828) and *Greece Expiring on the Ruins of Missilonghi* (1827). Roy Howard Brown, "The Formation of Delacroix's Hero between 1822 and 1831," *The Art Bulletin*, LXVI (1984), 244–249. Note the association of patriotism and popular historical victory with themes of victims and battlefields in contrast to the ghostly crowd in Ary Scheffer, *Allons, enfants de la Patrie* (1827) or J. Travies, *Peuple affranchi* (c.1830), which included a catalogue of social types but without historical mission. Jeanron's work of 1830, *A Barricade*, falls in between; it has something of the concrete, historical power of Delacroix but, without a hint of allegory, cannot effectively evoke the promise of the historical future. His corpses in the *Second Insurrection of Lyon* (1834) are far more telling; the treatment of *Le Peuple aux Tuilleries* (1830) is closer to the comic tradition. These and nine other works were reproduced as illustrations in Louis Blanc, *Histoire de dix ans* (Paris, 1849), 5 v., a setting that makes Jeanron's reliance on traditions of genre and battle paintings, even for the revolutions in Belgium and Poland, seem strangely indifferent to social interpretations.

erwoman and child shown as indestructible round lumps trudging wearily up from the Seine (and called simply *The Heavy Burden* [1850–1855])—all of these images are fixed in historical context. Willingness to predict history's direction makes his symbolic representation of the people in *Liberty of the Press* effective (Fig. 5). The central figure in a worker's blouse vibrates with the heroic stature of a classical nude (a perfect model for later generations' socialist posters). Standing guard against the agents of repression, the muscular proletarian defending freedom is a historical force. The contrast between Delacroix's oil painting and Daumier's lithograph includes a difference as to social solidarity and class conflict, but, independent of medium or social vision, they have in

Fig. 5 Honoré Daumier, *Liberty of the Press*, 1834.

common a confidence in history that brings the people to center stage.[30]

Western art until the nineteenth century really had no special vocabulary for presenting the lower orders beyond those signs—of occupation, place, or clothing—given them by society itself. Yet, we can see such a vocabulary beginning to be formulated in France in the period under discussion and by the artists already mentioned. Moreover, they were able to do so even though class analysis was not central to the art of this period. The caricaturists' cultural and ethical disdain for the bourgeoisie did not mean that they analyzed society as a whole in class terms; and, as Millet, whose work seemed so socially radical, always insisted, he was no socialist.[31]

The socially conscious art of this period is remarkable for its continuity within the great tradition of Western art. If classical art stressed universal aesthetic values, it could also provide models for a democratic vision of people from every class, a hint of allegory adding significance to heroic figures, forever healthy and young, while avoiding statements about social relations. If Christian art presented saints and Jesus as ordinary people, that tradition could be invoked to give ordinary people a timeless dignity. The socially conscious depiction of the lower orders thus began with an emphasis upon their universal human qualities, underscored by references to classical and Christian art. Although the poor were often presented in terms of what they did not have or could not aspire to (a middle-class perspective), such pictures were also understood to express the human frailties that they shared with their superiors.[32]

Emphasis upon the dignity of the poor logically followed, a step that led away from the easy communication of genre paint-

---

30 Compare the French Revolution's use of the figure of Hercules. Hunt, *Politics, Culture, and Class in the French Revolution* (Berkeley, 1984), 94–117. Courbet's *L'apôtre Jean Journet* (1855) is comparable not only in its image of the worker striding across the world but also in its echo of an image common in popular art, the wandering Jew.

31 Nineteenth-century artists rarely depicted the confrontation of classes (Clark, *Absolute Bourgeois*, 181) because few believed in it.

32 Contemporary religious art, however, so emphasized sentimental piety, order, and cleanliness that even when there were scenes of pilgrims visiting the Curé d'Ars or crowds at a Croix de Mission, everyone somehow looks bourgeois. Most popular religious images were disembodied from any clear tie to contemporary society. See Catherine Rosenbaum-Dondaine, *L'image de piété en France, 1814–1914* (Paris, 1984).

ings in which costume and setting were relied upon to establish a figure's social status. Unless made to seem funny, tattered clothes and dirty faces were likely to convey the wrong message and simply to seem repugnant. The sense of justice that underlay the caricaturists' slashing attacks on the July Monarchy made it easier to see peasants as the victims of a kind of permanent disaster. Socially concerned artists in turn came to focus more on the helpless feeling of poverty than its external signs; images of refugees or *saltimbanques* conveyed a poignancy that was social as well as psychological.

When it came to portraying the visually less dramatic situation of the worker, that approach proved less effective. The attention given to artisans, however, emphasized the dignity and satisfactions of skilled labor; and artisans had the additional appeal of being politically active, being threatened by social change (and thus also victims), and being craftsmen like the artists themselves. At the very moment when he was becoming less and less representative of urban workers, the artisan was made the symbol of the laboring man. In newspaper, pamphlets, and propaganda that image would live on as the symbol variously of the French Republic, the proletarian, the trade unionist, or the builder of a new society.[33]

By the 1860s, however, a change was taking place in what it would mean to depict the lower orders. Clearly, that was related to the experience of revolution in 1848, followed by the Second Empire and rapid industrialization—factors traditionally emphasized. But there was also a change more internal to art. The moral concern that many artists felt for the emancipation of the lower orders had as one of its most important effects a contribution to the emancipation of art. They expanded the subject-matter and the sources of inspiration accepted as legitimate for high art; they broadened the understanding of what constituted seriousness in art; and they added to a growing belief in the autonomy of an artistic vision, independent of social or political programs.[34]

Some of those who sought to make the lower orders a subject for art made use of the traditions and forms of folk art and hoped

33 Hunisak, "Images of Workers," 52–55. On the iconography of workers, Hobsbawm, "Men and Women in Socialist Iconography," *History Workshop Journal*, VI (1978), 121–138; subsequent discussion in *ibid.*, VIII (1979), 167–182.
34 Michael Fried, "Manet's Sources: Aspects of His Art, 1859–1865," *Artforum*, VII (1969), 30–40.

that their own art could reach the masses. At times, then, the art of this period reached, like a rainbow, from popular to high culture; but as a bridge it proved similarly evanescent. Both the borrowing and the lending were as limited as these nineteenth-century artists' own connections to and knowledge of the society below them. Ultimately more important was their willingness to violate old canons that restricted high art to beautiful subjects and permitted only the beautiful to represent the good.[35]

Popular theater probably contributed more than popular art to a visual vocabulary of social realism. Whereas the preferred images in popular art continued to be those of a world different from the one in which the people lived (a world of saints and heroes, strange animals and dramatic events, and decorative illustrations of popular wisdom), popular theater built on a different basis. Particularly vigorous in this period, it searched out illusionistic techniques for representing everyday life. Almost by definition, it dissected society into a limited series of assumed roles. From the traditional set-pieces of commedia dell'arte, it invented situations that seemed contemporary. Theater thus had a great deal to offer artists trained in the traditions of high culture who wished to depict life at the bottom of society and, in doing so, themselves had to overcome the distance between actor and spectator.[36]

Realism similarly offered justification for treating almost anything visible as a subject for art, including the lower classes; but that proved to be more radical aesthetically than socially. There were fundamental problems of communication. Literal representation of dirt and crime was more likely to look like a criticism of the poor than of society. The realistic portrayal of the lower orders on any grand and consistent scale required ideologies not yet available or a social indifference that few artists could feel. To escape the constraints of realism, some turned to expressionist

---

35 Schapiro, "Courbet and Popular Imagery," 175–179. Clark, *Courbet,* 81, finds a connection between the ubiquitous *Degré des ages,* a series of couples representing the various stages of life, and Courbet's *Burial at Ornans.* Cuisenier, *French Folk Art,* 294, sees a shift in folk art at just this time away from religious themes. Paulson, *Representations,* 203–204, notes the tendency to assume an analogy between ugly bodies and evil.

36 Even images of "Le Monde Renversé" stuck to reversing the roles of men and animals, showing dogs at table, an ox-cart pulled by men, a cow butchering a man, etc. Pierre Louis Dûchartre and René Saulnier, *L'imagerie populaire* (Paris, 1925), 13–14. Wechsler, *Human Comedy,* 42–44; Haskell, "The Sad Clown," 10–11.

techniques and the use of allegory. Horace Vernet made an elaborate effort to lend classical grandeur to modern civilization; he could (somewhat coldly) connect ancient myth to modern steam, but even that required omission of social context. That was one of allegory's virtues; Théophile Gautier felt grateful that the painting, *Misery the Procuress* (1860), was allegorical, for, "given its modernity, it could have led to realism in bad taste." Allegory, however, rests on a common culture; and the attempt to achieve through symbols an integration that social life did not provide was generally sterile. In its abstractness allegory expresses values and moods better than it describes social conditions; and where social comment really was the dominant intention such efforts risked turning into cartoons.[37]

Efforts to depict the lower classes may have been discouraged by disagreement over social issues but were probably inhibited more by that historical self-consciousness which conferred great prestige on history paintings and then suffocated them in official interpretations. From that perspective contemporary scenes were statements about the direction of historical change and therefore about the destiny of France. This consciousness of history was shared by the crowds that flocked to Louis Daguerre's dioramas; it determined the organization of museums, dictated the costumes that actors wore on stage, altered the illustrations in history books, and became a theme of the *Voyages pittoresques*. When Heine could see an apotheosis in Robert's painting of a harvest scene, it was because of his view of history:

> If we have contemplated . . . that history which rolls on so crazily in mud and blood . . . that which we call the history of the world; then in this picture . . . we read a history which is greater still . . . I mean the history of humanity!

Ironically, that awareness also undermined the expressive power of historical paintings, for sensitivity to period costume and pre-

37 Robert Beetem, "Horace Vernet's Mural in the Palais Bourbon: Contemporary Imagery, Modern Technology, and Classical Allegory during the July Monarchy," *The Art Bulletin*, LXVI (1984), 265–269. Commenting on Vernet's *The Scourges of the Nineteenth Century: Cholera and Socialism* (1848), Beetem makes an interesting comparison to Alfred Rethel's pictures of the 1848 revolutions; but note how much more convincing it is to place Satan in real towns than Vernet's classicizing figures. The painting of Misery was by Auguste-Barthélemy Glaize, cited in *The Second Empire*, 309.

cise moments in the past lessened the universality that such works were meant to express. Freedom from these pressures was one of the advantages of a turn to new subjects.[38]

At the same time, Courbet invested his paintings of contemporary scenes with something of the aura of history painting. As the boundaries that distinguished historical from other paintings ceased to be clear, it was difficult to find a way to depict many people from the lower orders (or to find an occasion for doing so) without suggesting some energy or purpose that, to a nineteenth-century French eye, would imply revolutionary change. Cartoons and caricature could also lessen the burden of history, but the irony that these forms required was more suited to exposing bourgeois hypocrisy than workers' misery. A desire to escape from this heavy historical seriousness may well have contributed to the popularity of genre paintings. These were not models likely to encourage an independent social vision. Often they depended for their effect on knowledge external to the picture itself, on some well-known piece of literature or famous anecdote; and the easier they were to read, the more conventional was their message. But the possibility of giving genre themes something of the serious intent associated with history paintings implied a liberation of artistic choice that went beyond the increased appropriateness of including the lower orders.[39]

The Bourbon and July Monarchies, the Second Republic, and the Second Empire each had its own program for the visual arts, with favored styles, themes, and artists. By the second half of the nineteenth century, however, the French artists most admired today generally avoided association with official politics. Their conception of art stressed its autonomy and sought the sort of complexity and ambiguity admired in literature, emphases associated with "modern" art ever since. Claiming sovereignty

---

38 Bann, *Clothing of Clio,* 26–31, 43–47, 54–58, 60–63,79–88; Benjamin, "Paris," 80–83. Heine is quoted in Holt, *Triumph of Art,* 313.

39 Schapiro, "Courbet and Popular Imagery," 181, sees Courbet as a transitional figure between the cultivated artist of historical painting carrying all the baggage of high culture and the artist of the second half of the century who "relies on sensibility alone." Delacroix associated his dream of a new kind of history painting with popularity among all classes. Clark, *Absolute Bourgeois,* 125. Farwell, *Manet and the Nude: A Study in Iconography in the Second Empire* (New York, 1981), 86–87, 68. The preoccupation with history could also sustain the assumption that Italian peasants were happy arcadians; in addition to Robert, note Jean Baptiste Corot's *Bridge of Narni Near Rome* (1826). Meisel, *Realizations,* 434.

over realms of their own creation, artists were more committed to a personal vision than conventional values. For that reason, too, depicting the world of workers remained a subordinate interest. That painters like Breton and Bonheur turned from pictures with a social bite in the era of 1848 to subjects socially safer has to do with an altered aesthetic as well as market pressures and political caution. In the Second Empire there were many who still hoped that culture could unify society; but when Courbet set on a single canvas figures representing all of society, he placed them in his studio with himself at the center.[40]

There had long been talk of the need for a new art; Heine had even suggested that, until a new age provided that art, artists would have to rely upon "the most self-intoxicated subjectivity." Hidden in that proposal was an admission that aesthetic values mattered more than social programs. The new art, when it came, would reveal the world in a scintillating play of light reflected from the surfaces of middle-class leisure more often than from those of lower-class toil.[41]

40 Boime, "The Case of Rosa Bonheur: Why Should a Woman Want To Be More Like a Man," *Art History*, IV (1981), 384–409; Anna Klumpke, *Rosa Bonheur: Sa vie et son oeuvre* (Paris, 1908), 175, 180, 201; Hollister Sturges et al., *Jules Breton and the French Rural Tradition* (Omaha, 1983), 7–19. On the serious impact of the Second Empire, Boime, "Official Realism," 31–123. Carol Zemel, "The 'Spook' in the Machine: Van Gogh's Pictures of Weavers in Brabant," *The Art Bulletin*, LXVII (1985), 122–137, analyzes the ambiguity that marks a new direction. Werner Hoffmann (trans. Brian Battersheim), *The Earthly Paradise: Art in the Nineteenth Century* (New York, 1961), 11–24. Cf. Boime, "Official Realism," 108–110.
41 For Heine's review of the Salon of 1831, see Holt, *Triumph of Art,* 313–315.

Peter Paret

The German Revolution of 1848 and Rethel's

Dance of Death   If we agree that art, as everything else, may contribute to historical understanding, we should also recognize that the imponderables of aesthetic quality and of the relationship between the artist's psychology and his work make art a difficult historical source. When art is studied not for its own sake but as an indicator of conditions beyond it, the artist's inner life may even seem, or in fact be, a distorting element. His psychological constellation and the aesthetic expression it finds in images or structures are always shaped to some extent by forces independent of the outside world. Even when the artist is encapsulated in a firm tradition, meets the specific demands of a patron, or in other ways functions according to external constraints, traces of individuality remain in his work. On the one hand, historians seeking evidence on social or political developments, or on changes in ideas and attitudes, may be deceived by this residue. On the other hand, recognizing the nature of the residue enables us to analyze links between particular and general elements, and makes possible an interpretation more accurately attuned to the special character of the material than one that categorizes the work of art simply as yet another document that mirrors its times.

We may believe that a landscape by Camille Pissarro or an abstraction by Piet Mondrian can help us explain the social and political world in which they were created, even if the artists consciously or unconsciously meant to paint merely a farm house and a meadow shaded by a few poplars, or an arrangement of lines and rectangles. Inevitably the application of such art to political or social analysis is marked by a high degree of subjectivity. Art that openly addresses contemporary developments, especially if it does so in a figurative manner—a lithograph by

Peter Paret is Professor of History at the Institute for Advanced Study, Princeton. He is the author of *The Berlin Secession* (Cambridge, Mass., 1980) and *Clausewitz and the State* (Princeton, 1985; rev. ed.).

This essay is a shortened version of a chapter from a work in progress on the history of German culture from the 1830s to the twentieth century.

Käthe Kollwitz, for instance—may appear less ambiguous. But if we use it as documentation of its nonaesthetic context, we are in large part interpreting an interpretation, and should take particular note of the artist's personal, subjective elements that helped shape the work.

This essay has as its subject a work conceived and executed in response to political events: *Auch ein Totentanz*, a cycle of woodcuts by Alfred Rethel. My discussion cannot touch on every aspect of the woodcuts, their iconography, and their thematic and psychological roots. I limit myself to tracing the more important links between the external world and the artist's emotions, social position, politics, and historicizing aesthetics which caused him to use motifs of the past to interpret the present.

I also explore the documentary character of the woodcuts. Almost from the day they were published it was recognized that they constituted an important political statement and, judging from the frequency with which they appear as illustrations in studies of 1848, they have retained their hold on the historical imagination. But Rethel's message may have been misunderstood. We gain a clearer perception of the woodcuts as an expression of the Revolution of 1848, and as one man's interpretation of the revolution, if we bring our knowledge of history and of the artist to bear on his art.

Rethel's *Auch ein Totentanz*, which may be translated as *Another Dance of Death* or *This, too, is a Dance of Death*, consists of six thematically linked woodcuts, each accompanied by brief explanatory verses. The cycle was published a few weeks after the May 1849 uprising in Dresden, which Rethel witnessed and in which several hundred people were killed, and it quickly became a popular and commercial success. Nearly 15,000 copies were sold within a year; a political organization—the Conservative Alliance of Saxony—brought out a special printing; and there may have been pirated editions. At the time, the woodcuts were certainly the best-known interpretation by an important artist of the German Revolution of 1848 and 1849.[1]

---

1 The verses accompanying the woodcuts were by Robert Reinick, a minor poet and painter. Rethel himself advised Reinick on the text, and changed some of the wording. On Rethel and on the history of the cycle, see above all Joseph Ponten (ed.), *Alfred Rethels*

The first plate, and because of its allegorical complexities the weakest, shows Death emerging from his grave, greeted by five female figures with claws instead of feet, who are sending him on his revolutionary mission. They have overpowered and robbed Justice. She is seen in the background, hands tied, on a throne the foundations of which are giving way. The central figure, Cunning, presents Death with the sword of Justice, Dishonesty holds out her scales, while Vanity puts a hat with a cock's feather and a revolutionary badge on his skull. Behind these three, Blood-lust waits with a scythe, and Fury leads a horse forward.

In the second plate, Death rides through open country toward the town that is to be the scene of his activities. Above the town walls rise narrow, steeply roofed houses and the spires of a Gothic cathedral, but also factory chimneys of the new industrial age. Death is now booted and spurred; he wears an eighteenth-century coat, which contrasts with his broad-brimmed hat, a contemporary symbol of nationalism or radicalism. Two peasant girls run off to the right, and by a milestone on the edge of the road two ravens watch the horseman, while a third flutters away.

Now in the town, Death has dismounted before an inn. Workers, a woman, and children have gathered round the stranger, who entertains them with a trick. He holds the scales of Justice by the tongue, not by the handle, so that the clay pipe of the common man seems to weigh as much as the crown. On the wall behind him he has posted a manifesto that calls for Liberty, Equality, and Fraternity. In the right foreground, an old woman with a rosary pushes a small boy away from the spectacle. Behind her, the horse of Death stares at its master and the crowd.

The crowd has become a mob. One man is raising his fist, another a stick, a third already has picked up a rock. From a wooden platform Death offers his sword, which is now engraved with the words "People's Justice," to the outstretched hands below. On the platform beside him, a stonemason or blacksmith (judging by his apron and hammer) holds a flag bearing the letters "Repu[blic]," and with his other hand points to an approaching

---

Briefe (Berlin, 1912); *idem, Studien über Alfred Rethel* (Stuttgart, 1922); Heinrich Schmidt, *Alfred Rethel, 1816–1859* (Neuss, [1959]), with a useful though not entirely accurate bibliography. Another interpretation of the Revolution by a major artist is Adolf Menzel's unfinished *Aufbahrung der Märzgefallenen*. The interesting links between Menzel's and Rethel's work cannot be discussed here.

Fig. 1 Alfred Rethel, *Another Dance of Death*, Plate 1.

Fig. 2 Alfred Rethel, *Another Dance of Death*, Plate 2.

Fig. 3 Alfred Rethel, *Another Dance of Death*, Plate 3.

Fig. 4 Alfred Rethel, *Another Dance of Death*, Plate 4.

column of soldiers; but Death ignores him. Violence has already erupted: smoke rises above the rooftops, and at the edge of the square a man has been lynched.

The fifth woodcut depicts the climax of Rethel's political dance of death, and the last draws the moral. A barricade of crates, lumber, and barrels filled with paving stones is being defended against soldiers. A cannon ball has just shattered a beam, and three men are falling. Others take their place; elsewhere on the barricade men continue to fire, supported by snipers from the windows of a house. Death stands on a mattress atop the barricade. In one hand he holds the revolutionary flag, the other lifts his coat to reveal not the body of a man but a skeleton.

This terrifying violence is followed by a scene of desolation. Parts of the town are in ruin; soldiers guard the square before the destroyed barricade, some are already marching off. A mother and her son weep for the dead. A dying man—copied from Eugène Delacroix's *Liberty on the Barricades*—raises himself on his arms and stares at the leader who has betrayed him and his companions: the bare skeleton of Death, riding over the barricade, a wreath of victory on his skull. His horse, now without harness and saddle, licks the blood from the chest of a corpse—or does its drooping tongue merely signify exhaustion?—and steps over the sword of Justice, which has been dropped on a door torn off its hinges. The times are out of joint, even if order has been re-established. The intense horror that emanates from Rethel's subdued rhetoric makes this last woodcut unique in European art.

Of the many strengths of Rethel's cycle we may, for the present, note the following: his use of an old and powerful motif—the dance of death—which he applies to an issue of great contemporary concern; and the dance-like continuity from image to image, created by the leading actor in his various roles. Other elements in the sequence further bind its separate stages together: the horse, for instance, which in several plates also serves as a surrogate for the viewer, and perhaps even stands for the artist reacting to his own work; the sword, the scales, the flag, and the revolutionary hat—elements that may change from image to image, and thus reflect the inconsistencies of life and the ambiguity of the event depicted; the various moods of the horse, ranging from horror to weariness; the hat, now with one feather, now with two, the brim folded on the right or the left; the sword,

Fig. 5   Alfred Rethel, *Another Dance of Death*, Plate 5.

Fig. 6   Alfred Rethel, *Another Dance of Death*, Plate 6.

with and without legend, and with a different hilt in the last woodcut; and many others. The richness of detail invites us to search through each picture, but we are never in danger of losing sight of the clearly defined major themes. The firm composition of each plate, and its dramatic and often emotional execution, are enhanced by the woodcut technique, easily legible and appealing even to the unsophisticated. Finally there is the message of the work as a whole, which interprets revolution in strikingly simple and hostile terms.

In his six woodcuts Rethel presents Death as an almost omnipotent seducer, who uses the illusion and rhetoric of equality to induce urban artisans and workers to rebel against the state. Death appears to be motivated simply by the wish to expand his realm, to quicken the dance of death. He is shown as a malevolent force, who does not have the interest of the common people at heart, but drives them to destructive and ultimately self-destructive behavior. His appeal to equality is a trick; what he means is not social, political, or economic equality, but merely the equality of death. This particular revolution at least has no ideological justification. Its outcome is presented as a tragedy, but also as inevitable and just: good people are misled into committing criminal acts and must take the consequences. In the spring and early summer of 1849, when liberal reform and the last revolutionary movements throughout Germany were faltering, this message could count on a strong reception among conservatives and also among many who a year earlier had hoped for political change, but now were disillusioned.[2]

The conventional interpretation of Rethel's woodcuts as an anti-revolutionary tract rests on a good deal of evidence, and it has dominated responses to the work from 1849 to the present. But if we shift our attention from the work of art to the person of the artist we encounter a puzzle: Rethel was not a conservative.

2 The verses under the last plate may be translated as:
  Their leader was Death!
  He kept his promise.
  Those who followed him lie pale,
  Brothers all, free and equal.
  See, he has unmasked himself!
  As victor, high on horseback,
  The mockery of decay in his eyes,
  The hero of the red republic rides away.

As we know, he witnessed the fighting in Dresden in May 1849. After the uprising was suppressed, he characterized it in a letter to his mother as a "magnificent effort for German glory, which was defeated by the sword of coldly calculating military force." He continued: "I watched the growth of this movement with suspicion, I expected a Red Republic—Communism with all its consequences. Instead, popular enthusiasm in the best sense of the term sought to bring about a great and noble Germany, a task God entrusted not to radical newspapers and agitators but to the people."[3]

Rethel's statement that in Dresden the barricade fighters carried out God's will is difficult to reconcile with his critical, accusing treatment of revolution in the six woodcuts. If we take this contradiction seriously enough to want to resolve it, we must look further into Rethel's life and politics, and also at his earlier work. We may then find not only that the *Dance of Death* is in harmony with his political beliefs, but that it is characterized by motifs and compositional solutions that he had experimented with for years.

Rethel, was born in 1816, the son of a French official stationed in Aachen during the Napoleonic Era who remained in Germany when the empire collapsed, married the daughter of a local businessman, and established a small chemical factory. At the age of thirteen the boy was enrolled in the Düsseldorf Art Academy. A self-portrait of the following year demonstrates his precociousness, but its introversion and sadness also sound a warning note. A later self-portrait, done at the age of twenty-three, reinforces the impression of emotional suffering, and indeed for much of his life Rethel experienced bouts of severe depression. We do not know their psychological content, but a preoccupation with death was a part of them. In the early 1850s his condition worsened, and he declined into a state of total apathy from which he did not recover. He died in 1859 at the age of forty-three.

When Rethel entered the academy, Düsseldorf, together with Munich, formed the center of historical painting in Germany. Historical painting was strongly affected by the increasing atten-

3 Rethel to his mother, May 2, 1848: Ponten, *Rethels Briefe*, 119. A modern example of the conventional interpretation of Rethel's woodcuts is the characterization of the cycle as "counter-revolutionary" by two left-wing scholars, Helmut Hartwig and Karl Riha, in their study of West German responses to the memory of the Revolution of 1848: *Politische Ästhetik und Öffentlichkeit* (Steinbach, 1974), 16.

tion that scholars paid to the Middle Ages, and by the more rigorous, scientific character that their research was assuming. From his student days on, most of Rethel's work addressed the past. At his first major project he painted a cycle of frescoes on the life of Saint Boniface, missionary to the German tribes. He made extensive studies for another cycle depicting Hannibal's crossing of the Alps, and painted a series of imaginary portraits of medieval emperors. He also illustrated books—he was one of the illustrators of Karl von Rotteck's *History of the World* (Freiburg i. B., 1812–1827), a standard work of early German liberalism—and contributed several woodcuts to an edition of the *Nibelungenlied*.

A serial concept, in which a narrative—usually on historical themes—progresses from image to image, characterizes much of Rethel's art. Among his individual works is a portrait of his mother, today in the National Gallery in West Berlin, one of the most searing character studies in German painting of these years, and several variations on the theme of death. One of his very few landscapes is an oil of a castle on the Ruhr river, which had been converted into a factory—a juxtaposition of old and new that is encountered again in the second plate of *Another Dance of Death*, which shows the scene of the coming insurrection as a town with a cathedral, old houses, and factory chimneys. That coexistence and confrontation of the old and the new defines not only the aesthetic theme of the dance of death and contributes to its political message; it is the central issue of much of Rethel's work.

In 1840, Rethel won a major commission to paint a sequence of murals on the life of Charlemagne in the medieval townhall of Aachen. Together with his sketches he submitted a detailed historical program to the jury, which explained his plan to trace the rise of Charlemagne from tribal king to German emperor. The wishes of many middle-class Germans for a more united fatherland were expressed in Rethel's program, and contributed to its acceptance by the jury. The cycle concluded with a symbolic appeal to the present—a scene in which Death happens to play a central role: a later emperor descends into Charlemagne's crypt to seek inspiration from his great predecessor, whose gigantic sitting corpse towers over the living like another Barbarossa awaiting the day when he will rise from his mountain tomb to redeem the Germans.

Because some remodelling of the townhall was required, and for other reasons, Rethel did not begin on his project until 1846. He was still at work on the murals when the revolution broke out two years later. For a time he proceeded undisturbed by outside events; by the end of 1848, however, after he had finished the fourth panel, he did not move on to the next but instead chose the political and social conflicts around him as a new theme, and began *Another Dance of Death.*

The documentary evidence for Rethel's politics is rather sparse, but surviving correspondence from the early 1830s indicates that as a young man he attended meetings of liberal clubs, hoped for German unification, and thought that Prussia should have constitutional government. These activities and sentiments were characteristic of bourgeois circles in the Rhineland.[4]

We do not know his ideas then and later on such specifics as the extent of the franchise; but it is certain that his desire for a united Germany was no passing phase. In a letter of April 1849 he continues to hope, as many liberals still did, that Frederick William IV would accept the imperial crown. The Dresden uprising a few weeks later, which he called a "magnificent effort for the glory of Germany," was in the main—the participation of Mikhail Bakunin and some Polish revolutionaries notwithstanding—a late, muddled protest against the refusal of the Saxon king to support unification.[5]

Even after the last insurrections in Saxony, the Rhineland, and Baden had been put down, Rethel remained loyal to the ideal of a new Reich, and expressed his allegiance openly in the arena that mattered most: his work. In the last two murals of the Charlemagne cycle, which he painted between 1849 and 1851, he introduced black-red-gold banners—according to legend the colors of the emperor, but also the colors of German unification that, before 1848, had been prohibited as subversive throughout Germany, and were then chosen by the Frankfurt Parliament to symbolize the new national unity.

What led Rethel to the motif of the dance of death? We do not know, but the idea could easily have arisen once he linked his

4 Rethel to his parents, Oct. 21, 1833: *ibid.*, 20, 23, 24, 26–29.
5 Rethel to Reinick, April 22, 1849: *ibid.*, 116.

interest in sequential images with the fascination that death as an aesthetic theme had long held for him. From 1847 on he experimented with personifications of death in a contemporary setting or in an undated, ahistorical environment.

One subject, suggested by a personal experience, he treated in at least two drawings, which he entitled *Death the Servant*. At a party that Rethel attended, another guest suffered a fatal heart attack. Rethel interpreted this event by drawing Death as a skeleton in servant's livery, pouring wine at a social gathering. A guest whose glass he has just filled has collapsed. Two whippets in the lower right corner of the sketch have the same compositional function as and similar postures to the raven in the second plate of *Another Dance of Death*. The one who turns and looks at Death raising the bottle to serve others is also the double in posture and expression of the horse in the fourth woodcut, craning to watch Death as he holds out the sword of Justice to the crowd.

Another motif, first treated in 1847 in a sketch entitled *The Cholera*, was developed into a woodcut with the alternate titles *Death the Murderer* or *Death as Enemy*. We see a hall, which only seconds earlier had been filled with masked dancers. In the center, surrounded by dead and dying dancers, Death plays on a violin made of two bones. Musicians and guests are rushing out of the hall. On a stone bench sits Cholera herself, wearing a vaguely Egyptian headdress and a flame-covered robe. Heine's account of the cholera epidemic of 1831 in Paris appears to have inspired this print, but the period depicted is left unclear.[6]

Of Rethel's separate graphic works that bring the figure of Death into scenes of everyday life, a third, the woodcut *Death as Friend*, had the greatest popular impact. High in the tower of a vast church, an old bell ringer has died peacefully in his armchair. Death, wearing the shell emblem of a medieval pilgrim on his hat and robe, rings the knell. Through windows and open arches we see the setting sun, Gothic finials, and a gargoyle, which resembles the whippet in *Death as Servant* and the horse in *Another Dance of Death*, and is repeated in simplified form in the back-

6 Heinrich Heine, "Französische Zustände," 6th article (Apr. 19, 1832) in *idem* (ed. Manfred Windfuhr), *Werke* (Hamburg, 1980), XII, pt. 1, 133–134.

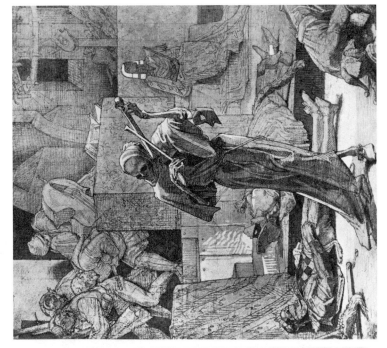

Fig. 8 Alfred Rethel, *The Cholera.*

Fig. 7 Alfred Rethel, *Death the Servant.*

Fig. 9 Alfred Rethel, *Death as Friend.*

ground of the last plate of the cycle. Again the historical era of the scene is not clearly defined.[7]

That Rethel personified Death in his work and placed him in a variety of settings—bell tower, dance, social gathering—must have been influenced by the increasing interest in the motif of the dance of death in Europe at that time. Modern scholarly literature on the subject began in the 1830s and 1840s, and earlier dances of

---

7 *Death as Friend* conveys an idyllic, apolitical aura of the sort often encountered in the woodcuts of Ludwig Richter, Rethel's Dresden contemporary, who incidentally also illustrated verses by Robert Reinick: a burgher's contented dream of rural and small-town Germany—encapsulated in sunshine and spider webs—existing almost unchanged from the Middle Ages to the last halcyon years before 1789. A few decades later, Wilhelm Busch, in the pen-and-ink illustrations to his stories in rhyme, provided an ironic gloss to this vision of timeless middle-class comfort and passivity. In our century, Theodor Heuss, in his edition of Rethel's *Auch ein Totentanz* (Stuttgart, 1957), 12, has likened *Death as Friend* to a folksong; but it would be more accurate to compare the woodcut to an *art*song of the 1830s and 1840s, in which the sophisticated and nervous sensibility of its creator employs an archaic vocabulary to develop a theme of sentimental appeal in unspoken opposition to the modern, industrializing world.

death were being published in more accurate editions, in particular the two great series of woodcuts by Hans Holbein: *The Alphabet of Death* and *Images of Death*. The very title that Rethel gave his work indicates that he wanted it to be understood in relation to its predecessors: like Holbein's woodcuts his were a dance of death, as was the revolution that they depicted.

The motif of the dance of death is documented from the second half of the fourteenth century on, first in the form of processions and dramatic performances, then in murals in churches and cemeteries, and finally in paintings, books, and graphics. The dance generally consisted of a procession or continuous chain of couples, a man and a woman, about to be carried off by Death, who was represented either as a skeleton or as a decaying corpse. Holbein adopted these two ways of depicting Death, but broke up the procession into self-contained images. Some show only Death and his victim; in others, Death singles out one individual from a group; and, in a few plates, several Deaths appear.

Some of the victims react with dignity, others struggle, and others still are taken unaware. Like its medieval models, Holbein's sequence conveys a message of inevitability, and his vigorous realism does not prevent him from echoing the medieval dance's appeal to the viewer to reflect on his approaching end, lead a better life, and die a holy death. Holbein reinforces the message that death levels all by stressing the vanity of human effort and by occasionally striking a note of social criticism: Death takes a nun from a cell that is a place of assignation rather than of piety; an attorney accepts a bribe while Death shows him that his time has run out. In each image the emotional as well as the aesthetic drama derives from the confrontation of men and women with the ultimate reality—death—and at the same time with an impossibility: a skeleton or moldering corpse that moves and acts like a human being but possesses absolute power. This terrifying encounter of the familiar with the unknown is absent only in a few introductory and concluding woodcuts, which provide an explanatory framework for the entire sequence: *The Creation, The Fall, The Eviction from Paradise, The Last Judgment,* and the woodcut entitled *The Bones of All Mankind,* which, in accord with the late-medieval wall paintings, opens the dance. It represents the vision of Ezekiel, but also the medieval celebration of All Souls' Eve when the dead rise from their graves, leave the charnel house, and go out into the world to attack the living.

Rethel's separate graphics on death and Holbein's woodcuts provide a clearer perspective on the character, themes, and political message of Rethel's Dance, and they make it easier to explore its historical significance. It may be well to begin with the element of realism in his cycle. To be sure, the woodcut technique that Rethel employs has an archaic, stylized quality that differs greatly from some contemporary lithographic representations of the revolution, which already approach the non-linear, atmospheric character of photography. Not his style but the content of the cycle is marked by the artist's search for realism, as a comparison with newspaper illustrations of the time reveals. For instance, lithographs of street fighting in Berlin in March 1848 and in Dresden in May 1849 show the same type of barricade that appears in the fifth and sixth woodcut: piled-up paving stones, barrels, and planks. From neighboring houses people are firing in support of the main body of insurgents, and on the barricade itself the attitude, postures, and, in some cases, the clothing of the defenders are similar to those of the men in the fifth plate.

Rethel gives contemporary attributes even to the fantasy element in his images—the personification of Death. In the spring of 1848 a revolutionary style of dress quickly developed. It is illustrated in a well-known portrait of Friedrich Hecker, the leader of the insurrection in Baden, which shows him wearing the broadbrimmed, feathered hat, long coat, and boots that are familiar to us as the uniform of Death in Rethel's woodcuts. Another illustration, this one of an insurgent who has been executed, again includes the familiar hat with the revolutionary badge. The firing squad marching off is the double of the soldiers that appear in the last three woodcuts of *Another Dance of Death*. Rethel's passion for recreating the reality of his time was as pronounced as Holbein's—with one highly significant exception that I note below.[8]

But in some basic respects the two cycles are dissimilar. For one thing, they ascribe different roles to the figure of Death.

8 Another contemporary political reference is worth noting: twice Reinick's verses refer to Death as "*Sensenmann*" man with the scythe. "*Sensenmänner*" was also a common term for rural revolutionaries, for example the Polish insurgents of 1831.

Fig. 11 Friedrich Hecker. Contemporary broadsheet.

Fig. 10 Fighting on the Barricades, Berlin, March 1848. Contemporary newspaper illustration.

Fig. 12 Executed Insurgent. Contemporary lithograph.

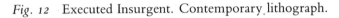

Holbein presents Death as an ever-present, natural force. In some cases the skeleton-surrogate of this force may act as judge, unmasking and punishing hypocrisy and evil; but Death strikes the just and unjust alike. Nothing in Holbein's woodcuts qualifies the basic truth that has always given the motif its fascination: the inevitability and evenhandedness of Death.

Rethel's view is more complex. As we noted earlier, he presents Death as a seducer. The strength of the seduction derives from the identity of the seducer: the seduced victim will die. But for the duration of Rethel's dance, Death is not a universal but a selective force. He and the female personifications of evil that send him on his mission have chosen a specific group of men and women that he must mislead if they are to die. In Rethel's woodcuts the skeleton gains his hold over the viewer because we recognize and accept him as a symbol of the impermanence of our existence; but his universality has been placed in the service of something specific and finite: a social and political message. Death advocates an ideology that is a malevolent force which ultimately destroys its followers. Yet we can defend ourselves against it. The old woman and the boy in the third woodcut, who leave the crowd that Death is seducing, will presumably escape the fate of those he tricks into believing that a clay pipe weighs as much as a crown. In reality it is the artist who performs the sleight of hand: the universal power of Death has become attached to a particular ideology, which is made terrible by it, but which need not be believed. Death is imminent only for those who are seduced into rebellion.

A further basic difference between Holbein and Rethel springs from this interpretation of Death as seducer. Rethel presents him as the leading actor in a tightly constructed narrative, in which he approaches his victims, and tricks and betrays them. In Holbein's dance only the framing images—*The Creation, The Fall,* and so on—lend a slight narrative continuity to the whole: Adam and Eve's sin has the dreadful consequences for the rest of us that will now be detailed. The main body of the cycle consists not of linked but of separate images. Each woodcut is a drama in itself; the impact of the work as a whole comes from the strength of the single theme, which is repeated and varied in dozens of images. The order of the plates is not fixed; even in the earliest editions their arrangement varies.

Rethel's sequence is much shorter and tells a story that depends on each image occupying a fixed place in the sequence. Compositionally, each woodcut is self-contained; but the first three plates derive practically all of their meaning from their function as essential steps in the narrative. The remaining three, continuing and closing the sequence, are equally necessary; but each can be and often has been shown separately, its meaning subsuming the message of the entire dance: Death and his message hold the dance together. Motifs that run through parts of the sequence help strengthen its continuity. We have already noted the purloined sword of Justice and the revolutionary hat. Other links are the presence of animals in five of the six plates, and of women—divided into good and evil forces—in four.

Unlike Holbein, then, Rethel presents his dance in the form of a narrative. But the mechanism by which Rethel turns his revolution into a morality play is borrowed from Holbein and

Holbein's predecessors. Rethel returned to the dance of death in its very early, fourteenth-century form, All Souls' Eve, when the dead rise from their graves to trick, frighten, and punish the living. The first woodcut of his cycle is a new version of this event, which usually opened the medieval dance of death. Rethel combines this old motif with an invention of his own, expressed in the idiom of nineteenth-century symbolism—the defeat of Justice by base emotions—to motivate the political role that he has given his leading actor.

The coming together of the old and the new, of reality and of fantasy, which is so prevalent in Rethel's work, is basic to his dance of death, starting with his decision to introduce a specter into a nineteenth-century town, and to interpret the politics of 1848 by means of a theme borrowed from medieval and Renaissance art. But Rethel also discovered the duality of old and new in his overt subject. He depicts a society in transition. Traditional values—symbolized by such Gothic remnants as the cathedral in the second plate, and the church and the statue of a saint in the last—coexist with the factory chimneys of a new world before the power of which they must bend. The people deceived by the ideology that Death promotes are victims of this transition. It is possible that some of the men in the crowd-scenes work in factories, but we cannot be certain. Everyone who is clearly identified belongs to the older, traditional society of artisans that is being pressured and displaced by the industrial revolution. The baker in the third woodcut; the young silver-miner behind him, identified by the traditional, tall embroidered cap of these aristocrats of early modern labor in central Germany; perhaps also the laughing man in the old-fashioned smock, who may be a waggoner; the blacksmith in the next plate—these are people peculiarly susceptible to revolutionary appeals because they are losing their economic security and their firm place in society to modern capital formation and new methods of manufacture and distribution.

Historians today would agree with Rethel's identification of this group as a driving force of the Revolution of 1848. But he ignores other kinds of participants. It cannot be accidental for an artist of Rethel's passion for detail to draw crowds in which we recognize neither industrial workers nor anyone who appears educated and well-to-do. We see no civil servants, no members of the professions, no students—groups that played a major role in the urban uprisings of 1848 and were again prominent in the fighting in Dresden in May 1849. Rethel's revolutionaries are artisans, journeymen, small shopkeepers—a German variant of the *sans-culottes*.

This narrowing of the social character of the revolutionary crowd is significant in itself; it also explains the apparent inconsistency between the pronounced conservative tone of *Another Dance of Death* and Rethel's liberalism. His woodcuts do not condemn all revolutions, merely populist movements of the lower classes whom a clever agitator can rouse to suicidal attacks on law and order. The slogan "Liberty, Equality, Fraternity" on the wall of the inn and the republican banner of the insurrection never reflected Rethel's politics. He supported the bourgeois revolution that sought a greater or lesser degree of national unification, constitutional government under a hereditary ruler or rulers, and an increase in the participation in public affairs by those who had an economic and cultural stake in the country. The radicalization of this revolution—demagoguery and communism, as he put it in May 1849–he feared. He rejected the extension of political rights to men that he regarded as unqualified, whether they were artisans facing ruin or peasants leaving the land to work in new factories. If Rethel's crowd is made up of *sans-culottes*, their interpreter is a Girondin.

The woodcuts thus express the views of a major segment of liberal and moderate bourgeois opinion in Germany, which wanted to be rid of absolutism and the more extreme forms of particularism, but supported neither republicanism nor the levelling of all class distinctions. Rethel did not intend his dance to be a critical parable of the Revolution of 1848 as such. His cycle should rather be seen as a forceful expression of one of several positions held by those who opposed parts or all of the status quo. It is only in accord with the historical realities of 1848 that the woodcuts are also representative of a more general development that transcends the events that inspired them. When we relate their message to economic and social change in the 1840s and to Rethel's political outlook, we see that the woodcuts are an early document of modern class conflict. Once more Rethel has enlarged the function of the skeleton in his narrative. From a symbol of death the skeleton has been changed into the symbol of an equally pervasive and permanent aspect of human experience: conflict.

From the time of its original publication, when it was adopted as useful legitimist propaganda by the Conservative Alliance of Saxony, the most immediate impact of *Another Dance of Death* has been that of a conservative morality play. But once we delve beneath the surface of its images, we encounter a specific liberal point of view which approves some parts of the Revolution of 1848 and rejects others. Probably this intermediate position of the artist, which from one perspective might appear ambiguous, contributed to the widespread misinterpretation of his work. Aesthetically, the woodcuts constitute a grandiose attempt to combine modern and traditional idiom, which permitted Rethel to comment on events of his day in a tradition that went back to the Renaissance and earlier.

Finally, the woodcuts confirm what we know well but what is always worth recalling: aesthetic statements, whether or not they refer to politics, derive much of their energy from their environment and background. Reactions to the present always have their roots deep in the past, not only in the political and cultural past, but also in the psychological history of the artist. Rethel's inner life remains largely closed to us. But we do know that death powerfully affected his imagination. We also know that in this cycle of woodcuts he took a symbolic image of the end of everything—the skeleton—turned it into a causal force, and applied his private fantasy that destruction is the father of all things to the Revolution of 1848.

This article has concentrated on two major issues: first, those elements in the artist's private life, his cultural and political environment, and in the art of his time that led to the creation of *Another Dance of Death*; second, the potential of the work for documenting events exterior to it. Some aspects of the aesthetic interpretation of the woodcuts may benefit from an enquiry into the work's non-aesthetic antecedents. So far as its character as historical evidence is concerned, the cycle illuminates one of the basic forces of the Revolution of 1848: the attitude of a large segment of the German bourgeoisie, which favored reform but supported only limited social change.

From some Marxist perspectives the middle classes' refusal to go further may seem a betrayal of the revolution, just as such historians of the great French Revolution as Soboul accuse the Committee of Public Safety, caught in the assumptions of pre-industrial society, of having betrayed the common man as he emerged into the light of history in the Paris Commune and the *sans-culotte* sections. But it is ahistorical to claim that the most extreme groups in any revolution invariably represent its true nature. Revolutions are made by factions, which will differ in their view of means and ends. It is also true that their disagreements offer targets for the forces of the status quo and introduce ambiguities into the political conflict.[9]

Interpreting Rethel's woodcuts as a tract against revolution as such is inaccurate. But if we consider the deep currents of conservatism that swept through the German middle classes for a century after the Revolution of 1848, it is not without historical significance that Rethel, the supporter of constitutionalism and unification, should depict the people in arms as victims rather than as heroes, misled agents of their own and society's destruction. The political and social conditions in which *Auch ein Totentanz* was created help to explain the work; but, with the intensity and precision that is unique to art, the woodcuts also illuminate a force that helped shape the history of Germany in 1848 and beyond.

9 See, e.g., Albert Soboul (trans. Remy Inglis Hall), *The Sans-Culottes: The Popular Movement and Revolutionary Government, 1793–1794* (Princeton, 1980).

Elizabeth Johns

The Farmer in the Works of William Sidney

Mount   In the 1830s in New York, the painter William Sidney
Mount, who was born and spent his career on Long Island, earned
a distinctive place among the emerging American genre painters,
artists who depicted scenes of everyday life. He was the first artist
to paint farmers as his subjects, a matter of considerable interest
to his audience, and he was recognized as technically superior to
his contemporaries. His career spanned the years 1830 to 1868,
an era when nationalist writers, critics, and artists worked to forge
a new art based on American themes, and his paintings were
judged by critics, patrons, and fellow artists to be of major importance in this enterprise.

   His audience was extraordinarily large and diverse. He exhibited his paintings annually at the National Academy of Design
in New York City, where they inspired generous critical comment. Critics, eager to boost the dignity of American art, wrote
of him as our "American Teniers," "American Ostade," and
"American Wilkie." In this enthusiastic climate of reception, New
York City's richest citizens—Charles M. Leupp, Charles A.
Davis, Jonathan Sturges, and Luman Reed, all of whom were
avid patrons of the arts and of such other cultural institutions as
the New-York Historical Society—sought his works. Engravers,
too, gave Mount patronage, increasing his audience by thousands
in their distribution of prints based on his paintings, both in single
form and bound in gift books. Indeed, one of Mount's images of
a farmer was engraved on bank notes that circulated from 1838
to 1860 in states from Georgia to Michigan.[1]

   Why were Mount's images so popular? What in American
life in the 1830s and 1840s did they draw upon and transform into
art?[2]

Elizabeth Johns is Associate Professor of American Studies at the University of Maryland,
College Park, and is a Fellow of the Woodrow Wilson International Center for Scholars.
She is the author of *Thomas Eakins: The Heroism of Modern Life* (Princeton, 1983).

1 John A. Muscalus, *Popularity of Wm. S. Mount's Art Work on Paper Money, 1838–1865*
(Bridgeport, Pa., 1965).
2 Questions of historical context have thus far been raised only superficially in the study

My analysis draws upon clues about the historical importance of Mount's work provided by the commentary of his critics— men of the self-conscious generation of writers for journals and newspapers eager to support a nationalist art. It will be a later task (to be developed in a book-length study) to look in detail at Mount's patronage, and to study the relationship of his themes to those of writers, printmakers, and other painters. But the critics provide an excellent starting point. Their assessments of Mount's cultural achievement fall into three categories. First, they praised the artist's choice of rural subjects. Second, they delighted that he rendered the "true American character" or the "essential American type," a character that they defined as "comic." And third, they invoked as essential to his paintings the Long Island location of his scenes. These are the contexts in which I investigate the meanings of Mount's works for his audience.[3]

First, however, I examine in detail the four paintings that illustrate my discussion, images that were and remain Mount's best-known works. They were painted in the clear, linear style typical of Mount (influenced by his early apprenticeship to a sign painter), a style that conveys expression, gestures, costume, and setting with directness and simplicity—and with a crispness that contributes a subtle humor to the images.

of American genre painting. The standard surveys are Hermann W. Williams, Jr., *Mirror to the American Past; A Survey of American Genre Painting: 1750–1900* (Greenwich, Conn., 1973); Patricia Hills, *The Painters' America: Rural and Urban Life, 1810–1910* (New York, 1974). On Mount specifically, the most recent book-length work is the compilation of archival documents by Alfred Frankenstein, *William Sidney Mount* (New York, 1975). A complete bibliography of earlier studies on Mount is David Cassedy and Gail Shrott, *William Sidney Mount: Annotated Bibliography and Listings of Archival Holdings of The Museums at Stony Brook* (Stony Brook, 1983). The Museums at Stony Brook, which hold the largest concentration of Mount paintings, drawings, and archival materials, have begun a cultural interpretation of Mount with *idem, William Sidney Mount: Works in the Collection* (Stony Brook, 1983) and Martha V. Pike et al., *Catching the Tune: Music and William Sidney Mount* (Stony Brook, 1984). However, the only fully developed study of the relationship of Mount's work to contemporary events is that of Joseph B. Hudson, Jr., "Banks, Politics, Hard Cider, and Paint: The Political Origins of William Sidney Mount's Cider Making," *The Metropolitan Museum of Art Journal*, X (1975), 107–118.

3 Criticism of Mount's work appeared in such journals as *The New York Weekly Mirror*, *The American Monthly Magazine*, *The Knickerbocker*, and *The Literary World*, as well as in such New York newspapers as the *Evening Post* and the Long Island newspaper, *The Long Islander*. Mount kept many of his reviews (unfortunately, few of them either dated or sourced) in a scrapbook now referred to as the Setauket Scrapbook, Emma S. Clark Memorial Public Library, Setauket, New York, a photostatic copy of which is at The Museums at Stony Brook.

The first of the four paintings, *Long Island Farmer Husking Corn* (1833/34), depicts a well-dressed farmer standing in a cornfield husking corn from the stalk (Figure 1). Behind him, in the right foreground of the painting, is a large basket nearly filled with healthy-looking ears of Indian corn. The golden yellow-brown of the corn stalks, the bright yellow kernels of the corn, the warm brown earth, the rich dark brown of the farmer's suit, and the saturation of the sky with the light of a warm sun contribute to a sense of the fruitfulness of the earth. Proud in his bearing, the farmer is the picture of well-being—clean, rosy-cheeked, sturdy. Although the figure of the farmer posed against his abundant field of corn would seem to suggest that he is an emblem of agricultural virtue, he is by no means a heroic figure. Underneath the jauntily turned brim of his hat we see a smiling profile with prominent, sharp nose and chin that suggest at once both amiability and sharpness. The face would seem to be a comic type, in its varied qualities an inventory of character. This man is Mount's equal—neither a peasant to be pitied (like the rural figures painted in France a few years later) nor an intimidating gentleman-farmer, but instead a fellow-citizen.

Long Island Farmer Husking Corn aroused a large, favorable response, first among the critics, and then among a wider audience. Shortly after its exhibition, Dunlap, a historian, gave it a high rating in his *History of the Arts of Design,* published the same year. Judging that the image would be meaningful to a large audience, the editor of the giftbook *Wintergreen* had it engraved for the annual in 1844. Finally, about 1838, it began to appear in bank notes, in which guise it was often placed side by side with a traditional female allegorical image of agriculture and/or an image of George Washington.[4]

In the painting *Farmer Whetting His Scythe* of 1848, Mount placed the farmer in the midst of a swath of grass that has just been cut for hay (Figure 2). The grass seems to be a mixture of clover and timothy. In this scene, in contrast to the *Long Island Farmer Husking Corn,* Mount posed the farmer against a landscape that catalogues much of a northern Long Island scene. One can see farmhouses and meadows sweeping down in the rear distance

---

4 William Dunlap, *History of the Rise and Progress of the Arts of Design in the United States* (New York, 1969: orig. pub. 1834), II, 451–452.

Fig. 1 William Sidney Mount, *Long Island Farmer Husking Corn*, 1833–1834.

SOURCE: The Museums at Stony Brook, gift of Mr. and Mrs. Ward Melville; reproduced with permission of The Museums.

Fig. 2 William Sidney Mount, *Farmer Whetting his Scythe,* 1848.

SOURCE: The Museums at Stony Brook, gift of Mr. and Mrs. Ward Melville; reproduced with permission of The Museums.

to Long Island Sound, two schooners in the Sound, and, on the horizon, the New England coast line. The long shadows suggest that it is late in the afternoon; and indeed, the farmer's jacket, a dark brownish-green with bright red lining, is dropped on the ground in the right foreground, where he perhaps laid it in the heat of the day. There it is wrapped around a bottle, no doubt to keep the bottle's contents cool. The picture, like *Long Island Farmer Husking Corn*, is happy in every respect. Reds dot the farmer's clothing, his jacket, a shirt that he wears under his white shirt, and the pulls to his black boots. The farmer's face is shadowed by the brim of his felt hat, but his cheeks have high coloring; his hands are unwrinkled and undirtied. Appearing to be in his mid-twenties, he looks smiling, innocent, and confident—a man as happy and as clean sharpening a heavy scythe at the end of a hot working day as he would be sitting in front of a fireplace on a Sunday. As in *Long Island Farmer Husking Corn*, we have a scene of agricultural abundance presided over by a figure who seems hardly to have had to work for it, and at the same time we have a celebration of that work.

The third painting is one of Mount's best known. *Farmers Nooning*, 1836, shows four farmers and a young "farmer boy" taking their noonday break in a field that has just been cut for hay (Figure 3). On a hay cock in the sunshine, a black (called a "Negro farmer" by one critic, a "negro" and "black fellow" by others) abandons himself to sleep, oblivious to the impudent tickling of a straw placed in his ear by a young boy of about ten. In the foreground, a shady area under an apple tree, three white farmers relax in significantly different positions. The one on the right stretches out on the ground on his stomach; the other two sit. Although we cannot make out the activity of the farmer in the middle, because he has his back to us, the figure on the left is busily preparing the strickle with which he will sharpen his scythe, which is hanging conspicuously from the tree over his head. In the left foreground is a lunch bucket, and in the center are a hat and jacket. Three of the figures are rich in expression: the black, relaxing in the sun on the haystack with a wonderful expression of pleasure on his face and ease in his body; the young boy, preoccupied in his mischief, with a tickled glint on his face; and the man to the left, bent over his task with the seriousness of one devoted to the work ethic, apparently oblivious to the

Fig. 3 William Sidney Mount, *Farmers Nooning*, 1836.

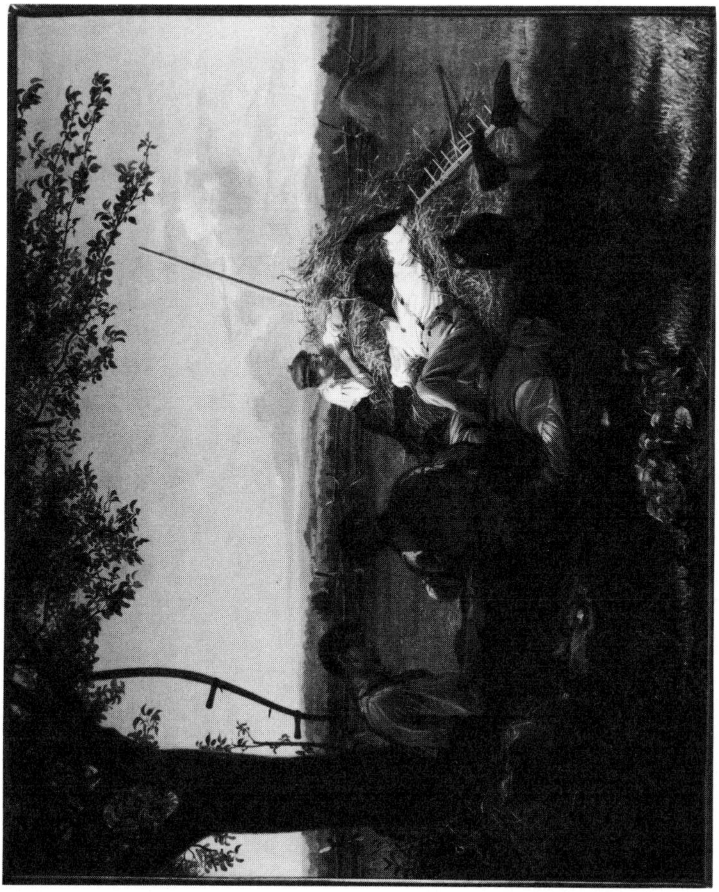

SOURCE: The Museums at Stony Brook, gift of Mr. Frederick Sturges, Jr.; reproduced with permission of The Museums.

pleasures of either the sun or the cool grass. In the relationships between these figures, at least two opposing motifs are suggested: that between childhood and adulthood (with the black occupying a middle role) and that between discipline and laziness. This second motif is additionally enforced by the shoddy condition of the apparel of the white man who is resting, as opposed to the neat, well-cared for clothing of the man preparing his strickle.

This painting had as diverse an audience as any that ever left Mount's easel: it was bought by Sturges, a wealthy patron; the Apollo Association had it engraved in 1843 for distribution to its middle-class membership scattered all over the nation; and another engraving was featured in the July 1845 issue of *Godey's Lady's Book,* a periodical devoted to female and home readership.

Finally, a fourth painting by Mount shows the farmer's character in another light. Originally called *Farmers Bargaining for a Horse* (1835), this picture shows two farmers in the midst of a bargaining session for a handsome horse that stands nearby (Figure 4). One farmer is white-haired and the other about thirty, but both indulge in whittling a stick to orchestrate their verbal maneuvering, a custom that had come affectionately to be seen as an American characteristic. The younger man, whom we see in three-quarter profile, looks up as though to check on the progress—and thus the mind-set—of his antagonist. He wears a battered top hat; perhaps it is he who is the visitor to this farm. The late-afternoon shadows are long and soft. In the left distance, hidden from the farmers themselves, a woman raises her hand at a fence, as though to call. Critics speculated that she was the wife of the old farmer, about to interrupt the negotiations with the call that dinner was ready. In this painting as in the others, the colors are bright, the technique clean, linear, and remarkably smooth. The details are at a minimum: it is the characters and the situation that speak. And, we ask, is the situation admirable, silly, or, in the vernacular understanding, characteristic? Certainly for the old farmer to have his conclusion to a bargain dictated by his wife's call to dinner is marvelously comic. This painting, like *Long Island Farmer Husking Corn* and *Farmers Nooning,* became extraordinarily well known. It was bought by Reed, a wealthy and distinguished patron of American art, and was subsequently engraved twice, first for the annual *The Gift* in 1840, and then for the American Art-Union in 1851 for distribution to its national membership.

Fig. 4 William Sidney Mount, *Bargaining for a Horse (Farmers Bargaining)*, 1835.

SOURCE: Reproduced with permission of the New-York Historical Society, New York City.

In these scenes, as in his other paintings, Mount distanced his figures with idealizing and simplifying effects. The farmers are not dirty, their clothes are neither soiled nor wrinkled (although there are instances in which they are frayed), their cheeks are pink and their skin without blemish. As though they are playing roles or illustrating stock situations, they lack psychological complexity, radiating instead good cheer and even amusement.

In terms of Mount's critical appraisals, what were the major currents in American farming during the 1830s and 1840s that illuminate Mount's treatment of farmers—and his audience's delight in it?

Although New York in 1830 had just begun an explosive growth pattern, America was still a rural society. In 1830, 90 percent of the American population lived in rural areas, with 75 percent of the people engaged in agricultural pursuits. Most farms were small (although there were spectacular exceptions, mostly in the South and in the area of New York state settled by the Dutch); a homestead averaged about one fourth of a section, a good portion of which a single farmer could cultivate by himself with the help of a hired hand at harvest time. Typically, the farmer owned his land, although tenancy in his young manhood, during which the farmer saved to buy his own land, was not unusual. The farmer saw himself as self-sufficient, which he largely was. By raising such crops as corn, wheat, barley, and oats, and by keeping cows, hogs, poultry, and perhaps sheep, the farmer met most of the needs of his family and could obtain the rest in his community. Humble as might have been the actual life of the farmer, in the agrarian ideology of American society during these years he was a figure of near-heroic significance.[5]

Thomas Jefferson, anxious to differentiate the developing American nation from her European counterparts, had first pro-

5 Hedrick, *A History of Agriculture in the State of New York* (New York, 1933); Paul W. Gates, *The Farmer's Age: Agriculture 1815–1860* (New York, 1960); Clarence H. Danhof, *Change in Agriculture: The Northern United States, 1820–1870* (Cambridge, Mass., 1969); Darwin P. Kelsey (ed.), *Farming in the New Nation: Interpreting American Agriculture 1790–1840* (Washington, D.C., 1972). For agrarianism, see Richard Hofstadter, *The Age of Reform* (New York, 1955); Louis H. Douglas (ed.), *Agrarianism in American History* (Lexington, Mass., 1969).

posed the ideals of agrarianism in his *Notes on the State of Virginia* (London, 1787). Agriculture, he wrote, was the economic base of the new nation, and the farmer, a freeholder working his own land, was its civic unit. In America the yeoman was the foundation of political life, Jefferson argued, whereas in Europe that position was occupied by the peasant, who had no political rights to exercise. To the ownership of land and the practice of agriculture Jefferson attributed all the virtues of the model citizen in a democratic society: political and economic independence, morality, stability, health, and the capacity for hard work.

Over the next half century Jefferson's ideals were touted by writers, politicians, and farmers themselves. Hector St. John de Crèvecoeur, an immigrant, answered Jefferson's famous question "What, then is the American, this new man?" by identifying him as having been from the very first settlement a farmer, whose governance of his crop according to the laws of nature made him the ideal citizen in a democratic government. Political parties based their rhetoric on the agrarian ideal, even after voters had begun to assume urban patterns of behavior. George Washington, at the conclusion of the Revolution, had conspicuously assumed the role of the Roman farmer Cincinnatus and returned to his farm. Andrew Jackson, in 1824 and 1828, in opposition to the party of John Quincy Adams that he alleged had been founded on financial rather than agrarian interests, conducted his campaign as a "man of the soil," stressing that his moral character had been formed through farming. William Henry Harrison's successful campaign against the Democrats in 1840 was formulated on precisely the same claim.[6]

Throughout the nineteenth century, governmental leaders formulated land settlement policies in the West on the assumptions that the pioneer was first and foremost a farmer and that the basic civic unit was the family farm. The agricultural press, which grew dramatically during the years 1830 to 1860, even praised the benefits of the agricultural life to personal health, printing statistical tables that showed that farmers lived longer than any other occupational group. As the rhetoric swelled in intensity, patriotic essays, political campaigns, and speeches at agricultural fairs con-

6 John William Ward, *Andrew Jackson: Symbol for an Age* (New York, 1955), 24–25, passim on Jackson, 95–96 on Harrison.

cluded with the universal tribute that the farmer was the "free son of a free soil."[7]

Yet, as any of Mount's city patrons—and certainly his sitters—would have known, farming was not necessarily idyllic, financially secure, or intellectually rewarding. Much as the yeoman might have treasured his independence, the labor on a one-man farm was exhausting, demanding work days of up to fourteen hours. Able to depend on little remuneration beyond subsistence during even the best years, the small farmer was the victim of violent storms or droughts that in some years wiped out his basic subsistence. His life was remote from the entertainments of the city, and worse, from political and social news. For many farmers the agrarian ideal was a cruel myth; discouraged, or bankrupt, or both, they migrated to cities in increasing numbers. Of farmers who stayed on their farms, a major lament was that they were losing their sons to the regular hours, less back-breaking labor, and social diversions of the city.

Moreover, as the national press discussed in endless detail in the 1830s, the character of farming itself was changing so rapidly that no one assessment could accurately reflect its basic conditions. For one thing, there was the problem of soil exhaustion. Eastern farmers had so severely depleted their soil with continuous planting that crop yields were only a fraction of what they had been. Although an increasing number of farmers had adopted the scientific techniques that Jefferson and others had imported from England in the late eighteenth century—techniques which replenished the soil with crop rotation, fertilizing (sometimes directly, by foraging livestock), and the introduction of grasses—a substantial core of farmers continued to work in the old ways. It was a matter of disdain to city experts, and of outrage to agricultural leaders, that farmers could be so hopelessly old-fashioned and stubborn.

As Mount's businessman-patrons knew firsthand, in addition to demanding new agricultural techniques, farming in the 1830s began to assume a new role in the economy, shifting from a self-sufficient to a commercial enterprise. Many eastern farmers who

7 Albert L. Demaree, *The American Agricultural Press 1819–1860* (Philadelphia, 1974; orig. pub. 1941); Richard H. Abbott, "The Agricultural Press Views the Yeoman: 1819–1859," *Agricultural History*, XLII (1968), 39, 42; *Transactions of the New York State Agricultural Society*, VII (1847), 138.

had exhausted their soil moved to just-opened lands in Michigan and Wisconsin, where fertile soil and a new system of canals and railroads enabled them to transport crops cheaply and quickly to eastern cities. Such farmers became businessmen, specializing in crops for the market. Even in the East, the typical farmer, who had earlier been almost autonomous, became part of a regional, even national market system, his livelihood subject to such impersonal forces as transportation complexes and price competition. The independent, self-sufficient yeoman became increasingly a memory.

Mount's images of farmers entered public life at a time when farming was in the very heat of change in its ideological associations, in its actual practice, and in its function in the economy. What is the relationship between this varied character and the content of Mount's paintings?

The painting *Long Island Farmer Husking Corn* is virtually a paean to agrarianism. The farmer is a single figure, presumably a yeoman reaping the fruits of his own hard work. In the nature of his crop, he is very much an American farmer, the origin of corn in the New World being a matter of national pride. In addition, Mount's audience may well have associated corn with all American settlements; because corn did not demand a completely cleared field, required as implement only the simple hoe, and provided food for both humans and animals, farmers inevitably grew corn first—in Plymouth and Virginia, slightly later on Long Island, and on the frontier as the nation moved west. Moreover, corn was a crop that the farmer could manage independently, harvesting it over a period of weeks, unlike other crops that demanded harvest within just a few days. Corn, therefore, was the clearest symbol not only of the anchoring of the agrarian ideal in the times of pioneer settlement, but also of the continuing ideal—whether matched by reality or not—of a farmer's self-sufficiency.[8]

Mount's image is not necessarily conservative, however. Beyond corn's implications as a fundamental New World crop, it also signaled new developments in scientific agriculture. Long before Mount began painting farmers, settled farms in the New York area—including many on Long Island—had turned to wheat

8 Hedrick, *Agriculture in New York,* 335; Danhof, *Change in Agriculture,* 204.

production because it was so much more remunerative. Wheat, however, drained the soil of nutrients, and in the effort to rejuvenate the land New York—and Long Island—farmers in the 1830s adopted a method of crop rotation known generally as the Chester method (from its origins in Pennsylvania). This method called for the rotation of wheat with corn, oats, and grasses. That Mount's farmer was growing corn potentially placed him in the most recent scientific tradition.[9]

Another element of the painting suggests two additional interpretations: Mount's farmer is husking the corn directly from the stalks, instead of carrying out the more complicated procedure, recently adopted in the 1830s, of cutting the stalks near the ground, stacking them in shocks, removing the ears of corn, and, finally, husking them at leisure. He may be interpreted as an old-fashioned farmer who husks his corn directly and alone; or as a new scientific farmer who lets his livestock forage in the harvested corn field (and thus fertilize it) or plows the stalks under for a richer soil. Either reading of the activity in these paintings is highly complimentary to the farmer.[10]

Both *Farmer Whetting His Scythe* and *Farmers Nooning* also convey agrarian values. The single farmer whetting his scythe is presumably a yeoman, his industry and prudence nicely conveyed by the care with which he prepares his agricultural tool. *Farmers Nooning,* too, celebrates the farmer who is always prepared; moreover, with its evocation of a warm rural noon, it sets forth the simple pleasures of the rural life. With these scenes, Mount may also have celebrated recent developments in agriculture. The farmer shown sharpening his scythe is standing in a field of the new scientific grass crop, a combination of red clover and timothy grass. Rotated with wheat, this grass restored humus and nitrogen to the soil. And the group in *Farmers Nooning* have taken a break from cutting a field of grass for hay. By the time of Mount's career, a large amount of hay was grown by Long Islanders, not only to restore their soil, but to meet the growing New York market for fodder for drayage animals. In both paintings, the messages of hard work and prudence are clearly set forth—not only with the crop grown on the land, but also with the activity

9   Gates, *Farmer's Age,* 169; Danhof, *Change in Agriculture,* 272.
10 Kelsey, *Farming,* 185.

of the farmers. The admirable care with which the farmers have nourished their soil, and the readiness with which they have adapted to new market conditions, are reinforced by the associations of keeping the scythe sharp, so that it too works well.[11]

Indeed, in their health, in their work, and in the fruitfulness of their farms, Mount's farmers are the very embodiment of the ideal yeoman described by Jefferson, other political leaders, and the agricultural press. Yet in Mount's images the farmers do not plow or use any new agricultural implements, they do not take care of animals, and they do not hurry to outpace a coming storm; their industry is more potential than actual. In the activity and personal expression in Mount's characters, and in the lighting and coloring effects of his painting technique, nothing conveys even a hint of sweat, disappointment, or hardship—the darker aspects of being a farmer. That both Mount and his large audience knew the many realities of farming, however, suggests that these pleasant images had a function quite distinct from that of peasants in the field painted at the same time on the other side of the Atlantic.[12]

That function derives from the close relationship that Mount's audience perceived in the images' rural character and what critics described as their comic, national character. On the one hand, Americans celebrated farming as the ideal democratic pursuit; on the other, they denigrated farmers themselves as rustic—even comic. What led Mount rather than anyone else to paint such an ambiguous image at this time? Part of the answer lies in the fact that the varied implications of the farmer for American national identity had begun to be explored in the "Yankee" theater, in which Mount was very interested. Referring to Mount's farmers again and again as "Jonathans" and "Yankees," critics linked his paintings with this developing comic tradition.

The central character of "Yankee" theater was Jonathan, the American farmer. First sketched out in 1787 by Royall Tyler in his play *The Contract,* and then developed in increasing detail by playwrights and actors from the 1820s to the 1840s, the Jonathan character evolved during a time when the American stage, belles

---

11 Danhof, *Change in Agriculture,* 269; Hedrick, *Agriculture in New York,* 344.
12 See John Thompson et al., *The Peasant in French Nineteenth-Century Art* (Dublin, 1980).

lettres, and the periodical press were dominated by British material. Early cultural nationalists, like Samuel Woodworth, the editor of the *New York Literary Mirror,* an ambitious cultural journal, Ralph Waldo Emerson, Nathaniel Parker Willis, and a host of others—including the critics who wrote about Mount's paintings—called for an American drama, literature, and art that would celebrate specifically national characteristics. On the stage, it was comedy that first served this purpose, a cultural expression aimed at, and thus drawing upon the values and tensions of, the largest possible audience. A succession of talented actors developed the "Yankee" character—a rural fellow with characteristics that differentiated Americans from the British.[13]

Mount had close connections to this theater. During its formative years, which were also the formative years of his career, Mount was a resident of New York, and throughout the rest of his life he lived on Long Island only a short distance from the city. Mount's uncle in New York, Micah Hawkins, although by trade a grocer and inn-keeper, was by avocation a musician and writer and an avid contributer to the emerging tradition in Yankee theater. In November 1824, during Mount's residence with him, Hawkins' *The Saw Mill: or a Yankee Trick,* the first comic opera in America, opened at the Chatham Theatre. One can imagine Mount being caught up in the excitement of its production and reception. His brother, Henry Smith Mount, a sign painter to whom Mount was at that time apprenticed, wrote to their brother, Robert Nelson, who was teaching in Georgia, that the music and songs were "very beautiful." With light music and comic dialogue, the action of Hawkins' play unfolded the successful scheme of two American characters pretending to be "Yankees" as they outwitted a stupid aristocrat. From the time of this early theatrical association, Mount took up his uncle's enthusiasm for the theater and became a theatergoer for the rest of his life. He made sketches of theatrical characters and costumes, commented in his journals and notebooks about performances, and

13   On the Yankee theater, see Arthur Hobson Quinn, *A History of the American Drama from the Beginning to the Civil War* (New York, 1943), 292–303; Francis Hodge, *Yankee Theatre: The Image of America on the Stage, 1825–1850* (Austin, Texas, 1964). The Jonathan figure eventually became Uncle Sam.

longed even late in life, after he became too ill to travel, to return to New York to see the theater.[14]

The pervasive agrarian idealism of American public discourse had a strong influence on the character of Jonathan, the archetypal stage Yankee. A farmer, Jonathan was a model agrarian: he owned his own land, worked hard, and had pure manners. But he was also simple on occasion, to the point of seeming doltish, and at these times his behavior was hilariously comic. Yet underneath this facade, Jonathan was shrewd, and he usually obtained precisely what he wanted. The Jonathan character was thus a fascinating composite: coupled to his agrarian virtues were the city audience's disdain for the farmer's remoteness and their half-admiration half-contempt for his reputation as a sharp bargainer (a characterization that probably stemmed from the association of the Yankee farmer with the New England peddler). And it was in this rich combination of virtue and slyness that Jonathan triumphed on stage over the representative of the Old World. That representative was a British aristocrat: a city-dweller (predictably from London), a dandy, and a smooth talker. The plots of the plays crackled on the oppositions of their characters: country/city, simple/pseudo-sophisticated, healthy/decadent, and free-holding democrat/parasitic aristocrat.

The most popular, and certainly the most long-lived, play of the Yankee theater was the "pastoral opera" by Samuel Woodworth called *Forest Rose: Or American Farmers,* which opened at New York City's Chatham Theatre on October 6, 1825, and played on the American stage for more than forty years. Both a panegyric to American rural character and life and an amused criticism of it, *The Forest Rose* extols farming with the same lightheartedness that we find in Mount's paintings. The play opens in the idyllic setting of the country, as the characters sing: "Here, in scenes of sweet seclusion, Far from bustling towns we dwell, While around, in rich profusion, Autumn's yellow bounties swell . . . What are city joys to these?" (Act I: 1). An endorsement of rural morality comes from the miller, who tells his daughter Harriet, a wholesome rustic girl: "The girl who

14   For an exposition of this material, and reproductions of Mount's drawings, see Peter G. Buckley, "The Place to Make an Artist Work: Micah Hawkins and William Sidney Mount in New York City," in Pike et al., *Catching the Tune,* 22–39.

would reject the honest heart and hand of an American farmer, for a fopling of any country is not worthy of affection or confidence" (I:1). Farmer William, who eventually wins Harriet, delights wholeheartedly in his role as an independent and as a provider: "Blest with plenty, here the farmer Toils for those he loves alone; While some pretty smiling charmer, Like the land, is all his own" (I, Finale). As foils to the miller and William, the male characters of Blandford and Bellamy provide the anti-aristocratic bias of the play; the American Blandford cannot marry William's sister Lydia because of the class consciousness of Blandford, Sr., and Bellamy is a "fop" from London, a dandy without good sense.[15]

Jonathan Ploughboy, the Yankee character, takes a vigorous place in the play between the pure rural virtue of William and the decadent stupidity of Bellamy. Jonathan is both stupid and shrewd. He speaks slowly, confuses the identity of the female characters, and makes an outrageously funny interpretation of lovers' initials that he finds on a locket, reading CB and LR as "Cows, Bulls, Lambs, and Rams." As a farmer he is honestly in love with the earth; but he is also a merchant, and on that account he is crafty and eager to make a bargain. He is in love with Sally, but she has no property; thus he sings to Harriet: "I love the ground you walk on, for 'tis your father's farm, Could that be mine without you, I'd be a happy man" (I:4). Silly as he is, however, Jonathan takes charge in righting the wrongs of the play and in so doing demonstrates both his shrewdness and his good heart.

The action ends happily, with William winning Harriet, Blandford getting a second chance at Lydia because his socially prejudiced father dies, and Jonathan united with Sally. Harriet, who has previously been discontented with farm life and longed for the entertainments of the city, learns her lesson. The songs that conclude the play celebrate farmers as "Lords of the soil," the farm as the locus of contentment, and the farmer's labor as the foundation of the economic health of the nation. Yet the lyrics place all these virtues in the context of a city society unappreciative of every aspect of farm life except the material: "Ye fair, who

15   This play is reprinted in Richard Moody, *Drama from the American Theatre, 1762–1909* (New York, 1966).

seek a splendid lot, Behold content, a richer prize, Within the humblest ploughman's cot, That rank and pride despise. And palace or cot, whatever your lot, The farmer your table supplies, my dear, The farmer your table supplies."

The tradition of the Yankee theater, with its combination of the serious and the silly, the ideological and the satiric, was integral to Mount in the creation of his works and integral to his audience in their assessment of them. Like the opening of *Forest Rose,* Mount's settings are rural idylls, with golden grain and pink-toned blue skies. The very techniques with which he rendered his figures—clean, linear, brightly colored—create characters that, like those of the Yankee theater, are happy and simple. His farmers stand still for our appraisal; as in *Long Island Farmer Husking Corn,* they are not so much "doing" as "being," for they are of interest as a character type. When there is slight action, as in *Farmer Whetting His Scythe* and *Farmers Nooning,* it illustrates stock rural virtues with the simple oppositions of the comic theatre, just as the painting *Farmers Nooning* places the rural work ethic of the farmer on the left in opposition to the stock laziness of the black and of the white on the right. And the painting *Farmers Bargaining for a Horse* illustrates the convention so popular on the Yankee stage that the Yankee farmer whittled all the time; laconic, especially in making a bargain, his plans could be "spied out" only by the speed with which he was coming to a point in his whittling. And last, the farmer's wife in the left background of that painting, presumably about to interrupt the proceedings, comically undercuts the dignity of the protagonists.

The treatments of the farmer in both the Yankee theater and the paintings of Mount convey the tensions in American agrarian idealism. These tensions were heightened poignantly by the rapid growth of cities and consequent fading away of the old farming life. New York audiences for Mount's work were particularly regretful of these changes and made explicit their delight in Mount's Long Island subject matter. Although the Yankee or Jonathan character in the theater was that of the New England farmer, Mount's paintings focused on Long Island farmers, and critics praised the perfectly American typicality—the perfect "Yankeeism"—of these Long Islanders.

What in the character of Long Island encouraged commen-
tators to identify it as paradigmatic of America and Long Island
rustics as the American national type?

In theory, Long Island was a perfect relic of the past. Whereas
in 1830 Manhattan seemed to its inhabitants to be burgeoning, its
development having reached all the way up to 4th street, Long
Island, just across the East River, was almost exclusively rural.
Brooklyn, by that time a modest suburb, was only a short ferry-
ride away, but the eastern parts of Long Island were virtually
remote. Setauket was a six-hour steamboat ride from Manhattan
or a five-hour ferry and coach ride. Nearly all of the eastern Island
population pursued agriculture or fishing, and there were many
areas of the Island that were still wilderness. And yet Long Island
was stunningly close to the nation's financial, commercial, and
industrial center. A symbol of the fact that in 1830 New York
state was both the largest agricultural producer and the financial
and industrial center of the nation, Long Island's proximity to
New York City created a kind of time warp.[16]

Not only in its rural nature, but in its political, economic,
and religious history, Long Island came to be seen during Mount's
career as a microcosm of the nation's past. The first histories of
Long Island were written during this time; historian Benjamin F.
Thompson, of Long Island, was Mount's patron and avid supporter; historian Nathaniel Prime, of New York City, was an
intellectual and cultural leader and a strong supporter of the arts.
Both Thompson and Prime, recounting the settlement of the
island by the Dutch and the English (the Dutch on the western
end and the English on the eastern end), emphasized the early
leadership that Long Island had given to the province of New
York. Noting that on Long Island Americans had pursued the

16 For accounts of Long Island, see Benjamin F. Thompson, *History of Long Island* (New
York, 1839; rev. ed. 1843); Nathaniel S. Prime, *A History of Long Island* (New York,
1845); Richard Bayles, *Historical and Descriptive Sketches of Suffolk County* (New York,
1873); Ralph H. Gabriel, *The Evolution of Long Island* (Port Washington, N.Y. 1960; orig.
pub. 1921); Marilyn E. Weigold, *The American Mediterranean: An Environmental, Economic
and Social History of Long Island Sound* (Port Washington, N.Y., 1974); James E. Bunce
and Richard P. Harmond, *Long Island as America: A Documentary History to 1893* (Port
Washington, 1977); Joan D. Berbrich, *Three Voices from Pasumanok: The Influence of Long
Island on James Fenimore Cooper, William Cullen Bryant, and Walt Whitman* (Port Washington,
1969).

two major occupations of the early Colonial settlers, farming and fishing, they identified as important in the development of the Island virtually every aspect of public life that Americans connected with the strengths of the country: the traditions of free-holdership (with small farms rather than the large patroon holdings along the Hudson River), of strong self-government, of freedom of worship and resistance to persecution, and of early common education.

Prime drew particular attention to Suffolk County, the eastern part of Long Island, from which Mount drew his subjects. The settlers there, he hymned, "had no royal charter or proprietary patent as the foundation of civil government. Having purchased their lands of the original proprietors of the soil [the Indians], and secured a corresponding grant from the patentee, without any restrictions to their civil rights, they found themselves absolutely in a state of nature, possessing all the personal rights and privileges which the God of nature gave them. . . . they founded a pure democracy." Praising eastern Long Island as the first part of the state to be "occupied by actual immigrants for the purpose of a permanent settlement and agricultural pursuits," Prime observed that "In no part of this republican country is there so great an equality, and such a strong sympathy and perfect fellow-feeling, among the whole mass of population, as in Suffolk County, especially in the eastern towns." And yet, even more than their republicanism, Prime admired the country folk for their piety: "[The] chief glory of old Suffolk . . . [is the] primitive puritanism" of her people. As his climactic illustration of the morality of these Long Islanders, Prime gave the information that "till of late years, not a single lawyer would live by the exclusive exercise of his profession, within Suffolk County. . . . this arose, not from any prejudices against the profession, but from the peaceable disposition of the inhabitants, that entirely superseded, except in a few rare instances, the necessity of their learned assistance."[17]

17 Prime, *History of Long Island*, 77, 78, 75, 79, 84. Thompson, too, emphasized the integrity of the early settlers in buying their land from the Indians: "Motives of honor, justice, and humanity, as well as true policy, dictated the propriety of such a course by strangers coming to settle in a country already occupied by a people, the undisputed tenants of the soil," *idem, History* (1839), 65–66.

Suffolk County, in short, was the microcosm par excellence of the best of American character; it had been and still was the very realization of the agrarian ideal.

In terms of the agriculture practiced on Long Island, farmers had reason to be proud. The Island had been the first area in the state to grow wheat and subsequently the first to turn substantially to the production of hay. Long Island farmers had an admirable record in employing scientific techniques to replenish their soil, especially in the use of fish for fertilizer.

But Long Islanders, alas, suffered from the same disdain for their rural life that farmers across the country experienced and that was so vital a part of the humor of the Yankee theater. New Yorkers were relentless in their contempt, claiming that many Long Island farmers, especially those from the eastern end of the island, did not leave the island even once in their entire lifetime. Some, the jokes had it, did not go farther than their small community. Stories satirized Long Island dialect. Long Island farmers on occasional jaunts to New York were ridiculed for their clothing and their slowness. Yet Long Island was a vacation paradise. New Yorkers took pleasure trips to Long Island to get away from the city—but they breathed sighs of relief on returning to "civilization." And even though Mount was the darling of the New York critics, presumably because of what he *did* paint, they felt it obligatory to note that the delightful manner in which he painted prevented his audience from lamenting too much that the subjects were not suitable for a "genteel" taste.[18]

As a Long Islander himself, and an eastern Long Islander at that, Mount was in as ideal a position to convey the contradictions between attitudes toward Long Island as he was to convey the richness of the Jonathan character. Coming from an Island lineage that reached back to the seventeenth century, Mount had been born to a freeholding farmer of substance and had spent his own youth as a "farmer boy" on the family homestead at Setauket in

18 Found throughout contemporay and retrospective literature, and referred to especially by Prime, Thompson, Weigold, and Berbrich, above, these attitudes of disdain for rural life are more powerful in cumulative effect than in individual citation. Their emotional power is particularly clear in such instances as Thompson's impassioned refutation in 1843 of Timothy Dwight's comments in 1804 ("Journey to Long Island," *Travels in New England and New York* [New Haven, 1821], III, 198–235) that Long Islanders had "confined minds" and a "regular [and boring] life" (II, 298–303). For comments on Mount, see clippings in Setauket Scrapbook, 3, 22.

Suffolk County. On being apprenticed as a sign painter to his brother in New York City, Mount learned to enjoy thoroughly the pleasures of city life. And yet, except for the years of his training at the National Academy of Design, he never stayed long in the city. He fled the noise of New York for Long Island in 1827, yet later stated disdainfully that he had retired to "paint the mugs of Long Island yeomanry." And although the newspapers occasionally announced Mount's imminent return to full-time residence in the city, he never again lived there for longer than the few months of the winter exhibition and theater season. His journals are full of laments over the tension he experienced between living on Long Island and living in New York: he was bored in the country and nervous in the dirty, noisy city. He needed the quiet of the country to paint, but the stimulation of the city to come up with ideas. Most of all, he needed the patronage of the city. Of all the patrons for his genre subjects, virtually no one was a Long Islander. It was the city patrons, Long Island's New York City neighbors, who delighted in what Mount's subjects offered.[19]

But Mount's rural prison/paradise was not static. Long Island, like other areas of the United States, was changing rapidly. Farming on the island had begun to change character, as many farmers had turned from self-sufficiency farming to providing hay, oats, wood, and vegetables for the New York City market. The population on Long Island was moving eastward from Brooklyn at an alarming rate. After a long and bitter battle, construction on the Long Island Rail Road had resulted in a line from Brooklyn to Jamaica by 1834 and all the way to Greenport in 1844. Although the railroad made it possible for farmers to get their produce to the market, it also brought citizens from the market—from New York City—out to the eastern stretches of the island and stimulated land speculation that greatly harmed the farmer. Manor houses and "country estates" were springing up with increasing frequency, weekend residences of city merchants and financiers who knew nothing about the soil; Long Island was on its way to becoming a place of ersatz farmers. And the past was being obscured in more insidious ways as well. James Fenimore Cooper, Thompson, and others complained that Islanders,

19   The quotation is in Frankenstein, *William Sidney Mount,* 18.

eager to please the new residents from the city, were changing the historical names of their communities to bring the Island "up to date"—replacing "Oyster Pond" with "Orient," and "Hallet's Cove" with "Astoria," "Success" with "Lakeville" and "Musketo Cove" with "Glen Cove."[20]

Relic and microcosm of the past that Long Island had been at one time, the evidence of this past was vanishing fast. In addition to the tension between ideal and comic that Mount's paintings convey, an important part of their significance was his celebration of activities, traits, and simple natural scenes that were rapidly disappearing—in rural life, in national character, and on Long Island.

On a more abstract level, Mount's paintings offered his audience direct and indirect reminders of ideals of national life that also were being destroyed. These ideals were associated with farmers. Freeholding, for instance, by the 1830s was no longer a requirement for voting, and an increasingly urban population had little opportunity to acquire land, much less to enjoy its benefits. Andrew Jackson's seizure of Indian lands for public sale ignored the premise on which freeholding was based—the purchase of one's land from its owner. So extensive had been the empires built by large landholders in western New York state that barely one fourth the voting population in 1835 were freeholders; the rest were tenants, renters, or even squatters, and the rent abuses of landlords led to violent anti-rent wars in the 1830s. Land speculation in the disposal of public lands in the American west meant that in few instances did those lands go directly to the yeoman.[21]

Other values that had been part of the agrarian ideal were overturned, too. Jackson's introduction of bank notes meant that wealth no longer inhered in the results of "real" work, such as that of the farmer (and thus the irony was great that many of the bank notes carried Mount's image of the farmer husking corn, "real wealth"). Workers crowding into the city enjoyed none of

20 Berbrich, *Three Voices*, 35–36; Thompson, *History* (1843), II, 302.

21 Studies of the economic, social, and political complexities of the nation during Mount's career include Marvin Meyers, *The Jacksonian Persuasion: Politics and Belief* (Stanford, 1957); Foster Rhea Dulles, *Labor in America* (New York, 1960); Edward Pessen (ed.), *New Perspectives on Jacksonian Parties and Politics* (Boston, 1969); idem, *Jacksonian America: Society, Personality, and Politics* (Homewood, Ill., 1978).

the advantages of the farmer, poor as his circumstances might have been: they were not independent laborers, they were not self-sufficient, and they were not stable. It was not only the lower classes that lived uncertain lives in the city. More comfortable citizens, if they were engaged in commerce, were subject to devastation during financial panics. Finally, as increasing disparity marked the distribution of wealth, class divisions became more and more pronounced; an egalitarian American society of yeomen could no longer be held up as even remotely realizable.

Thus an investigation of the contexts invoked by Mount's critics—the yeoman ideal and agricultural practices, the Yankee theater, and the setting of Long Island—yields insight into the complex relationship between national ideals and changing realities in the 1830s and 1840s, especially as perceived in New York, that formed the themes of Mount's paintings. This study also reveals that for Mount's images at least, the American audience for art felt it appropriate that the disparities between national ideals and changing realities form the subject matter of a new national art.

Barbara Miller Lane

Architects in Power: Politics and Ideology in the Work of Ernst May and Albert Speer

This article has a twofold purpose. First, by comparing some aspects of the lives and works of Ernst May and Albert Speer, it illuminates the special experience of architects in power in the twentieth century. Throughout history, architects have had a greater need for wealthy patrons than have other artists because of the great expense of buildings. And government buildings, because of their size and visibility, have always been the most attractive of commissions. Thus, architects have always been involved to some extent in politics, and have nearly always sought positions of power and influence. But never before the twentieth century, when the scale of government building has often transformed architecture into planning, and the relative democratization of politics has vastly increased the size of the audience, has the need for power among architects been so great. Both May and Speer held positions of authority which enabled them to make decisions as planners and as architects. Both were strongly supported by powerful patrons, but both also had to deal with the realities of politics and public opinion in a democratic, or at least a populist, era. I have written before about the work of both men, but have never attempted a direct comparison in order to examine the phenomenon of the architect in power.[1]

A second purpose is methodological. In the process of explaining the goals of their work to their patrons and to the public, May and Speer often made statements which were not entirely true. They described themselves as creators of an architecture

Barbara Miller Lane is the Andrew W. Mellon Professor in the Humanities and Director of the Growth and Structure of Cities Program at Bryn Mawr College. She is the author of *Architecture and Politics in Germany, 1918–1945* (Cambridge, Mass., 1968; new ed. 1985). This article is dedicated to Franklin Lewis Ford, teacher and friend, on his sixty-fifth birthday.

1 Lane, *Architecture and Politics in Germany, 1918–1945* (Cambridge, Mass., 1968; new ed. 1985); *idem,* "Albert Speer," *Macmillan Encyclopedia of Architects* (New York, 1982), IV, 115–116.

which was uniquely expressive of a "new era," and each defined this expression in both aesthetic and political terms. But the roots of their inspiration were more complex than either they, their patrons, or their audience believed. By illustrating this point, I hope to offer some guidelines for historians who wish to explore the relationships of architecture and politics in the twentieth century.

May was *Stadtbaurat* (municipal architect) and *Dezernent für Bauwesen* (overseer of city planning) in Frankfurt am Main from early 1925 to mid-1930. During those years he had almost absolute power over all architecture and urban design within the city. He exercised most control over projects supported by municipal funds, but, since his office was empowered to issue what we would call building permits, his influence on style was widespread. May's office, during his term in power, had jurisdiction over such varied projects as the installation of storefront signs, plans for the revivification of the old city center, and the design of tombstones in Frankfurt's graveyards. It is not surprising that some of his opponents accused him of "*Stildiktatur*" (aesthetic dictatorship).

The most constructive aspect of May's administration, however, was the development of an extensive green belt plan for Frankfurt, and the planning of a series of new satellite cities. In the five years of his administration, approximately 10,000 housing units were erected, and plans were set forth for many more. His office also laid the basis for an ambitious regional plan, which has only achieved its full impact in the post-war period. The satellite towns which were completed between 1925 and 1930 were not just housing areas; they included new kinds of street layout and new community facilities of all sorts, including schools, shops, entertainment facilities, parks, and gardens. In writings of the time, May claimed to have created for Frankfurt not only a new dwelling form, which he thought would revolutionize human relationships, but also a model of a "new city."

In 1930, May, together with a number of his staff, left Frankfurt for Moscow, hoping to build many "new cities" in Soviet Russia. By the time he discovered that Stalinist Russia was far less welcoming to his ideas than Weimar Germany had been, Adolf Hitler had come to power in Germany and had condemned all "art bolshevists," including May. Leaving Russia in 1934, May was unable to reenter Germany, and became a stateless person until 1945. During the war years, he took refuge in Kenya; thereafter he returned to Germany, settled in Hamburg, and awaited the call to achieve the "new city" on a large scale. But, by the 1950s, the specific circumstances that had lent appeal to his work in the 1920s were forgotten, and the call never came. During his last years, May was active in some important housing organizations in Germany and served occasionally as a planning consultant, but he never regained a position of real prominence. He died in 1970, an embittered man.[2]

Under Hitler, Speer held a position not unlike May's in Frankfurt, with the significant difference that Speer could, at times, aspire to control design in the Reich as a whole. From 1934, when the young Speer succeeded Paul Ludwig Troost as Hitler's principal architect, to 1942, when he took over the Ministry of Armaments and War Production, Speer occupied a position of unique power in the history of architecture. He was personally responsible for the most important of the new buildings and projects of the new Reich: the Nuremberg Party Congress Grounds, the New Chancellery in Berlin, and the replanning of Berlin. In addition, as the Führer's most favored architect and close personal friend, he was able, in theory at least, to name architects for any public building in Germany (under Hitler, during the depression, nearly all buildings were public), and to oversee and influence their designs as much as he wished. In practice, as so often in the Third Reich, Speer's power was contested by many other officials and by the other Nazi leaders, together with their favored architects. His power was also often undermined by the whims of Hitler himself. Nevertheless, Speer was able to set his stamp on a large number of buildings and projects, to the extent that many people then and now see his work as synonymous with Nazi architecture. Speer encouraged, and himself believed in, this identification: he saw himself as seeking a new style which would embody or represent the political ideals of the Führer and of the thousand-year Reich.

2 Justus Buekschmitt, *Ernst May* (Stuttgart, 1963); Reginald R. Isaacs, "Ernst May," *Macmillan Encyclopedia*, III, 126. On May's reception in Russia and on the general development of Soviet architecture and planning, see Anatole Kopp, *Town and Revolution: Soviet Architecture and City Planning, 1917–1935* (New York, 1970); idem, *L'architecture de la période stalinienne* (Grenoble, 1978). My remarks on May's last years are based on personal interviews in 1960, and correspondence thereafter.

Because of his role as minister under Hitler, his imprisonment for war crimes at Spandau (1946–1966), and his series of apologias and public appearances after his release from Spandau, Speer is far better known as a political figure and as an architect than May. His career is still the subject of bitter debate in Germany and elsewhere. Speer himself, in his writings and in his many television appearances, was often unable to separate his architecture from his role as Hitler's confidante and, ultimately, as one of the most powerful Nazi officials in the German war effort. Thus it is not surprising that public debate about the merits of Speer-like architecture is often mired in pro- or anti-Nazi denunciations. This tendency to see Speer's architecture as uniquely representative of Hitler's government has become a particular problem recently, when post-modernist architects have increasingly felt a fondness for a historicist architecture somewhat akin to Speer's. I do not discuss Speer's architecture without relation to his politics, but I show that the relationship between the two was more complicated than many people think. I restrict my discussion almost entirely to the years when Speer served Hitler as an architect, rather than as a minister.

The careers of May and Speer can be viewed sequentially, in order to see how and for what ends they used their unusually powerful positions. Before he headed the Frankfurt building administration, May (1886–1970) had been a designer of small housing developments, known in German as *Siedlungen* (colonies). May had spent some of his early career working in England with Raymond Unwin, one of the leading architects of the garden city movement. In the early 1920s, May's housing designs still resembled Unwin's: small, village-like dwellings, with steeply pitched roofs. May's city planning continued to display the influence of garden city ideas throughout his career, but his architecture, by 1925, had undergone a transformation into what would soon be known as the International Style.

The International Style, as defined first by Walter Gropius at the Bauhaus, and then later by Henry-Russell Hitchcock and Philip Johnson at the Museum of Modern Art show of 1932, was an austere, cubic architecture, altogether devoid of historical references. Characterized by a balanced asymmetry, unlike most of the Western architectural tradition; by thin skin-like surfaces, often (but not always) executed in reinforced concrete; and by extensive window areas set flush in the surface of the building and often bearing a considerable burden of abstract patterning, the new style was startling in appearance. It appeared particularly startling in Frankfurt am Main, one of Germany's oldest, most history-laden cities.

Frankfurt's origins begin with the Romans and the Franks. One of Germany's leading financial centers since the later Middle Ages, it was the site of momentous events in German history: the election and coronation of the Holy Roman Emperors on the Römerberg; the early declaration of adherence to a reformed religion in 1530, near the Lutherecke; and the framing of a constitution and parliament for a united Germany in 1848, at the Paulskirche, which, though unsuccessful, left some imprint on the Bismarckian constitution and remained as a memory of hopes for national union under liberal auspices. Historically, Frankfurt was Roman, Imperial, Protestant, nationalistically German, wealthy, and liberal. Although it was absorbed into Germany via Prussian hegemony, the memory of these various traditions remained. The long and complex history of the city left a physical legacy as well: the small medieval core of the city was ringed by lavish parks and boulevards dating from early modern times. These parklands and newer residential areas were in turn ringed by neighboring towns which, with the progress of industrialization, began to grow inward toward the old city.

By the beginning of the twentieth century, Frankfurt's wealth was augmented by the growth of late industrial organization there; the city had come to be one of the principal sites of Germany's chemical and electrical industries. It was also, by that time, an important center of Social Democratic influence and an early locus of working-class housing reform movements. Frankfurt entered the Weimar Republic, therefore, with a population that was conscious of its history, but also extremely cosmopolitan, liberal, relatively well-to-do, and receptive to social reform. It had also recently entered a period of extremely rapid growth. As May grew up in Frankfurt, he must have been aware of these different traditions and contexts.

In 1924, Ludwig Landmann, city councillor and head of the office of housing policy in Frankfurt, became mayor. Landmann, who has been described by his biographer as more of a technocrat than a politician, was nevertheless a leading member of the Democratic Party in Frankfurt, and was brought to power by an overwhelming majority of Democrats and Social Democrats in the municipal elections. His stated program was the modernization of all aspects of municipal functions, but especially the improvement of transportation and housing conditions. He also planned and achieved the incorporation of many outlying towns and suburbs into an enlarged metropolitan area. In 1925, Landmann combined all of the older city offices concerned with planning and housing, extended them to the enlarged metropolitan area, and appointed May as the director of the whole. At this time May was known as a designer of public housing in Breslau, and as a recent convert to the architectural ideas of the Bauhaus. When May was called to Frankfurt, however, he had not yet executed a significant number of the buildings in the new style, nor had it been widely employed elsewhere in Germany.[3]

Landmann charged May with the task of improving transportation conditions within the city while retaining as much as possible of the historic character of its inner precincts. Above all, however, he was asked to develop a vast public housing program and to plan for current and future growth. May and Landmann began, shortly after the new appointment, to speak of the creation, in architecture and planning, of a "New Frankfurt," an embodiment of a "new era," suited to fast-moving traffic, high technology, and social reform.[4]

May's architectural response to his task can be summarized by a brief look at the house which he designed for himself in Frankfurt in 1926 (Fig. 1). An austere cubic structure, executed in white stucco to resemble reinforced concrete, it looks like a module for prefabricated mass housing. Inside, the walls are bare plaster, also white; there are no moldings to obscure the sharp, apparently machine-made edges. Furnishings are sparse and geometric appearing, and the whole is flooded with light. Tillich said

3 Dieter Rebentisch, *Ludwig Landmann, Frankfurter Oberbürgermeister der Weimarer Republik* (Wiesbaden, 1975), 306, 133; Lane, *Architecture and Politics*, 89–90.
4 See *Das Neue Frankfurt* (Frankfurt am Main, Nov. 1926–July, 1931), esp. Landmann, "Zum Geleit," I (1926), 1–2. May was sole editor until 1927, and then shared the editorial tasks with others until 1931. Subtitles varied. From 1931 to 1934 (when it was closed down by the Nazis) the magazine continued as *Die Neue Stadt,* edited by Joseph Gantner. Many issues are reprinted in Juan Rodríguez-Lores and Günter Uhlig (eds.), *Das Neue Frankfurt/Die Neue Stadt* (Aachen, 1977).

Fig. 1 Exterior and Interior Views of May's House, 1926.

SOURCE: Walter Müller-Wulckow, *Deutsche Baukunst der Gegenwart* (Leipzig, 1929), pt. II, 42, 45.

of this kind of architecture that it represented a religion of every-day life; for May this religion included, in addition, a deification of simplicity, which he saw as working class.[5]

But the main impact of May's ideas upon Frankfurt was in the satellite communities designed by him and his staff to the north of the old city, with a greenbelt in between. My examples are drawn mainly from two of these satellite communities, Römerstadt and Praunheim, both located in the Nidda valley to the northwest of the city. From a distance, these communities look like piled up and strung out versions of the housing module described above. To our eyes, accustomed to Moshe Safdie Habitats and the megastructural urban visions of the Japanese Metabolists, they are not so shocking, but in 1925 they looked like alien visitors at the edge of the older city. On closer examination it becomes clear that the kind of patterning which in most buildings of the International Style was created by the massing of a single building, or just by fenestration on a single facade, was in Frankfurt extended to whole communities (Fig. 2). Each community was built up from simple geometric forms to a series of high points, creating an overall asymmetrical balance which gave the community stylistic coherence. This design coherence was reinforced by color: different streets were painted in contrasting colors, so that the overall effect was of a kind of three-dimensional Mondrian, writ very large. The street pattern reinforced the integrity of each community, which was bordered by broad, trolly-served boulevards, linking it to the old city. Within each community, winding and increasingly narrow streets and footpaths created a unifying pattern (Fig. 3).

The dwellings in these new communities were very small. Reflecting the lingering effects of his garden city training, May chose to build not the more economical high-rise structures with which others in Germany were beginning to experiment, but low-rise buildings, never more than four stories, and as often as possible only two or three. One corollary of the rather lavish use of land necessitated by this practice was to make the dwelling units small in order to keep them economical. Since these dwellings were also intended from the start to provide low-cost housing for

5 Paul Tillich, "Kult und Form," *Die Form*, V (1930), 578–583.

Fig. 2 Siedlung Hohenblick: Color, Massing, and Patterning Unite Two Blocks.

Fig. 3 Siedlung Praunheim: Narrow Streets Create a Village-like Effect.

SOURCES: Lane, *Architecture and Politics*, Figs. 54, 56.

the working classes, an additional impetus for cost-efficient planning was introduced.

Many of the Frankfurt dwellings consisted of only two or three rooms: a main room convertible for both dining and sleeping, and one or two additional rooms with folding beds or bunk beds. Furniture was very simple, and much of it was built in (Fig. 4). The Frankfurt dwellings also usually contained a largely prefabricated pullman kitchen, which came to be known as the *Frankfurter Küche*, and a very small, prefabricated bath unit, the *Frankfurter Bad*. These were the elements of what came to be known in Germany as *Die Wohnung für das Existenzminimum*, the minimal dwelling, the solution to Germany's (and the industrialized world's) housing shortage and to the demographic crisis then seen to be approaching. The minimal dwelling, and May's solutions for it, were widely appreciated, and formed the subject of the first and second organizational meetings of CIAM (*Congrès Internationaux d'Architecture Moderne*) in 1928 and 1929. May was one

Fig. 4 Plan of Minimal Dwelling.

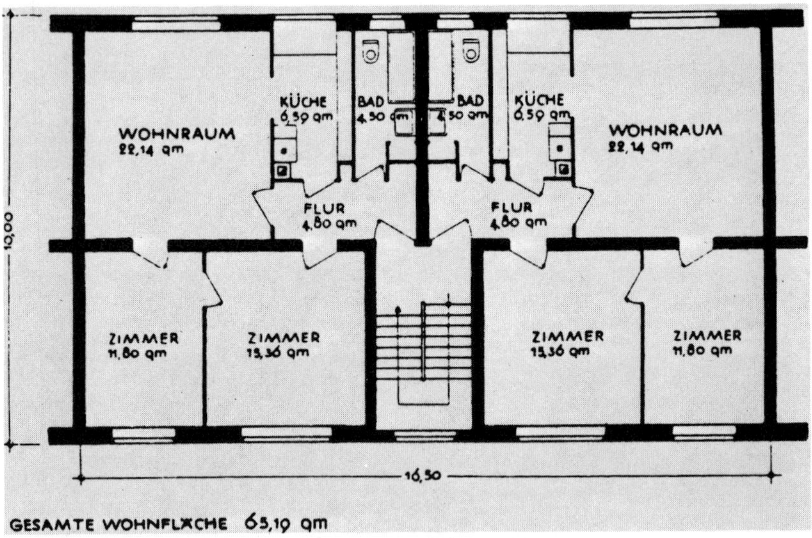

GESAMTE WOHNFLÄCHE 65,19 qm

SOURCE: *Das Neue Frankfurt*, II (1927), 116.

of the principal founders of the organization, which has been identified by historians almost entirely with Le Corbusier.[6]

For May, and for many others in Germany in the mid-1920s, minimalism in housing was not just a response to economic necessity, but was also an act of faith. As Taut put it in 1924, "only in freedom from disorder can the personality develop freely." The simplicity of new kinds of dwelling design would, he said, produce a new "mental attitude, more flexible, simpler, and more joyful." Taut's words were part of a larger plea for a "spiritual revolution" aided by a new architecture and by the machine and industrial production.[7]

May expressed similar views: "Architecture has left behind it the path of decadent imitation and now recognizes the laws of form appropriate to our time. . . . The altered spiritual attitude of mankind has resulted in a new dwelling form . . . [in] the crystal clear, often intentionally humble, spatial arrangements of modern architecture." And, "Our co-workers in Frankfurt have drawn together in a philosophy of building . . . [intended] to provide housing for the masses. . . . They seek . . . architectural and planning goals that grow out of our own era. They know that the forms of Frankfurt's housing not only succeed in embodying a new style, but also that their labors are essential as milestones on the road toward an architecture which is specifically expressive of the twentieth century."[8]

For May, Taut, and others, the minimal dwelling meant a rejection of *things,* a concentration on the simplest and most universal *forms,* and the erection into an aesthetic dogma of a way of life simple enough for the poor and therefore appropriate for all. Ironically, many of May's dwellings turned out to be too expensive for the working classes, and were populated by middle-class intellectuals and professionals.

Apart from these innovative dwelling designs, the Frankfurt *Siedlungen* were held together formally by overall massing and pattern, and by a complex street pattern which was both urbane

6 News item, *Die Form,* V (1929), 124; May, "Kleinstwohnungen," *Zentralblatt der Bauverwaltung* (May 8, 1929), 297–300; *idem,* "Die Wohnung für das Existenzminimum," *Das Neue Frankfurt,* IV (1929), 111–114.

7 Bruno Taut, *Die neue Wohnung* (Leipzig, 1924), 104, 90. See also Lane, *Architecture and Politics,* 66.

8 May, "Das neue Frankfurt," *Das Neue Frankfurt,* I (1926), 2–11, 4; *idem,* "Grundlagen der Frankfurter Wohnungsbaupolitik," *ibid.,* III (1928), 113–125.

(on the broad boulevards) and neighborly (on the smaller streets). Each settlement also included a variety of community facilities. In addition to shops, churches, restaurants, and central laundries, innovative educational institutions were incorporated into nearly every development. Martin Elsaesser's schools in Praunheim and elsewhere implemented the ideas of Johann Heinrich Pestalozzi and of more recent educational reformers, such as Hermann Lietz, by emphasizing manual labor, outdoor gymnastics, and training in horticulture as part of their curriculum. One *Siedlung* included a community building which housed a pre-school day care center; others had rooftop nurseries for infants.[9]

In addition, each *Siedlung* had gardens. Row houses had their own gardens to the rear, and apartment dwellings had individual garden plots grouped together. The gardens were originally conceived as truck gardens, for raising fruits and vegetables. In a few cases, additional large plots were set aside nearby, so that larger crops could be cultivated. Surrounding the gardens, lying behind the rows of buildings, were parks: parks for playing fields, parks with romantic walks along the Nidda River, adapted from a long tradition of English landscape design. And, leading down from the main boulevard of Römerstadt, a large swath of open land served as a sheepfold. The shocking appearance of the grazing sheep next to the abstract geometry of the housing highlights some of the tensions and ambiguities that lay beneath the surface of May's "new architecture" for a "new Frankfurt."

The imagery of May's architecture and urban design was not merely that of a socially conscious or even socialist housing reform. The layout of the new communities depended partly on the tradition of broad boulevards developed in Frankfurt from the fifteenth to the eighteenth centuries, and partly on the narrow, winding streets of the oldest parts of the late medieval inner city. The greenbelt arrangement was related to the British garden city movement and to its German offshoots of the early twentieth century; the sheepfold and the park paths had a similar origin. The prominence of gardens, particularly the larger scale truck gardens, demonstrated the thinking of Adolf Damaschke, an early

---

9 On educational institutions in the new Frankfurt, see Städtisches Hochbauamt Frankfurt am Main (eds.), *Frankfurter Schulbauten* (Frankfurt am Main, 1929); Fritz Wichert, "Die neue Baukunst als Erzieher," *Das Neue Frankfurt*, III (1928), 233–235; May, "Die Architektur der neuen Schule," *ibid.*, 225–233.

twentieth-century land reformer of considerable interest to the Nazis, who believed that each municipality should hold large areas free for cultivation in order to ensure food and health to future generations. A consultant in the planning of the Nidda Valley development was Leberecht Migge, a leading landscape architect of the 1920s and a disciple of Damaschke; Migge's ideas came rather close to Nazi *Blut und Boden* theories.[10]

Thus, May's ideas as realized at Frankfurt were a mixture of historic references to Frankfurt itself, garden city and English landscape traditions, reformist central European educational theories, some authors of which were politically very conservative, German land reformers of whom the same could be said, community organization ideas of a generally left-wing stamp, a working-class aesthetic of a sort, and a particularly rarified version of avant-garde art. The Frankfurt housing of the later 1920s uniquely illustrates the cauldron of conflicting ideas and political allegiances which characterized the Weimar Republic. But what does it tell us about the architect in power?

Most of us will admire the accomplishments of May in Frankfurt, even though we may realize that they could not have been achieved, in a democracy, without a very strong authority—stronger in fact than most democracies are willing to allow their architects and planners. May's powers were more akin to those of André Le Nôtre and Baron Georges Eugène von Haussmann than Edmund Bacon; indeed, for the term of his office, he had a more independent authority than any past architect dependent upon the whim of an absolute monarch. May himself took this authority for granted: it was necessary in order to achieve what he wanted to achieve, and nothing less would have done. And what he wanted to achieve, he said, was not merely a solution to Frankfurt's housing problems, but a new community, in which a new architecture would have an educational effect on people's lives, and on their relations to one another. He believed that architecture shapes human beings, their beliefs, and their society, and he saw no difficulty in the notion of imposing the forms of

10 Walter Creese, *The Search for Environment: the Garden City Before and After* (New Haven, 1966); *idem, The Legacy of Raymond Unwin* (Cambridge, Mass., 1967); Kristiana Hartmann, *Deutsche Gartenstadtbewegung: Kulturpolitik und Gesellschaftsreform* (Munich, 1976); Leberecht Migge, "Grünpolitik in Frankfurt am Main," *Der Städtebau*, XXIV (1929), 37–47; Christiane C. Collins, "Leberecht Migge," *Macmillan Encyclopedia*, III, 195–196.

a new society on people for their own good. He was content to be a dictator.[11]

May felt obligated, by virtue of his appointment in Frankfurt, to join a political party for the first time in his life. Inspired by the Fabian ideals that he had learned to admire in England, he entered the Social Democratic Party in 1925. Like so many of his generation, May was extremely naive about practical politics. He liked Mayor Landmann, and he shared the idea of many avant-garde artists of the time that artists had a special role to play in the post-war years in helping to bring about a spiritual revolution. He was glad to have his designs sponsored by a socially conscious municipal government; he would have been equally glad to have had them realized in Soviet Russia. Whether, if given the opportunity, he would have accepted the patronage of Hitler, we cannot know; in any case the opportunity never arose, and could not (given Hitler's aesthetic preferences) have arisen. But if May had been asked whether, in retrospect, the presence within his work of right-wing as well as left-wing influences troubled him, I think he would have said no. Nor do I think it would have bothered him to have been told that his work retained links to the past, as well as previews of the near future. May believed that he had assembled talent under the rubric of his own vision—that this vision was absolute and in a sense unrelated to specific political circumstances. Most architects, fundamentally, share this attitude. The ultimate sources of their creation is personal, and—to them— absolute. Most architects, therefore, like power, and its source is less important than the extent to which it aids in the realization of their aims.[12]

Speer (1908–1981), a far less complicated figure than May, and a poorer and less interesting architect, was a young and relatively unsuccessful architect in Berlin during the depression years. He held a good teaching post as assistant to his mentor, Heinrich Tessenow, at the Berlin Technische Hochschule, but commissions to build were unobtainable. In the politically volatile atmosphere of Berlin at the beginning of the 1930s, Speer joined the Nazi

11 May, "Das soziale Moment in der neuen Baukunst," *Das Neue Frankfurt*, III (1928), 81–87. It should be noted, however, that May's opponents were relatively few before 1928, and that he continued to be well liked by most residents of the city even after 1930.
12 Rebentisch, *Landmann*, 133.

Party. Soon, he received from the local party leaders some interior decoration work and a few other minor commissions. The decisive turning point in Speer's career came as a result of a personal meeting with Hitler in July, 1933; Speer was apparently genuinely mesmerized by the magnetism of the Führer. Hitler, in turn, was attracted by Speer's youth, engaging personality, malleability, ambition, and willingness to build at "the American tempo." Speer received commissions for a temporary Party Congress Grounds building in Nuremberg and for the remodelling of the Chancellery in Berlin. Promises of larger commissions quickly followed, and a strong bond was forged between Hitler and Speer, both frustrated architects.

After the death of Troost in 1934, Speer became principal architect to Hitler and, in 1937, *Generalbauinspektor für die Reichshauptstadt* (general supervisor of building for the imperial capital). In these positions, he was in charge of the replanning of Berlin and Nuremberg and either designed new buildings for these cities, or supervised the choice of architects. He also played a part in vast plans to restructure many other German cities and here too often influenced the choice of architects. Many of these plans remained unexecuted, but they were repeatedly displayed as models and photographed for Nazi publications as evidence of the new Reich's will to build and of the creation of a new, National Socialist architecture, one which was designed "for the people," but which also embodied a specifically national and Germanic tradition.[13]

Because Speer worked so closely with Hitler it is still difficult to come to an unbiased decision as to whose ideas were whose. One case in which it is clear that Hitler played a major role was the project for rebuilding Berlin, a plan of which both were very

---

13 Speer's exact title, and the actual limits of his power, continue to be unclear. According to his *Erinnerungen* (Berlin, 1967), trans. by Richard and Clara Winston as *Inside the Third Reich* (New York, 1970), he was named *Sonderbeauftragter für Bauwesen* in 1936 and *Generalbauinspektor für die Reichshauptstadt* in 1937. Contemporary publications, however, often referred to him as *Generalbauinspektor für das Reich*, or simply as *Generalbauinspektor*. His powers were legally limited to Berlin, but were informally extended in a variety of ways, not least through his influence on Hitler. On the relative roles of Hitler, Speer, and competing architects, see esp., Jost Dülfer, Jochen Thies, and Josef Henke (eds.), *Hitlers Städte: Baupolitik im Dritten Reich. Eine Dokumentation* (Cologne, 1978); Thies, *Architekt der Weltherrschaft. Die 'Endziele' Hitlers* (Düsseldorf, 1976). For additional bibliography, see the preface to the 1985 edition of my *Architecture and Politics*.

proud. The plan envisioned the construction of two great transportation axes which would meet in the Platz der Republik (the
former Königsplatz), the site of the recently burned Reichstag.
The east/west portion of these axes would join Unter den Linden,
the Pariser Platz, and the Charlottenburger Chaussée, in a new
grand boulevard reaching out to a new system of ring roads
around Berlin. The north/south portion of the axes would be
shorter and more ceremonial. It would join the old Lehrter and
Anhalter railroad stations (remodelled and part of a revised rail
network) by a great street along which would be monumental
new administrative buildings for the new Reich. Extensions of
the north/south axis, beyond the railroad stations, were also to
have joined the ring road. Bridging the lower end of the north/
south axis was to be a 400-foot high version of the Arc de
Triomphe, which Speer says was Hitler's design. At the head of
the axis was to be another giant building, a great domed hall for
gatherings of the Nazi faithful.[14]

The domed hall was to be part of a huge complex of buildings
encasing the Platz der Republik, which would include a mammoth
residence and chancellery for Hitler and administrative buildings
built up around the Reichstag, the ruins of which were to be
preserved as a memorial. South of the domed hall, which appears
in models to have been a version of the United States Capitol,
inflated, like the triumphal arch, to gigantic size, were to be new
ministries and offices, museums, an opera, and "palaces" for some
of the other Nazi leaders. Speer also claimed that Hitler had a
hand in the design of the Great Hall, but that he himself was the
principal architect of the rest of the scheme. In retrospect, he was
most proud of the ways in which the plan would have facilitated
transportation. But he also remarked, in one of his post-war
efforts to understand his own actions, that at the start of his
association with Hitler, "[I] would have sold my soul . . . for the
commission to do a great building." These were great buildings
indeed, if size is a criterion of greatness: so "great" in fact that

---

14 Lars Olof Larsson has differentiated the ideas of Hitler and Speer in the replanning
of Berlin with considerable success: *Die Neugestaltung der Reichshauptstadt* (Stockholm,
1978). For a discussion of the historical context of the Berlin plan, see Lane, "The Berlin
Congress Hall, 1955–1957," *Perspectives in American History*, I (1984), 131–185.

Speer, and perhaps even Hitler, must have known that they were unbuildable.[15]

It seems likely that Hitler's main contributions to Nazi architecture, at least in the public sphere, were these projects for buildings of great size. In addition to the buildings on the north/south axis, Speer and Hitler spoke of mile-wide railway stations and new urban centers "for infinite numbers of people." Speer's executed buildings, in contrast, were relatively modest in scale, rather consistent in style, and very different in most respects from the buildings planned for the new Berlin. The buildings which Speer completed for Hitler between 1934 and 1942—a new chancellery in Berlin (but not the giant one of the plan), a German pavilion for the Paris World's Fair of 1937, and the Zeppelinfeld Stadium for the party congresses at Nuremberg—were certainly monumental, but not in the sense of gigantic size (Figs. 5 and 6). All were clad in masonry and were massed symmetrically around exaggeratedly large central entrances. These entrances, and, in the case of the Chancellery, the windows also, were set down close to street level, providing passersby with a sense of visual accessibility unlike most government buildings of the past. Repetitive vertical elements, as at Nuremberg and in the Paris Pavilion, gave a sense of a link to tradition, in that they distantly resembled classical colonnades. At Paris, a simplified cornice also offered some suggestion of a link to the past, as did the rustication on the exterior of the Chancellery. Yet overt and specific references to the classical tradition were rarely present: the garden side of the Chancellery had real columns and capitals, but on the front the columns were so reduced as to appear as only symbols of columns, and this was even more true at Paris and at Nuremberg.[16]

Although he never acknowledged it, Speer, like other architects of the 1930s, was deeply influenced by the Modern Movement. The pared-down, abstract geometric forms of the Nurem-

15 Speer, *Third Reich,* 74–75: according to Speer, the idea of the width of the axes was also Hitler's, for whom Paris, in this case, was the main inspiration. *Ibid.,* 78–79, 31.

16 Hitler's taste in private life, as exemplified at the Berghof, inclined toward the rustic: *ibid.,* 46, 86. Hitler, speech at the cornerstone ceremony of the House of German Tourism, June 14, 1938, in Max Domarus (ed.), *Hitler: Reden und Proklamationen* (Würzburg, 1962), I, 873–874.

Fig. 5 Zeppelinfeld in Nuremberg, by Speer.

Fig. 6 German Pavilion, Paris World's Fair, 1937, by Speer.

SOURCE: Library of Congress, Prints and Photographs Division.

berg Party Congress grounds, for example, owe a great deal to the passion for simple geometric forms, without ornament or explicit reference to history, of the avant-garde architects of the 1920s. What set Speer apart from this movement was his insistence on masonry cladding and on axial symmetry in the arrangement of spaces and masses: his apparent rejection of steel and concrete and of asymmetrical arrangements. Buildings like the Zeppelinfeld differed from those of the Modern Movement by a narrow, yet visually significant margin. And despite his own predeliction for Baroque and strongly neo-classical motifs in architecture, Hitler was pleased with Speer's buildings. Hitler may have continued to wish for unbuildable versions of the United States Capitol and the Arc de Triomphe, but he came to see the combination of modernity, reference to tradition, monumentality, and accessibility in Speer's executed buildings as uniquely expressive of National Socialist goals.

In retrospect, Speer was most proud of his designs for the party congress grounds at Nuremberg. Here bright flags by day and searchlights by night echoed and dramatized the vertical piers of the grandstand, and framed the complex marching patterns of thousands of Nazi delegates inside. Speer called the vertical columns of the searchlights his "cathedral of light," and wrote, in the first of his memoirs, that this "cathedral" was his "most beautiful architectural concept." How curious that he should have remembered as his favorite great building an ephemeral nonbuilding. But Speer's talent was above all a theatrical talent, and it was this that most fundamentally endeared him to Hitler, who regarded architecture as a stage setting and as instant propaganda.[17]

The overriding interest of the two men in the question of *appearance* in architecture, as opposed to the integrity of materials or to social utility, is underlined by what Speer called the "ruin value" of architecture. In their snowy walks above the Berghof and in their more intimate conferences in Munich, Nuremberg, and Berlin, Speer and Hitler often discussed what Nazi buildings would look like in ruins. On these occasions they also spoke of the ancient empires, of Babylon and Karnak, and of Rome, agreeing that these empires still expressed their power even as their

17 Speer, *Third Reich*, 59.

buildings lay in ruins. Their hope was that the buildings of the Third Reich, when and if that Empire fell, would also express its lasting power. This macabre preoccupation helps to explain their dislike of reinforced concrete as a building material: both believed that it would appear undignified in ruins. Yet Speer nearly always used reinforced concrete, under limestone cladding, because it helped him build at the speed Hitler wanted. And it did look undignified in ruins.[18]

These conversations about the ruins of ancient empires also shed some light on the nature and development of Speer's beliefs about the relationship of architecture and politics. Many of Speer's buildings, insofar as they made reference to the past, appear distantly classicizing. Speer himself, in the first memoir that he published after his release from Spandau, stated that the principal historic inspiration for his work was Greek architecture of the Doric order—this was, he thought, the most noble of past architecture. In addition, he said, Hitler thought, and he himself believed at the time, that the Greeks were the ancestors of the Aryans; if Speer were to attempt a truly Germanic architecture, the Doric was the appropriate model.

There were many sources for this curious idea. Hitler did conflate the Greeks and the Aryans, as some archaeologists had already done early in the century. The association of Greece and German nationalism had long roots in German architecture, especially in Bavaria: it influenced, for example, the patronage of Ludwig I and the work of Leo von Klenze. Speer himself may have picked up the association not from Klenze, but from reading German literature of the Romantic period, which he liked. But Speer was also interested in archaeology. Like other German architects of his time, his training in architectural history was imparted mainly by archaeologists. Of his teachers in that field he especially admired Daniel Krencker, Roman archaeologist and excavator of the Imperial Palace at Trier, and Walter Andrae, assistant in German excavations at Babylon and himself the principal excavator of Assur.[19]

---

18 *Ibid.*, 56, 154.
19 See Klenze's Walhalla at Regensburg. On varying interpretations of Greek architecture in the nineteenth century, see Peter Collins, *Changing Ideals in Modern Architecture* (Montreal, 1967). On Klenze, and on nationalism in German nineteenth-century architecture

There is persuasive visual evidence that Andrae's reconstruction drawings of the main buildings at Assur, the early capital of the Assryian Empire, formed the most direct influence upon Speer's designs (Figs. 7 and 8).[20] Speer need not have known much ancient history to have realized that Assur was the center of a Semitic empire, and that the peoples who produced these buildings could not by any stretch of the imagination be supposed to have been Aryan or Indo-European. (The two terms were often used interchangeably, even by reputable ancient historians.) Yet in his *Spandau Diaries,* published in 1975 but supposedly written while he was still in prison, Speer admitted the possible importance of Assyrian models as influences on his designs. How are we to explain this contradiction?[21]

It is always wise to regard an architect's explanation of his work with a healthy mistrust, and this principle is even more useful in the case of a man like Speer, who had so many explanations to make. Most architects draw upon a variety of visual sources in a relatively unconscious way. When Speer saw Andrae's drawings he had not yet met Hitler or joined the Nazi Party; hence he had not yet learned to believe that architecture should have some ideological content. Probably he retained from his memories of Andrae's teaching images of an especially old, and newly discovered old, empire, which, by association, suited the idea of "ruin value" in architecture. Probably he did not bother to think through the ideological implications of taking for his

more generally, see Thomas Nipperdey, *Gesellschaft, Kultur, Theorie: Gesammelte Aufsätze zur neueren Geschichte* (Göttingen, 1976), 133–173.

    Krencker (1874–194?) published, among other works, *Das römische Trier* (Berlin, 1923) and *Vom Kolossalen in der Baukunst* (Berlin, 1926). Andrae (1875–1956) was Krencker's assistant and, therefore, Speer's teacher. He was the author, with Heinrich Schäfer, of the standard volume in the Propyläen Kunstgeschichte series on Egypt and the Near East (*Die Kunst des Alten Orients* [Berlin, 1925]), a book which Speer would certainly have used as a textbook while studying with Andrae. Andrae was also head of the Near Eastern Division of the Berlin Museum, the author of many publications on Assur, and the most influential figure in German Near Eastern archaeology after the death of Robert Koldewey in 1926.

20 I first developed this thesis in my review of *Inside the Third Reich* in *Journal of the Society of Architectural Historians,* XXXII (1973), 341–346. I sent a copy of my review to Speer; it seems possible that the passage in the *Spandau Diaries* referred to in n. 21 below represents a response to the review.

21 See, for example, V. Gordon Childe, *The Aryans* (New York, 1926); Lane and Leila J. Rupp, *Nazi Ideology before 1933* (Austin, 1978), xv–xvi. Speer, *Spandauer Tagebücher* (Berlin, 1975), trans. by R. and C. Winston as *Spandau: the Secret Diaries* (New York, 1976), entry for March 16, 1949.

Fig. 7 Luitpoldhalle in Nuremberg, by Speer.

SOURCE: Werner Rittich, *Architektur und Bauplastik der Gegenwart* (Berlin, 1938), 27.

Fig. 8 Reconstruction Drawing of the Temple of Tukulti-Ninurta at Assur, 1921.

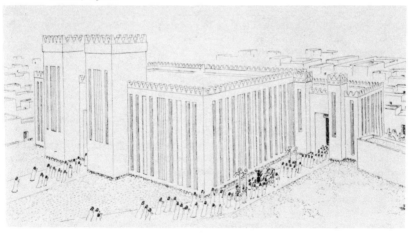

SOURCE: Walter Andrae, *Der jüngeren Ischtar-Tempel in Assur* (Leipzig, 1935), Fig. 3a.

models the products of a Semitic people. His protestations of admiration for Greek architecture, however, must have been conditioned by some notion of what he thought he ought to say, as a Nazi, and by a belief that this was what Hitler would like to hear. For Hitler's sake, and, one must assume, for his own sake too, Speer was committed to finding some expression for the nationalism of Nazi ideology, as well as for its references to populism. He explicitly rejected the "Germanic" styles of some Nazi architects. In the search for a rationale, it was the link between German, Aryan, and Greek which seemed to fit. Clearly, though, Speer's overriding desire was to create an architecture which looked durable and old.[22]

In this desire Speer was not alone. The concluding irony of this account of Speer's work is that, despite his genuine nationalism, his buildings closely resembled a widespread international movement in architecture in the 1930s. This movement created countless massive stone buildings characterized by repetitive vertical elements which suggested a link to some tradition, but also marked by an absence of ornament which tied them closely to the Modern Movement. Marcello Piacentini, Paul Cret, Charles Holden, Leon Azéma, Giuseppe Vago, Alexei Shchusev, and B. M. Iofan, to mention only a few, shared in an effort to create dignified, formal, yet accessible-looking official buildings in the 1930s and early 1940s. Examples include Cret's Federal Reserve Board Building in Washington, Piacentini's Senate building at the University of Rome, and the Palais de Chaillot of Azéma and others in Paris (Figs. 9, 10, 11). All, like Speer's buildings, are characterized by extreme axiality and centrality, exaggerated emphasis on the apparent thickness of the wall (which was usually masonry over steel and concrete), vertical proportions, and visual accessibility resulting from a formal emphasis on the central entrance. These were all, obviously, public buildings, commissioned by governments, but not by a Nazi government. In the United States this kind of architecture was so widespread that virtually all urban public buildings of the Public Works Administration closely resembled one another, and the buildings of Speer. Yet in the United States no single *Generalbauinspektor* gave direction to

22 Speer, *Third Reich* 11; Albrecht Haupt, *Die älteste Kunst, insbesondere: Die Baukunst der Germanen* (Berlin, 1923); Lane, *Architecture and Politics*, 137, 256, n. 34.

Fig. 9   Federal Reserve Building, Washington, D.C., by Paul Cret.

Fig. 10   Palais de Chaillot, Paris, by Leon Azéma and others.

Fig. 11   Il Rettorato, University of Rome, by Marcello Piacentini.

SOURCE: For Figs. 9, 10, 11—Lane, personal photographic collection.

architects, no Hitler ruled, and both Nazism and Fascism were unfamiliar movements. Government officials described the buildings of the PWA as modern temples to democracy.[23]

Speer's work was part of a more widespread international style than May's. Does this mean that Speer lied about his buildings, or that he and Hitler perpetrated a giant hoax about the ideological content of Nazi architecture? Or was it simply the case that Speer was taking inspiration from other contemporary architects and transforming their ideas to his own ends? I think that none of these statements is true. Speer had not travelled much when he became Hitler's architect, and there is little evidence that he knew of buildings similar to his own outside of Germany. There is also no evidence that he was other than sincere in his belief that he was developing a style which was specifically national socialist.

Instead, I suggest that the resemblances among public buildings in almost every Western country during the 1930s and 1940s were parallel developments, spurred by similar underlying political and social needs. These were depression years in every Western country. Each government felt the need to assure its citizens of its strength and durability, and each wanted a building style which was both modern and somehow old. Each government also appreciated a building style which seemed both universal and national. American, British, French, Italian, and Russian architects doubtless arrived at the rationale for their buildings by a different route than Speer's contorted reasoning about Greeks, Aryans, and ancient empires. But the impetus behind their reasoning, although in no sense Nazi, may nevertheless have resembled Speer's in certain particulars.

Ellenius has argued that, in modern Western societies since the early nineteenth century, the twin forces of nationalism and democracy have had a common effect upon the forms of public art. All Western societies, he writes, attempted in the nineteenth century to find historical references for their public buildings and monuments, references which satisfied the demands of increasing nationalism, yet were, at the same time, intelligible to an increasingly untutored popular audience in an increasingly democratic

23   Charles W. Short and Rudolph Stanley-Brown, *Public Buildings: A Survey of Architecture . . . completed between . . . 1933 and 1939 with the assistance of the Public Works Administration* (Washington, D.C., 1939), 1.

era. The result in architecture, according to Ellenius, was an ever greater abstraction from history: toward the end of the century a number of national monuments suggested their tie to a continuous national identity by massive masonry alone.[24]

Although I see some problems in applying Ellenius' argument to all government-sponsored architecture since the beginning of the nineteenth century, his reasoning helps us understand the public architecture of Western democracies and pseudo-democracies in the depression era. Everywhere, the effort to find a national style, clearly dependent on some tradition, clearly intended for the service of the people and intelligible to them, resulted in the style which has been termed "stripped classicism," but might better be described as "modernized antique." Speer was no less sure that his work was national socialist than was Cret that his was democratic, Piacentini that his was fascist, or Azéma that his was republican. All of these architects were responding to underlying political and social realities, but they were mistaken about the nature of their expression of specific political programs. This conclusion sheds considerable light on the political role of architects in power, and on the difficulties confronting the historian in interpreting the political significance of architecture.[25]

In comparing the careers of May and Speer, I have not offered a complete biography of either man, or a complete account of their works. Rather, I have called attention to certain common themes in the role of architects in public life in the twentieth century, and have suggested problems, and some solutions, in discussing the relationships between architecture and politics. The evidence of these two cases, at least, suggests that architects are not necessarily men of high political principles, or even people who are very intelligent about politics. It is clear that for May and Speer, the building or buildings came first, resulting from a specific creative vision, and the rationales came later and were less important. Underlying both the rationales and the formal vision was, in each case, a deeper guiding idea, which remained

24 Allan Ellenius, *Den offentliga konsten och ideologierna* (Stockholm, 1971).

25 Lane, "Government Buildings in European Capitals 1870–1914," in Hans J. Teuteberg (ed.), *Urbanisierung im 19 und 20. Jahrhundert. Historische und Geographische Aspekte* (Cologne, 1983), 517–560. Giuseppe Vago and the other architects of the League of Nations complex in Geneva must have believed that the best modern national style was also the best expression for a building which would assemble nations together.

relatively inarticulate. May's deepest desire was to build a new society out of the best of the old; Speer's, to preserve the appearance of the old in the service of a new monumental architecture.

Both cases also show (and evidence for this point could easily be multiplied) that, to achieve major commissions in the twentieth century, great power, or the patronage of great power, is necessary. Major architectural commissions in the twentieth century tend to be government buildings, and they tend often to be part of a larger planning process. To achieve the realization of an architect's goals, it would seem almost necessary that he either become a dictator of style himself, or find a dictator as a patron. In the process, he will also almost necessarily become a planner, because of the scale of modern building needs and the nature of government response to them. In short, to carry through large-scale projects, both May and Speer, men of radically differing views of the good society, were altogether willing to set aside the democratic process: to plan on a large scale for people's own good, whether they liked it or not. It is worrying that both were naive about politics, but not about power.

The careers of May and Speer also provide ample evidence of the difficulties confronting historians who seek to interpret the political or ideological content of buildings. Historians cannot necessarily believe what the architect himself has said about his work, or what his patrons say about it either. It is also unwise to infer the political significance of a building or building style from the reactions of its audience: right-wing groups in Frankfurt thought May was a Bolshevik, intent on destroying all tradition, which he was not; his Russian patrons came to believe that he was a Fascist, intent on importing Western capitalist politics into Soviet cities, which he was not. German admirers of Speer's work in the 1930s and 1940s would have been shocked to see its close analogues in France, England, and the United States; Americans are still unwilling to hear the public buildings of the Public Works Administration compared to their counterparts in Germany and Italy.

Two approaches to the question of the political significance of architecture are possible, however. First, one must believe that the architect meant what he said, as did his patrons and audience. Looking at this kind of evidence, one can gauge the short-term political intent and effect of a building or buildings. The statements of patrons and architects as to their intent, and the reactions of their audience, are themselves historical facts, which affect later observers in their own views about the political implications of architecture. Second, one can infer a larger political (and social) significance from the context of the buildings and of the architect's life. The "international style" of the 1930s and 1940s can be seen from this perspective as a product of the effects of the depression on government patronage in the industrialized countries, and also as a response to the long-term problem of relating architecture to history for a nationalist and popular audience. The International Style of the 1920s, in May's version, was the product of the political, economic, and intellectual turmoil specific to the first years of the Weimar Republic, when visionary hopes for a new society were first raised and then dashed. More broadly speaking, May's work was also a part of a modern movement in architecture which, among other things, celebrates the ability of modern technology to serve the needs of all members of society equally. The implications of this set of values are egalitarian and anti-nationalist, but not entirely ahistorical.

In studying the relationships between architecture and politics, historians must be willing to consult every kind of historical evidence: the nature of the creative process at a given historical moment; the public statements of intent by both architect and patron; the buildings themselves; the reactions of the users to both statements and buildings; the context, architectural and political, of the works and the writings; and the fundamental social and political conditions under which both appear. Since architects in power, at least in the twentieth century, seek to please many masters, and since buildings do not speak for themselves, the task is particularly complex. The rewards, however, are correspondingly great, since they include a fuller understanding of all the levels of life and consciousness, from the most public and programmatic, to the most private and irrational.